CHEERS FOR MARY KAY BLAKELY AND

American Mom

"Witty and piercing . . . Blakely takes on theorists whose edicts leave little room for common sense. She also attacks the 'family-value evangelists,' who, even after thirty years of social change, still expect Donna Reed perfection."

—Michele Ingrassia, *Newsweek*

"Affecting, wry. . . . There are countless moments, phrases, insights in this outlaw's odyssey that I will happily remember long after my own son turns twenty-one. . . . You can almost hear a nation of weary mothers cheering her on."

—Susan Pelzer, *Washington Post Book World*

"Any mother who has veered or, like Ms. Blakely, careened off the path of traditional motherhood . . . will find solace in *AMERICAN MOM*. . . . There are so many passages underlined in the first twelve pages of my copy that it looks like one of the freshman textbooks I read before I realized I didn't have to underline everything. This is the sort of book one ought to take to bed with a forgiving mate who lets you read all the good parts out loud."

—Anita Shreve, *The New York Times Book Review*

". . . serves up one good tale after another of the frazzling, frustrating but ultimately fulfilling life and times of a divorced, working mother. . . . Blakely's struggles and stresses . . . relate to challenges universally faced by mothers. Her wry and witty handling of them is satisfying medicine for maternal distress."

—Francesca Lyman, *Los Angeles Times Book Review*

"With her light touch, her middle-American roots and her radical honesty, she's the perfect person to bring some reality to the fractured debate over family values. We tend to give books on infant care to new mothers; this brave report on raising infants to be decent human beings could be more helpful and more fun."

—Suzanne Ruta, *Newsday*

"Blakely writes with an honesty bare as bone, truth that spreads your thinking."

—Ruth Moose, *Greensboro News & Record*

"Blakely has no use for self-appointed critics who look on as Mom tries to steer her children through a minefield of social pathologies, and then blame her when anything goes boom."

—Amanda Heller, *Boston Globe*

"Blakely speaks for many of us who grew up in one world and graduated into a society that was changing so fast it made our ears pop. . . . She speaks and writes well about both the limits of motherhood and the transforming effect it has on a woman."

—Lois Blinkhorn, *Milwaukee Journal*

"Warm, thoughtful, and funny. . . . For many boomer women, reading these essays will be like looking at a road map of their lives. . . . Blakely writes with a great deal of frankness and not a little irreverence."

—Joanne Wilkinson, *Booklist*

"Blakely's voice is seasoned and confident."

—Leslie Brody, *Elle*

"Blakely's warm, candid, touching, fiercely loving account of raising two sons will strike a chord with parents in this age of post-nuclear, extended families."

—*Publishers Weekly*

"*AMERICAN MOM* captures the private joys and pains of mothering. And it brilliantly illuminates America's odd public attitude of simultaneous mother worship and mother disdain. . . . Blakely has accomplished a very difficult feat: a book that both warms the heart and provokes thought on one of today's most debated topics—the family."

—Audrey Knoth, *Virginian-Pilot and Ledger-Star*

Also by Mary Kay Blakely

Wake Me When It's Over

AMERICAN MOM

Motherhood, Politics, and Humble Pie

MARY KAY BLAKELY

POCKET BOOKS

New York   London   Toronto   Sydney   Tokyo   Singapore

I am grateful to my editors Amy Gross, Julia Kagan, Mary McNamara, Nancy Newhouse, Evelyn Renold, Susan Seliger, Anne Mollegen Smith, Ellen Sweet, and Pat Towers for all the talking, thinking, patience and, not least, superb editing they have committed on my behalf over the last decade. Several pages of the following chapters were adapted from essays which first appeared in these publications: Portions of chapters two, four, and five first appeared in *Vogue* in May 1983, December 1981, and July 1983, respectively; portions of chapters six, twelve, and fourteen first appeared in *Ms.* in July/August 1987, December 1986, and March 1987; portions of chapters nine and eleven first appeared in *Working Woman* in February 1985 and August 1988; and portions of chapters fifteen and seventeen appeared in *Lear's* in September 1989 and August 1991. Chapter sixteen, "A Wrestling Mom," was adapted from "Breaking the Hold," published in the *Los Angeles Times Magazine* in May 1992.

In the epilogue, Phyllis Theroux's brief conversation with her son is paraphrased from her inspiring book, *Night Lights: Bedtime Stories for Parents in the Dark.*

The following writers fired my imagination with these turns of phrase, which appear without footnote in my text: For the concept of "the motherhood learning curve," I thank Carrie Tuhy; for the image of families as "small civilizations," I thank novelist Pat Conroy; for the description of myself looking like a "gut-shot bear" in chapter eight, I thank Kurt Vonnegut; J. D. Salinger described American slang with the sentence in chapter sixteen, "It was army." Dort Rudek invented the Scotch-tape pacifier in the prologue. Poet and author Adrienne Rich had the vision of women becoming the "makers and sayers" of our culture.

POCKET BOOKS, a division of Simon & Schuster Inc.
1230 Avenue of the Americas, New York, NY 10020

ISBN: 0-671-53520-X

First Pocket Books trade paperback printing November 1995

10 9 8 7 6 5 4 3 2 1

POCKET and colophon are registered trademarks of
Simon & Schuster Inc.

Cover design by Tom McKeveny
Cover photo by Dorothy Littell Greco
Inset photo courtesy of the author

Printed in the U.S.A.

to my prime movers,
Ryan and Darren

Contents

Acknowledgments

I am profoundly grateful to my sons, Ryan and Darren, for their intrepid independence and solid affection during the long months I was sequestered in my office, preoccupied with our past; to my parenting ally, Howard, for his continued affection and wit despite an ex-wife-who-writes; to my friend, Larry, not only for saving my life but also for admirably braving the ups and downs of the subsequent years; and to my parents, Kay and Jerry, who ushered me and my four siblings through childhood with skill and intelligence, then gave us a lifetime of ever-richer humor and love.

I thank my Fort Wayne friends, Joan Uebelboer, Cathryn Adamsky, Mary Ann Wanush, Carolen Collins, Ann Raber, Alice Gillam, and Jeanette Clausen, the war buddies and soul mates who taught me during my formative years that motherhood was not only a private passion but a political job. They opened my eyes, inspired my courage, and made me laugh when jokes were in shortest supply.

I am arguably the luckiest writer in America to have Phyllis Wender, my longtime agent and dear friend, as my first reader, dauntless critic, and indefatigable supporter. My editor Elisabeth Scharlatt managed to get this manuscript out of me with her patience, wisdom, huge affection, and unflagging faith. Nancy Nordhoff and the wonderful staff at Collages at Hedgebrook, a writer's retreat of the most sublime order, provided the peace and solitude I needed to begin the first stage of this work.

Acknowledgments

For taking time out of their own hectic lives to concentrate on mine, I am indebted to the loyal friends who gave me thoughtful readings, tough questions, and invaluable advice on the manuscript: Gabrielle Burton, Jane Myers, Patricia O'Toole, Carrie Tuhy, and Mary-Lou Weisman. My conversations with these word-smiths and truth tellers invariably restored my faith that writing is not a futile endeavor.

Although working in a one-woman office meant that I was often unable to keep apace with my correspondence, I thank my readers for their many moving letters—cheering me on, sharing their stories, and conducting their own motherhood with passion and nerve.

A book is never a solo effort and mine employed a large supporting cast of thinkers and writers who have sustained me for twenty years. I feel humbled, and elated, to share this result of their investment in me.

—Mary Kay Blakely

xii

Prologue
Who Are We This Time?

With swelling regret and a kind of damp pride, I traveled twenty-five hundred miles to Arizona State University the summer of 1992 and left my son Ryan, a high school wrestler and English-class con man, to fend for himself in the desert. I was excruciatingly aware that by the same time the next year my younger son Darren, then in the process of shedding his reputation as "the good child" and revealing his wilder self, would begin a similarly expanded independence. The mental countdowns that began on New Year's Day for the past two years—"nine months to go before he leaves home"—were like reverse pregnancies. The deep breathing exercises I learned twenty years ago in preparation for having a baby came in handy again, during the prolonged psychological contractions of letting my sons go.

Then, as now, wild speculations and vague worries about what to expect invaded my sleep with a barrage of questions: Who *is* this person coming along next? What kind of mother am I supposed to be *now*? The questions never stopped coming, and the answers, from year to year, were never the same. In the ongoing dialectic of motherhood, opposite realities could be simultaneously true: Two decades ago, my sons were the most lovable and stimulating creatures on the planet; they were also the most draining and fractious human beings I'd ever known. Now I didn't want my grown sons, my daily buddies, to leave home; I also couldn't wait for their ravenous appetites and deafening music to go. The cultural myth that mothers universally dread the "empty nest" is only half-correct. "The truth is," said my friend M-Lou, my reliably blunt reporter of what was just ahead on the motherhood learning curve, "they leave home just before you would kill them."

By the time my babies were ready to leave, they had acquired the muscled bulk of young giants and tended to travel in team-sized packs. My heavily trafficked nest was straining at the seams. A twenty-year labor, for even the hardiest of mothers, is one long, sweaty haul. While I welcomed retirement from active duty, I nevertheless found it difficult to turn off old habits of mind. The closer we came to the delivery date, the more frequent my examinations—I kept scrutinizing their behavior, their manners, especially their "attitude." One week I would be astounded by signs of growing confidence and ingenuity; the next I would be alarmed by gaping holes in their socialization. ("Only three months to go—is that enough time to clean this kid up so he'll pass for civilized?") Were they ready for independence? Was I?

In those pregnant months before they left, I had to keep resisting the urge to have another go at them, to commence a crash summer course in morals and manners. Every time I heard an alarming story on the news about male violence or saw them watching a raunchy video on MTV, I wondered how the values I had tried to pass along would weather the next transition. I knew I faced little chance of inspiring them with any sermons about life now. My sons had both reached the cool, isolating summits of late adolescence, when children are convinced they know everything. Would they eventually learn that nobody, ever, can possess all of the truth—that as long as they are human there will always be more thinking and striving to do? "Dominance makes a ruling group stupid," the late columnist Sydney Harris once wrote about the privilege that's bestowed at birth on certain white, heterosexual men. Would my sons resist stupidity?

AS I packed the car trunk last summer with Darren's clothes, computer, barbells, and books—the sum of his material parts—I realized I was approaching that impossible state my friend Joan, a mother of five, dreamed about twenty years ago when we were both frazzled working mothers in a county auditor's office in Indiana. After squeezing in too many errands during her lunch hour and fielding phone calls from squabbling kids all afternoon, she sighed deeply and uttered a fervent wish for the day she would "become unnecessary." To be unnecessary, of course, one has to accept not being in control.

Fortunately for me, my motherhood has been out of control for most of my sons' lives. First by choice, then by circumstance, we have lived like "outlaws from the institution of motherhood," as the poet Adrienne Rich described those who drift—or flee—from traditional rules and expectations. I became an official member of this irregular band a few years after my sons were born, when their father lost his job and we became what my friend Marti calls "economically challenged." My tenure as a full-time mother was necessarily brief. Since then, I have been a working mother, a divorced mother, a poor mother, an almost remarried mother, a comatose mother, a long-distance mother, and, finally, a deliberately single mother. The editor-in-chief of a national women's magazine added "unnatural mother" to my long list several years ago, after I published an essay in the *New York Times* about the mind-bending months I spent coming to terms with Ryan's request, at age thirteen, to live with his dad for a year.

"I can't understand any woman who would voluntarily give up custody of her children," the editor told her staff, calling my behavior "appalling." And she didn't even know the half of it.

By the time Ryan had proposed this domicile arrangement, our family had been through so many transformations and permutations that neither his father nor I could legitimately claim "custody" of the boys, although it took us several harrowing years of ballistic negotiations to comprehend this reality. In the early custody battles, our ultimata to each other reflected the same mentality as the National Rifle Association slogan that appeared on Indiana bumpers that year: "You can have my gun when you pry my cold, dead fingers from the trigger."

Our first custody agreement, translated from legal jargon, was essentially this: "Divorce me, and I'll make you regret it the rest of your life—and if you think you've seen the worst of me, just wait." Still smoldering with resentment, Howard and I were almost never talking that first year about "the best interests of the children"—although we used those words. When two wounded people coming out of prolonged marital strife talk custody, the negotiations are really about money and power, and why-don't-you-*love*-me? No one should actually try to live under a treaty drafted by the newly divorced. The initial attempts are rarely more than purging exercises. Our embattled period raged on for nearly five years—the national average, Professor Judith Wallerstein reports sadly, having studied the breakdown of small civilizations such as ours. It took time, and thousands of words, before Howard and I put an end to the acrimony and finally realized we were both in love with the same two boys.

However much the courts and lawyers have mangled the language—and therefore the attitudes—governing custody, we eventually understood that raising sons, like bearing arms, was less a right than a responsibility. A mother can legitimately be said to "have a baby"—but in a civilization such as ours, she can never claim to own a teenager. As our sons entered their second decade, I had to keep reminding myself of the note that Salinger's Zen poet wrote in his diary about the necessary detachment a parent must strive to achieve: "A child is a guest in the house, to be loved and respected—never possessed . . . How wonderful, how sane, how beautifully difficult and therefore true."

If I had admitted suffering terribly as a consequence of giving up custody, the women's magazine editor might have tolerated or even forgiven my departure from her norm. Martyrdom and self-sacrifice are still going concerns in the institution of motherhood. My public admission that I actually enjoyed my year of long-distance motherhood was apparently the most nettling part of my unnatural behavior. She was shocked by my admission that I would probably do it again with my younger son—which I did. Quite accidentally, I'd discovered that periodic separations helped all of us, including me, keep in vital touch with who we were and what we needed. This was a deeply threatening notion to the keepers at the gates of traditional motherhood.

All of my job titles, from Working Mom to Unnatural Mom, were deliberate career moves—with the notable exception of Coma Mom, when my illness and near-death in 1984 introduced us to a new reality none of us had anticipated. Our family values may have looked odd or painful to those who still believed there could be only one kind of family, but once we'd split from the nuclear mold, cooled off and expanded, squeezing ourselves back in would have been painful for us. My sons, taking their greater independence largely for granted, were surprised to hear, in the overwrought speeches at the Republican convention during the summer Howard and I took Ryan to Arizona State, that obedience and parental consent were the operative values in "the true American family." In ours, where the hierarchy kept shifting from year to year, an abundance of mercy and nerve were the saving graces.

"If you guys aren't a real family," Ryan said, getting depressed as he listened to Rush Limbaugh on the car radio, "I guess that makes me illegitimate."

"Don't worry—we were real enough when you were born," I assured him. "We just got more and more unreal over time."

Like most middle-class women who married in the early '70s, I started out with the expectation of being the kind of traditional mother that editors-in-chief everywhere could admire. Since then— through natural, unnatural, and outright supernatural events— those expectations have changed. Although I never planned to have such a checkered career as a mother, and certainly managed some stages more gracefully than others, each stage was critical to the next: the charmingly chaotic, physically affectionate years of our young nuclear family; the emotionally explosive and slightly radioactive period of our postnuclear family; the surprisingly fluid and eventually peaceful transition into two long-distance single-parent families. A critic in the *Times,* noting the radical changes so many families have made in the last twenty years, asked recently: "Is this dysfunction or are we all just highly evolved?"

"Change takes time," the cultural adage warns those of us who long for speedier, less antagonistic evolutions. Among the outlaw mothers I know who are trying to raise children, work demanding jobs, teach husbands and bosses that women are not happiest when out running errands, the eagerness for change is an almost physically felt pain. True, it took me many years to learn, and unlearn, what it meant to be a mother in contemporary America. But once I had those truths, I burned with the desire to live them. When I couldn't, and was paternally reminded that "change takes time," I would think: No, not true. I have changed. If you haven't—given exactly the same facts over exactly the same period—it's because *resistance* takes time.

TIME IS never more relative than when it is stretched across the full span of childhood. When my sons were toddlers, sticky and close, omnipresent and ever-needy, I measured my days out in two-hour spoonfuls between meals and naps and baths and stories. As our lives moved forward in these minute increments, I did not think it possible they would one day be leaving home—"before you know it," as innumerable friends told me. After serving them some twenty thousand meals, lowering the toilet seat thousands of times, issuing countless reminders that cars need oil to run, how could a mother so centrally engaged in their growth not know it?

Can a woman really forget cooking two and a half tons of macaroni and cheese? Can she forget playing solitaire until dawn on snowy nights, waiting for the sound of tires crunching into the driveway? Can a mother really not notice that her former baby's life has changed completely when he receives, among his high school graduation gifts, a pair of purple silk boxer shorts and a scented card written in a dainty, still Palmerized script? No, I think a mother always knows these small incidents are adding up to

Something Big. We just understand, like the fans who come faithfully to the Indy 500 every year, that it's going to be a long day.

Lurching and stalling through the early years, time moved slowly as the rookie drivers tested their limits, learned to take the curves, conferred with their pit crews. I got used to the whining noises and oily fumes, paying only half-attention through each repetitive cycle until a warning flag or frightening accident snapped my mind back on the track. Then, in the riveting final laps, time suddenly accelerated. Fixed solely on the finish line, convinced they knew all they needed to know, my sons hit the pedal to the metal and ignored any further signals from the pit. They barely stopped home long enough to refuel with a favorite pot roast, never mind windy sermons about life.

While they forged ahead with a speed that bordered on recklessness, I found myself falling back in time, seized with a ferocious desire to remember everything about this long day at the track. As twenty years of effort compressed in those final laps, I felt the stirring excitement and lumpy throat I often get in movie theaters. The musical score that kept playing in my head as I watched them fling themselves into the world was not Mozart's Clarinet Concerto or Pachelbel's Canon, but the theme song from *Rocky*. I know I should be far beyond the moist, sentimental lumpiness of motherhood by now. But as it turns out, I'm not.

In those zoom-lens months before Ryan and Darren left home, a familiar gesture or facial expression would trigger a sudden onslaught of memories. I would see the faces and hear the voices of all the "gone children" in the family album, all the little guys who used to people my life but who, inevitably, have now disappeared. This happens whether a mother willingly gives up custody or not. Whenever I caught a certain provocative smile, a long-suffering frown, I would be suddenly infused with a peculiar clairvoyance. I would travel back and forth in time, remembering the first time that look appeared, knowing how often it would return to delight or haunt me. Throughout the final countdown months, so many voices, stories, feelings kept flooding my brain.

I was swamped by one of these mind floods in a shoe store last August, as Darren tried on a pair of loafers in a size that could have comfortably fit both of my feet in one shoe. I remembered the first time I saw those astonishing appendages eighteen years earlier, then attached to the smallest, most fragile human legs imaginable. Once more, I was standing woozily next to his crib in the preemie intensive care nursery, leaning against his incubator for support as I watched his labored breathing. This impatient son, who had crashed into being two months before his due date—very nearly killing us both—lay unconscious amidst his tangle of wires and tubes while I tried to suppress my fears about his underdeveloped lungs and heart muscles.

He was tininess itself, his delicate pink form stretched nakedly under sunlamps to cure his jaundice, his skinny limbs covered with dark, prenatal fuzz—cilia hair for the amniotic sea he had just been forced to leave. I watched him take a wet gulp of air and then, suddenly, stop breathing entirely. My own breath stopped as the line on his heart monitor flattened. Hearing the alarm, the nurse jumped up and rushed to his incubator, flicking his tiny heel a few times until the rhythmic beeps of his heart returned again.

"Apnea," she said, sighing with relief. "They get so tired they forget to breath." She then went back to her paperwork at the nursing station, little Darren Oliver went back to sleep, and I worried about brain damage for the next five years.

DARREN'S TRAUMATIC birth was my first brutal encounter with the reality that motherhood was not and would never be entirely under my control. With two sons born eighteen months apart, I operated mainly on automatic pilot through the ceaseless activity of their early childhood. I remember opening the refrigerator late one night and finding a roll of aluminum foil next to a pair of small red tennies. Certain that I was responsible for the refrigerated shoes, I quickly closed the door and ran upstairs to make sure I had put the babies in their cribs instead of the linen closet. It was in this same period that Howard would come home from work to find his cherished domestic order dissolved in a rubble of Lincoln Logs and Legos. He would raise his eyebrows to ask, "What have you been *doing* all day?" I would shrug my shoulders to reply, "Hey—they're both still alive. I've done my job."

After I discovered the real life of mothers bore little resemblance to the plot outlined in most of the books and articles I'd read, I started relying on the expert advice of other mothers—especially those with sons a few years older than mine. This great body of knowledge is essentially an oral history, because anyone engaged in motherhood on a daily basis has no time to write an advice book about it. Women's magazines generally feature experts like Marie Osmond or Cher, who can get through motherhood without wrinkles. I learned my most useful survival tips mainly from friends during "coffee-klatsches"—as outsiders dimly regarded our informal motherhood training seminars.

Most of these tips were too insignificant for the pediatricly educated to bother with, but for those of us stationed on the front lines they saved countless lives. I remember trying to talk with Joan one afternoon while Ryan fussed in his playpen, flinging his rattles, teething rings, even his beloved pacifier overboard, and then wailing loudly until I retrieved each item. Undoubtedly recognizing the homicidal glint in my eye as I got up for the fiftieth time, Joan asked if I had a roll of cellophane tape. I immediately thought she was going to tape his mouth shut—a thought that had begun forming darkly in my own mind—but instead she gently wrapped it, sticky side out, around his fingers on both hands. For the next half-hour, he became totally absorbed, testing the tactile surface on his shirt, his nose, his hair, his toes. A toy that cost almost nothing, couldn't be thrown overboard, made no rattling noises—it was the perfect pacifier. I kept rolls of cellophane everywhere for the next three years—next to the phone, in the glove compartment, in my purse.

"Where did you learn this stuff?" I asked Joan, who possessed a wealth of small but effective techniques for preventing child abuse.

"I don't know," she said. "I guess after five kids, I now think like one: 'What would be fun?'"

I also relied on my friends whenever I needed a sanity check. One year, I'd completely lost my bearings trying to follow potty training instructions from a psychiatric expert who guaranteed success with his methods in three efficient days. I was stuck on step one, which stated without an atom of irony: "Before you begin, remove all stubbornness from the child." After reading this suggestion, I knew it only could have been written by someone whose suit coat was still spotless at the end of the day, not someone who had any hands-on experience with an actual two year old. I should have questioned this authority, but there's something about being an inept toilet tutor that has a dampening effect on self-esteem. And so I plodded impossibly on as the three-day plan stretched into the fifth interminable week.

"What's wrong with you?" Joan asked, when I walked numbly into the faculty lounge fresh from losing another round with my baby alligator. I described the trouble I was having "removing all stubbornness." At the rate we were going, I confessed, Darren would be ten years old before he was out of diapers. "I feel so shitty—and, apparently, so does he."

Joan laughed, deeply familiar by now with "the guilties." Mothers breathe guilt on the job every day, like germs in the air. She recommended I pitch the book, forget about arbitrary deadlines, and accept stubbornness as a fact of childhood. ("Powerlessness corrupts," she often said.) She then clued me in on a game using toilet paper rolls; Darren found it so amusing, he practically lived in the bathroom for three days. Quite painlessly, he mastered another level of civilization. Joan's theory of motherhood—the harder the developmental task, the more comedy it requires—became my own.

Every time I told Joan what a terrific mother she was, she would just smile and say, "You should know." Those words invariably prompted the story of a bad mother day. She told me about waking up once, in the middle of the night, foggy brained, unable to remember putting her two year old to bed. None of the usual details about the bath, the sleeper pajamas, the goodnight kiss would come into focus. She got up to check on the baby and was horrified to find her crib empty. Racing frantically through the house turning on lights, she finally found Patty in the kitchen, sound asleep in her high chair, her head slumped down on the tray. "At least I'd strapped her in," Joan said. "She had her seat belt on."

Nobody's perfect, we knew, but mothers are somehow expected to exceed all human limits. This ideal is especially preposterous since mothers are likely to have more bad days on the job than most other professionals, considering the hours: round-the-clock, seven days a week, fifty-two weeks a year. Fathers provide only irregular relief, and you can't call Kelly Girl for a potty trainer. You go to work when you're sick, maybe even clinically depressed, because motherhood is perhaps the only unpaid position where failure to show up can result in arrest.

Given the punishing rules—and the contemptuous labels for any mom who breaks them—mothers are reluctant to admit even having bad days, let alone all the miserable details leading up to them. We all have bad days, of course, a secret that only makes us feel more guilty. But once my friends and I started telling the truth about how far we deviated from perfection, we couldn't stop. Joan and I regularly got together with a raucous group for Friday afternoon happy hours at the Old Gashouse downtown, where we laughed and howled like outlaws around a campsite, regaling each other with our narrow escapes.

One mother admitted leaving the grocery store without her kids—"I just *forgot* them. The manager found them in the frozen foods aisle, eating Eskimo Pies." Another spooned Calamine lotion into her toddler late one night, thinking it was Pepto Bismol— "Can you *believe* it? If he hadn't gagged, I might have poisoned him." My frank and witty friends, my incredible Guilt Busters, rescued me whenever the slime hit—which happened a lot, since "mother" is the first word that occurs to politicians and columnists and popes when they raise the question, "Why isn't life turning out the way we want it?"

Most of our bad mother stories didn't look so awful in retrospect; some, however, looked much worse. Every one of my friends had a bad day somewhere in her history she wished she could forget but couldn't. A very bad mother day changes you forever. Those were the hardest stories to tell, shocking tales of gin in the afternoon or broken dishes at dawn, of riveting moments when we suddenly knew, *something's wrong here . . . this isn't who I want to be.* Leaning in close and lowering our voices, passing Kleenex around our huddle, we never laughed off the guilt described in those heartbreaking confessions. Only a survivor can afford to own up to such difficult truths, so we always knew how each story had to end. But none of us breathed freely until the final resolution was spoken: "I could still see the red imprint on his little bum when I changed his diaper that night. I stared at my hands, as if they were alien parts of myself . . . as if they had betrayed me. From that day on, I never hit him again."

HOWEVER PAINFUL or compromising the reality of motherhood, we preferred it to the national game of Let's Pretend—the fantasy in which we are all supposed to pass for perfect mothers, living in perfect families. This public pretense not only feeds private shame but, worse, it keeps women fearfully ignorant and immobile. The players of Let's Pretend must read the daily newspapers and remain convinced that their own kids have nothing to do with the statistical population who are gay, have sex, need abortions, get AIDS. The winners make it all the way around the board back to square one, Deny It, without blowing their cover. The losers have to quit the game, of course, if they draw a Chance card revealing one of their kids is pregnant. Or dead.

Getting bounced from the game into actual life is invariably traumatic because it is so much more impossible to deny a real dead kid than the statistical ones in the papers. A woman doesn't have to commit a bad mother day to lose her innocence. A bad mother day can also happen to you. Phyllis Schlafly had one during that same frenzied convention over family values in Houston—not a fatally bad day, but a hard one for her nonetheless. Just after she'd finished her victorious campaign for a party platform that was anti-gay, anti-choice, pro-gun, and pro-death penalty, a gay publication dropped a retaliatory bomb and "outed" her son.

It was a gross misuse of both mother and son, a political war crime by activists who let an urgent end justify the foulest means. It put the mainstream media in a fuzzy ethical dilemma, since facts illicitly obtained—whether from a purloined file from the Pentagon, or a stolen list of porn shop customers for "Long Dong Silver"—must first be put legitimately on record before they can be publicly dissected. Cornered by reporters who kept asking if she'd heard "the news" about her son, Schlafly finally said yes, of course, she'd heard—that was the point, wasn't it?

Once on record, the Sunday morning television pundits could jaw over the outing, speculating on whether it bounced Mrs. Schlafly from the leading position in Let's Pretend. Some critics righteously judged that she had "asked for it"—the same people who would argue that committing inhuman acts damages the perpetrators as much as their victims. Others rationalized that the facts were bound to come out anyway—too many people knew, too many of whom Schlafly had deeply offended. Why not release the information when it could have the greatest political impact? Because using a son—or daughter or brother or wife—to get to the real target is the cheapest kind of opportunism. The hypocrisy exposed by the outing was not Mrs. Schlafly's.

Interestingly, Schlafly, who is never at a loss for words before a microphone, remained almost mute on the subject. When pressed, she would say only this: She wasn't going to feed her son's private life to the bloodthirsty piranha in the media. For the first time in my long acquaintance with her, I felt like applauding her. Maybe she had never needed my compassion before, or maybe that's what twenty years of motherhood does to you: when someone you don't even like has a truly bad mother day—whether it happens because of her or to her—you feel her pain. In motherhood, where seemingly opposite realities can be simultaneously true, being the Christian mother of a homosexual son—let's say a very devout mother and a much-loved son—could induce a cognitive headache that might last for years.

I am more familiar with Schlafly's loopy vision of reality than I wish, since I had to live in it for so long. We were both raising sons in the early '70s—though on opposite sides of the Mississippi and of just about everything else. It was largely thanks to her, a popular speaker and successful campaigner from Illinois, that mothers in Indiana had so few day-care centers, sex education programs, school desegregation plans, or women's shelters. She thought "battered women" were part of a feminist plot to shame men and that shelters could only lead to the breakdown of families, which made sense to Indiana legislators. At the many hearings we both attended, I was frequently stirred by her speeches, though never to applause. When Schlafly talked, men listened. State representatives nodded and took notes, finding her vision of the Totaled Woman exactly in line with their own. Meanwhile, women on my side of the aisle would look at each other and wonder, "Is Phyllis Schlafly a female impersonator, or what?" She may have favored a staunch hands-off policy for government, but as a neighbor, she was in-your-face.

Schlafly may well remain mute on quite a few issues for a while, if her unwelcome news survives the initial barrage of denial. A lot of mothers with homosexual sons, Christian or not, go through many agonizing stages before accepting reality—maybe seeking therapeutic cures, extracting promises of celibacy, or arranging dinners with one "right girl" after another. After reading about the homosexual sailor aboard the *Belleau Wood* who was beaten to death in 1993 by his crew mates, so brutally, according to the *New York Times*, "that his mother could only identify him by the tattoos on his arms," you could understand why a mother would attempt to change a homosexual son. If change takes time and you've got only one life, wouldn't changing your son be easier than changing the entire navy?

Eventually, however, one bad mother day can produce more growth than a thousand good ones. That's why they're so memorable. Once we learn *something's wrong here . . . this isn't who I want to be,* the hard work of figuring out who we *do* want to be begins in earnest. One unwelcome but deeply personal revelation about sexuality can shake up a whole lot of other long-cherished facts about biology, motherhood, religion, jobs, housing, health care, discrimination, on and on. When certain cultural and biological facts are involved, it doesn't matter which side of the Mississippi you live on. With six growing children, Mrs. Schlafly invited a lot of Chance cards into her life. By the summer of 1992, homosexuality didn't even make the list of major things a mother had to worry about.

A "SNAPSHOT" feature in *USA Today* a few years earlier briefly listed the five greatest concerns parents and teachers had about children in the '50s: talking out of turn, chewing gum in class, doing homework, stepping out of line, cleaning their rooms. Then it listed the five top concerns of parents today: drug addiction, teenage pregnancy, suicide and homicide, gang violence, anorexia and bulimia. We can also add AIDS, poverty, and homelessness. Change takes time? Between my own childhood and the advent of my motherhood—one short generation—the culture had gone completely mad.

While my sturdy support network saved my sanity during my sons' early childhood, it was indispensable during the mind-racking years of adolescence, when the stakes rose precipitously and upped the guilt ante beyond any individual woman's resources. In an ideal society, mothers and fathers would produce potty-trained, civilized, responsible new citizens while government and corporate leaders would provide a safe, healthy, economically just community. But it was not our luck to live in an ideal world. Given the violence and greed and myopic leadership of the past two decades, a young man coming of age in the United States today faces treacherous curves and dangerous potholes on the way to every destination.

By the time my sons entered the second half of high school, every one of the grim realities in *USA Today* had shown up in the lives of their classmates and friends. It was impossible to assure myself that I didn't have to worry about my sons getting involved with guns or drugs. They and I both knew kids in our neighborhood, kids who regularly sat around our own kitchen table, who were. The scary reports about racial tensions and domestic violence in America were not abstractions to us. We have always lived right down the block, right next door to them, in our "good neighborhoods" as well as the bad.

Raising sons forever changed the way I read the newspapers. Desperate for an answer to "How could this *be?*" I would read and reread stories about the six teenage "wilders" from the Bronx who brutally assaulted a jogger in Central Park and left her in a coma; the half-dozen members of the California Spur Posse who proudly tallied their sexual conquests—including that of a twelve-year-old girl; the four high school athletes in Glen Ridge, New Jersey, who gang-raped a mentally retarded young woman with baseball bats and broom handles while nine others looked on. These stories *seared* me.

Invariably, my imagination would heat up and I would see six poor mothers in the Bronx, nine middle-class mothers in California, thirteen well-to-do mothers in New Jersey: I felt certain I knew exactly how their hearts must be breaking. I could also imagine what might be going on inside the tortured mind of Joel Steinberg's mother, after the bloody images of Hedda Nussbaum and five-year-old Lisa Steinberg convinced a jury of her son's guilt. To the bitter end of the trial, his mother refused to believe her son capable of such violent battery and murder. She built a case against Hedda, portraying her as a lousy mother, a drug abuser, so out of control she must have been "asking for it"—something, anything, to explain this alien son in the news, not the boy she once knew, not the son she so carefully raised. The choices I saw for her, listening to long months of shocking testimony, were these: Deny reality, or start weeping and never stop.

"You raise your children knowing them intimately," novelist

Rosellen Brown said, "but then you reach a point where that's no longer true." It takes twenty or so years before a mother can know with any certainty how effective her theories have been—and even then there are surprises. The daily newspapers raise the most frightening questions of all for a mother of sons: Could my once sweet babes ever become violent men? Are my sons really who I think they are?

Struck dumb with horror by the Glen Ridge trial—the four athletes, the baseball bats, the defense's insistence that sexual violence wasn't a crime if the retarded woman "asked for it," the neighbors' and relatives' rationalization that "boys will be boys"—my friend Elisabeth became suddenly panicked about what her own son regarded as normal. Home from college the week the story hit, he was riding the subway with her one morning when she asked—trying to sound casual as she pointed to a headline across the aisle—what he thought of the case. Whose argument did he identify with? He looked at her, dumbfounded, then caught her drift.

"Mom!" he fairly shouted. "Are you really asking if I know whether it's wrong to rape a retarded girl with a baseball bat???"

She was; she could hardly believe it herself. How could she, of all people, doubt his regularly demonstrated integrity? Because she knew, as most mothers who take the news personally do, that the integrity of every young man is under constant assault. Before reaching maturity, our sons will have been exposed to more than two hundred thousand episodes of televised violence. Professors Neil Malamuth and Edward Donnerstein, in a college sample of "regular guys, normal men," determined that 66 percent had a "conquest mentality toward women." Even if I'd had the money to afford private schools and expensive neighborhoods—which I didn't—there was no place in America where rape, battery, and violence weren't daily occurrences. Since we live in a culture where so many smart, successful, educated people from New York to California, so many high public officials all over the nation, could mistake a conquest mentality for normal, couldn't our sons make the same mistake?

I WISH it were true that a mother is the most powerful influence on her children. Unfortunately, her singular power lasts a limited time during early childhood, when most of us are half out of control ourselves. However diligent she may be, however dedicated, no mother can escape the larger influences of culture, biology, fate. Culture shapes the human mind through television, books, films, friends, teachers, coaches; biology governs the body with genetic codes, some imprinted with preset timers for schizophrenia or juvenile diabetes; and fate, through a motorcycle accident, a bullet, a broken neck, can change a young life completely, instantly. Even within the remaining quarter's worth of family influence, a mother shares her fraction of power with fathers and siblings and, especially in hard economic times, live-in relatives and friends. Until mothers become the sayers and the makers of the culture, until we can actually live in a society where mothers and children genuinely matter, ours is an essentially powerless responsibility. Mothers carry out most of the work orders, but most of the rules governing our lives are shaped by outside influences.

The stricken mothers in the Bronx or Glen Ridge may be responsible for less than a fraction of a fraction of the blame for the violent eruptions of their sons, and yet women habitually receive the major share of the blame. Long before the family-values folks damned us, we had years of practice chastising ourselves. A friend whose daughter was diagnosed with a learning disability spent a year wondering: Was it my fault? Was it the two glasses of wine I had at a party, decades earlier, before the warning labels about pregnancy appeared on liquor bottles? Another friend whose three-year-old son developed muscular dystrophy spent the next decade searching her soul: Was it my fault? Did his disease begin when I stepped on the fluoroscope in the shoe store, a child myself, to admire my toes in my Mary Janes? Had the X rays I playfully turned on, again and again, forever damaged my son's genes? The same questions bombarded my own mother, when my eldest brother manifested his first symptoms of manic depression: Was it my fault? Did his mental illness begin when he was three, when I tried to sleep through his cries from the nursery one night? The same questions invaded my life, after medical science finally pardoned my mother by uncovering genetic factors. As my sons approached the trigger age, it was my turn to worry: Was it my fault? Were they more vulnerable because of the dangerous chromosomes I brought to their gene pool? There is almost an arrogance in the outsized guilt these questions raise—as if a mother could bend biology, culture, and fate to her will, if only she were smart, attentive, dedicated enough.

WHEN I was "having a baby" two decades ago, I was only dimly aware that I was entering a partnership for life. If life expectancy statistics apply, my sons and I will spend more years in our future adult relationship than all the years I spent with them as babies, toddlers, young boys, and teens—all those loved "gone children" who exist only in memory now. Ultimately, it's absurd for a mother in one stage of development to throw judgmental grenades at women who have moved on to another stage. If we succeed in the job, all of us will eventually become out-of-control mothers, noncustodial mothers, very likely long-distance mothers. Today, only a fool would offer herself as the singular role model for the Good Mother. Most of us know not to tempt the fates: The moment I felt sure I had everything under control would invariably be the moment right before the principal called to report that one of my sons had just driven somebody's motorcycle through the high school gymnasium.

Once I'd given birth to my sons, there were no guarantees about where they would wind up, with whom, in what condition of health or sanity. "Each child represents such risk, such blind daring on its parents' parts—such possibility for anguish and pain," novelist Sue Miller wrote in *Family Pictures* (1990). The burst of love that began with childbirth expanded over the next two decades, along with the growing realization that I could not possess my sons for long, keep them safe, guarantee them a happy life. Joy/pain, joy/pain . . . the heartbeat of motherhood.

The shocks and goose bumps and passion of raising sons often caused in me that aching, delirious sensation Einstein once described as "the deep shudder of the soul in enchantment." For Einstein, this ache was relieved with tears when he heard the sweet swell of violins echoing through velveted symphony halls. For me, those tears often flowed in less elegant settings—frequently in emergency rooms, when the doctor finally emerged from behind the white curtain where one of my sons lay unconscious and announced, "He's going to be all right." I could be wearing a ratty sweatshirt splattered with blood when that quivering shudder came, but in that moment I understood what love—maybe even redemption—felt like.

For me, motherhood was a constantly humbling experience. However global I strove to become in my thinking over the last twenty years, my sons kept me rooted to an utterly pedestrian view, intimately involved with the most inspiring and fractious passages in human development. However unconsciously by now, mother-hood informs every thought I have, influencing everything I do. More than any other part of my life, being a mother taught me what it means to be human.

If I've taught Ryan and Darren something about women and jus-tice, my jock sons have taught me something about being a sport. In our ongoing discussions of gender politics, I've looked at the issues as urgently as ever, but through the lens of love and hope rather than anger and despair. By encouraging their greater com-passion and maturity, I have grown and changed myself. Raising boys has made me a more generous woman than I really am. Undoubtedly, there are other routes to learning the wishes and dreams of the presumably opposite sex, but I know of none more direct, or more highly motivating, than being the mother of sons.

PART ONE

THE MOTHER

Not to know what happened before one
was born is always to be a child.

—Cicero

1

Maternal Bondage

The first clue, certainly, that motherhood was going to be far more provocative and complicated than anything I'd imagined came the night I went into labor with my first son, as Howard began coaching me in the deep breathing techniques we'd practiced in our natural childbirth classes. In 1974 enthusiasm among our friends in Fort Wayne for all things natural approached an almost religious fervor. We bought natural fabrics, ate natural grains, wore natural blown-dry hair, distancing ourselves as much as possible from the lime-green leisure suits and creamed mushroom casseroles of the generation before us. Craving a less neon and more wholesome existence, we were heading back to nature by the Volkswagen busload. "But natural *childbirth?*" Lily Tomlin had asked, incredulous. "What a time to give up drugs."

According to our Lamaze instructor that winter, my body was supposed to "self-anesthetize" during labor and delivery, allowing me to remain wholly alert for the miracle of birth. She assured our class of hefty, plural-bodied women that our cervix muscles would become "naturally numb" as they swelled and stretched, and deep breathing would turn the final explosions of pain into "manageable discomfort." This description turned out to be as accurate as, say, a steward advising passengers aboard the *Titanic* to prepare for a brisk but bracing swim. If my self-anesthesia took at all, it packed the power of two baby aspirin.

Before I lost my innocence in the maternity wing of Parkview

Hospital that winter, I imagined facing my biological destiny as calmly as the natural mothers in the homebirth movies, issuing a low moan now and then but never screaming insensibly or savagely biting the hands of the gentle attending fathers—all bearded, naturally. In a cool ninety minutes flat, the homebirth moms went from calisthenic huffing to tears of joy to cogent monologues about birth as a spiritual experience. According to eyewitnesses, my own performance as a saint was brief.

After six hours of unremitting pain, I was nearly blind with sweat and exhaustion when the transforming moment arrived a few minutes before dawn on February 24, 1974. Looking down on my chest where someone had placed the wet, squirmy mass I dimly recognized as my son, I raised my head to offer a limp welcoming smile and immediately passed out. Both of my sons, as it turned out, were required to spend their first hours in the brave new world without me, as I struggled to regain consciousness in another room. This surreal relationship might have been the best introduction they could have had to living with a writer—but it was hardly intentional. From day one, it was clear I'd never be one of the movie moms. Both of my sons would be obliged to live with the real thing.

"After going through this once, whatever made you decide to do it *four more times?*" I asked my mother when I called that morning with news of her first grandson. She laughed. "You'll be surprised," she said, "how much that baby boy will make you forgive and forget." She chose not to mention just then, on my fragile first day, how much this baby would also shake me down to the barest truths about myself, as her own firstborn son had, exposing an unimaginable capacity for love and rage I would have the rest of my life. There would have been no point in her telling me the full, harrowing details of this life-altering journey then. With this son and, as she correctly anticipated, another one a mere eighteen months later, I was already committed. Although none of us could know how the strands of biology, culture, and fate would spin out of control in the years ahead, the web was begun.

My mother was right, too, about the general amnesty a newborn is granted after the ordeal of birth. When the nurse came into my room with the tiny creature responsible for the violent seizures the night before, now quietly subdued and bound in a blue receiving blanket, mercy and gratitude tied a hard knot in my throat. I thought Ryan Blake, four hours old, was beauty itself. His pictures from this period reveal that, in fact, he was puffy-eyed and nearly bald, his chubby face registering the same blank amusement Oliver Hardy might have worn as an infant. That morning, however, I saw only his uncanny resemblance to the air-brushed perfection of a Gerber baby. Here he was—dreamed about and yearned for—an actual son. *My* son? Our son. A living, breathing, hungry, wanting, healthy, gorgeous son.

The laryngitis that set in after my loud labor prevented speech, but I remember laughing and crying in soft, congested little barks. Howard, back in civilian clothes after turning in his green hospital scrubs, started laughing too and peered in closely as I unwound the tight swaddling to free the baby's limbs. We counted fingers and toes, came up with all the right numbers, marveled at the tininess of hands and feet, thought ourselves extraordinarily lucky. After months of searching for exactly the right name to put on the birth certificate, a series of nicknames spontaneously occurred to us: I held my sweet Lamb Chop while Howard poked his Little Buddy. "Hey, Bub . . ." we whispered. "Wake up . . . let's see who you are." Bubber, as we called Ryan that first year, opened his eyes briefly and squinted at us, as if sizing up his situation: "Hmmm . . . must be the screamer and the coach."

Satisfied that we posed no immediate threat, he drifted back to sleep. After we admired his somnolent beauty for a few more minutes, the nurse excused herself to continue her rounds, promising to return after we had our first hour of "bonding" together. Then Howard, having concluded his duties as a natural father with splendid success, kissed us both and went home to catch up on a night of lost sleep. Although fathers had finally regained access to labor and delivery rooms that year, the business of bonding was still largely regarded as a maternal matter.

Alone with the baby for the first time, I suppressed a small wave of panic. Clearly, everyone expected me to know how to keep him alive—a confidence I did not wholly share. Cradling the tiny, nearly weightless bundle in my arms, I waited anxiously for my maternal instincts to kick in. In times of mortal stress, one clings to comforting myths.

THE MOMENT, of course, never came. The naive notion that a mother naturally acquires the complex skills of childrearing simply because she has given birth now seems as absurd to me as enrolling in a nine-month class in composition and imagining that at the end of the course you are now prepared to begin writing *War and Peace*. It would be years before I would comprehend "maternal instinct"— the effortless knowledge women allegedly acquired with birth—as a cultural invention that kept the hard work of motherhood invisible to anyone outside the field.

The absolute dependence of a newborn infant inspired many things in me, but it did not activate any magical knowledge about what to do for the next twenty years. I soon began to understand that nothing would be automatic or easy again. Instead of the natural instincts I longed for, I was invaded with a wild sense of fraud: *I'm* in charge here? Overwhelmed by simultaneous waves of love and terror, I was besieged with the fear that I would ruin him somehow. One wrong move, according to prevailing theories, and the perfect baby asleep in your arms would be wide open to future bedwetting, reading problems, short attention spans, nail biting, even murder (police blotter profiles attributed the Boston Strangler's behavior to a cruel and withholding mother). I wanted desperately to make no mistakes. Yet I was certain that I would.

There is nothing natural about this pervasive guilt that besieges mothers. It was culturally manufactured by all the spin-doctors and psyche handlers who have an interest in motherhood. Preparing for a psychology seminar once, I counted more than one hundred passages in the *Psychological Abstracts* describing some form of neuroses mothers had or had caused in their children: They ruined their sons' sex lives and created unhealthy dependencies in their daughters. They warped creativity with overdiscipline and produced spineless soldiers with overpermissive "momism." In the literature of our culture, from *Portnoy's Complaint* to *The Cinderella Complex,* mothers seemed responsible for every nervous tic in the human psyche. Right there in the maternity wing, months before I did anything that merited real regret, I had my first bout of guilt. My claim to this perfect son felt so shaky and illegitimate that I fairly stole out of the hospital in 1974, holding my blue bundle so close to my chest I must have looked like someone who expected to be picked up for shoplifting.

A woman could get tangled in the far-reaching nets of maternal guilt for decades—and few women of my generation escaped the insinuating reach of the famous bonding theory launched in 1972, when pediatricians John Kennell and Marshall Klaus published "Maternal Attachment: Importance of the First Postpartum Days." I have to suppose now that the bonding metaphor that so dominated thinking of psychologists back then was coined when, after witnessing the intense physical relationship between new mothers and infants, men searched their own experiences for a parallel image and came up with epoxy glue.

The maternal bond, fierce in its possession and impervious to all known solvents, was alleged to happen instantly, almost chemically, within the first few minutes after the elements of A made contact with the stuff of B. If this powerful adhesive was timed and mixed properly, the mysterious properties of B caused A, the progenitor, to secrete infinite quantities of milk, patience, forgiveness, and compassion. A woman's impulse for lifelong sacrifice was thought to be born in that moment. Once set, this psychological bond was supposed to endure decades of assault—the sleep-deprived years of infancy, the notoriously terrible twos, the mother-loathing teens—without seriously compromising a mother's capacity for "unconditional love."

The grim results of faulty bonding had received wide attention when a growing body of evidence from animal studies suggested that mothers separated from offspring immediately after birth never successfully recovered their nurturing skills. Mother goats were especially lackluster in their maternal duties, butting away hungry kids who'd been taken away and returned only for dinner. In a study to determine whether similar behavior might occur in humans, twenty-eight single mothers were rated for their bonding and mothering habits on a three-point system from good to bad.

The three-point mothers had sturdily bonded in the maternity ward and earned high points by rarely leaving their babies at all during the first month and by fretting whenever they were apart over the next five years. The bond-deficient mothers were capable of leaving their babies for hours at a time, without so much as a phone call home. Since the study subjects were all single mothers, they could be forgiven for going to work, given their natural impulse to eat and feed their young. But those who had no remorse about leaving their children with baby-sitters did not rate well with the pediatricians.

These working mothers seemed to love their children somewhat conditionally, the way a father would, relying on help from other people and spending a portion of their days on other pursuits. If the pediatricians had thought to measure mothers' behavior against the norm for most fathers, these working moms would have all achieved above average scores. But there weren't even any animal studies of fathers back then, let alone human ones. So these remorseless mothers were classified as the most deeply disturbed and earned a zero rating.

Once launched, the bonding theory held powerful sway over the public imagination. As the distinguished pediatrician T. Berry Brazelton explained to Bill Moyers as recently as 1988, "the child gets a sense of being important" in the critical first years of life, or doesn't get it at all. "These kids that never get it . . . they'll make everybody angry. They'll become delinquents later and eventually they'll become terrorists."

"And you think that goes back . . . to this bonding period?" Moyers asked gravely.

"Yes," Dr. Brazelton answered solemnly.

For those so inclined, it was not a great leap from these scientific findings to decide that a guiltless working mother bore an alarming similarity to a mother goat.

IT'S HARD to believe, but the bonding theory actually represented more freedom for mothers. It "helped loosen up some of the maniacally tight restrictions on mother–infant contact in hospitals," *Newsweek* journalist Laura Shapiro noted, but added that it soon became "a weapon . . . a theory that quickly turned into a demand." At first, successful bonding was thought to take an hour, then a few days and finally, upon further study, a whole year. In the end, it was decided that a perfectly natural mother could ensure a sturdy bond and nonviolent offspring only if she stayed home—stone grinding her own wheat, as it were—throughout the critical "first five years." Imagine: Five years, without leave or furlough.

After the celebratory attention of "having a baby" subsides, the next five years of often terrifying isolation can destroy a woman's soul. Was the high incidence of postpartum depression among the bright young mothers I knew in 1974 a temporary hormonal imbalance, or did their blues come from the constricted social choices for mothers? During those first five years, I thought a lot about pioneer women on Midwestern farms. Since they had to help with the harvest (without John Deere combines), cook huge buffets for thrashing days (without microwave ovens), milk the cows at dawn/churn the butter at noon/dip the candles in the evening, when did they manage to bond? With new babies born in rapid succession, under the community supervision of sisters and aunts and older siblings, were those early working mothers responsible for producing the terrorists of the wild Wild West? Or was all this bonding and fretting and remorse demanded of three-point moms a kind of psychological terrorism of mothers?

Joan, who had five kids in the '60s before she became a recovering Catholic ("We used the rhythm method for the last three"), spent ten years working at home before returning to her job at

Bishop Luers High School. She said that whenever she read stories in the paper detailing the psychological ordeals of prisoners of war—which was so much in the news as the Vietnam veterans returned home—she wept uncontrollably. Their haunting descriptions of loneliness, aphasia, forgetfulness, minds running continuously over the same track, going a little nuts, sometimes fearing complete insanity—all these symptoms had been her own.

IT'S AN old trick now, God knows, but it works every time: At the very moment women start to expand their place in the world, scientific studies deliver compelling reasons for them to stay home. We all know what happened to Rosie the Riveter—all those inspiring posters of her confident grit, with her no-nonsense red bandanna and rolled-up blue sleeves exposing a nicely flexed bicep, disappeared immediately after V-Day. When jobs were needed by the homecoming boys and babies were needed to replace the "collateral damage" of war, Rosie the Riveter no longer provided a useful role model for the culture. Images of Tract Home Mom began flooding the public imagination shortly after the war. Outfitted in a flared skirt under a ruffled apron, she appeared in television sitcoms and ads, as the logo on angel food cake mixes and PTA bulletins, looking pleased as punch next to her foolproof meat loaf in magazine photographs. After two hundred years of American working moms, from the pioneer women right up to Rosie the Riveter, the "traditional mother" sprang up practically overnight. Not coincidentally, this new tradition emerged in the same decade that the field of child psychiatry was born.

The beauty of the bonding theory was that it not only persuaded women to remain home for long stretches of time or face a firing squad of guilt, but it also provided employers with a rationale for paying them less when they did return to work. Because motherhood was a matter of pure instinct, it was no more necessary to acknowledge than it was to thank someone for eating or peeing. At the Catholic high school where Joan and I taught, for example, veterans were awarded one year of teaching experience for every year of service, but women who spent a decade raising small children received exactly zero credit for teaching experience. A mother became Zero Mom whatever she did: Go to work early, and pediatricians flunk you as a worthless mom; go to work later, and employers think you've been wasting your time.

The salary policy was a bald statement of social values; perhaps it was a prescient sign that war experience would one day be more valuable than teaching experience in future high schools. No one noticed the absurdity, however, until Joan, whose growing feminism was becoming a hair shirt to the Franciscan friars running our school, pointed it out at a faculty meeting. Once she did, proposing that mothers should qualify for combat pay, it was she the administration thought absurd.

This attitude was not unusual in 1974.

I WAS relieved of my "good mother" status early on by returning to my teaching job when Ryan was still a babe, but I was bound to lose the title anyway. I already knew it was a transitory honor. Like Miss America's crown, I knew it could be taken away if a buried piece of history came under unfavorable scrutiny later on. It happened to my own mother after almost twenty years of exemplary service, during a traumatic clash with the authorities at the Illinois State Psychiatric Institute (ISPI) in Chicago. It was during her trial as a "schizophrenogenic mother" in the late '6os that I lost my innocence about the wisdom of following expert opinions when they conflicted with your own.

My mother had read about a research experiment being conducted at ISPI by two doctors from the University of Chicago, who were on the brink of some important discoveries about the overproduction of certain muscle enzymes during severe episodes of schizophrenia and manic depression. When Frank—her firstborn, most sensitive, most intelligent child—manifested his first severe symptoms, my mother enrolled our family in the research program in the desperate hope that there would be a cure in time to help him. But because psychotropic drugs were still in test stages—and because doctors have a hard time remaining passive during emergencies—we spent the interim months relying on old theories and old treatments, and searched for the cause of my brother's madness through psychotherapy. It gave us all something to do.

Before I ever read about the one hundred-some possible problems the *Psychological Abstracts* blamed on mothers, I was part of a zealous search for them on the locked ward of a Chicago hospital. Every week on Thursday nights, two therapists took my family on a safari through my mother's past, searching for the roots of my brother's illness. I remember in particular the evening my mother was grilled relentlessly about "overmothering" or "dominance" or "aggression" or "neglect." She answered the questions honestly, willing to investigate all possible causes in her search for a cure— even if the fault were hers. It was a luckless search, however, and the therapists seemed ready to move on to more promising candidates when a question was raised about "rejection."

My mother remembered a night in 1949, when my brother was three, which still caused her some regrets. That afternoon, she had seen the pediatrician, who'd applied bindings around my brother's head to flatten his ears a bit. Frank's tiny ears stuck out at what my mother thought was an adorable angle, but the doctor convinced her that they wouldn't be so adorable when he was a young man. They would mar his attractiveness, possibly threaten his sex life.

That afternoon, as the bindings were applied, I imagine the pediatrician caught my mother wincing. I'd seen that wince a hundred times—when my hand got stuck in the wringer of the washing machine or when one of my brothers had his head stitched in the emergency room. She usually followed the wince with a hug of sympathy, a pat of comfort—her usual formula for pain. The pediatrician, an authoritative man, disapproved of her soft-touch approach. He warned her of the dangers of coddling, especially of coddling boy babies. There were plenty of stories back then about how many young men's lives were wrecked by homosexuality because their mothers kissed them too much. The pediatrician seemed to believe that between my brother's ears and his mother, he had only a very narrow chance of living a normal life.

My mother reported being awake that whole night, listening to cries from the nursery, wrestling with her urge to scoop the baby up and comfort him. It took tremendous discipline, she said, but she accepted the punishment of the doctor's orders and resisted. She told the therapists that she could still hear those cries, twenty years later. Once more, she winced.

Detecting the fresh scent of guilt, the therapists probed deeper. Maybe she did indeed think my brother was homely, they suggested; maybe she really was unconsciously rejecting him. My mother considered this possibility for a moment, and then shook her head. No, she said simply, without further explanation. She looked across the room at my brother. Even ravaged by illness, even with something untameable coursing through him, he was clearly, electrically, a beautiful young man. My mother thought anybody could see that.

The therapists brought up one ulterior motive and then another, until finally they asked the question I'll never forget: "Why, then, did you follow the pediatrician's orders—why didn't you trust your own judgment?" The enlightened psychiatrists at the University of Chicago regarded my mother's postwar pediatrician as an ignorant soothsayer. Studies now prove, they said with authority, that too little nurturing does far more damage than too much. They supplied my mother with their facts, two decades after she needed them.

I was not quite twenty when I attended my mother's hearings, as the therapy sessions seemed to be. My knowledge of psychology was limited to college textbooks, and my late adolescence made me distinctly unsympathetic toward my parents. As the middle child in my devoutly Irish Catholic family, I was not raised to question authority. Even so, I knew the therapists were wrong. Even being predisposed to be critical of my mother—we had just recently emerged from the long, dark tunnel of mother/daughter conflict, and there were still a few touchy places between us—even with those dark spots clouding my vision, I knew my brother's madness wasn't her fault.

DURING FRANK'S lucid periods, my philosopher brother used to say he liked to think in dialectical fashion that all things are true, but only partly true—more true than what came before, less true than what will come later. By the time of my mother's psychiatric trial, scientific theories about "schizophrenogenic mothers" had replaced religious beliefs in demonic possession and witchcraft. Although such theories look preposterous from the vantage of today's more enlightened understanding of mental illness, they weren't laughable to the women whose lives they affected. Without apology to the thousands of women maimed by the label "schizophrenogenic mother," it was finally filed away in the dustbins of disreputable theories. ("I suppose we were lucky you weren't burned at the stake," I told my mother later. "In Salem, you'd have been cooked.") Although scientists and theologians have argued bitterly since the Reformation about which profession had the power to cure human dysfunction, both fields agreed on this much: The cause somehow lay with women.

Instead of receiving the compassion she so sorely needed during the long years of my brother's illness, my mother was probed, chastised, and ultimately blamed. As I learned that evening at ISPI, mothers should approach authorities with extreme caution. That night, an unconscious idea began gathering weight in my mind and, through the years, has developed into this rule for myself: "Never accept an expert's opinion if it violates your own because the experts can change their minds. Obedience to your own truth is the only safe ground to stand on, for only your own explanations will be defensible in court someday." Ironically, it was my law-abiding mother who prompted my first interest in becoming an outlaw.

There was no way to know which complexes my sons would develop—there were at least one hundred of them to worry about. And there was no way to know what books they might have to write someday to revenge themselves. There would be grievances, of that I was sure. But my mother's "trial" convinced me that when trouble comes, no mother should have to plead guilty alone. The pediatricians, psychologists, therapists, goat herders, fathers, and peer groups should all be called to the bench as well—not as witnesses but as co-defendants. It cost my own mother dearly for me to learn this truth. I reminded myself often over the next two decades: Be all you can be for your sons, but remember you aren't all there is. A mother is but one stamp on a life . . . very likely the one that hopes for that life, and loves it, the most.

2

"Just a Housewife"

The odds were never even in the contests between the credentialed professionals and the mothers like Kay, my own mother, who thought of themselves as "just housewives." The low self-esteem that handicaps so many mothers in their negotiations with the fathers and lawyers and politicians of the culture—for child support, health care, good schools—is most often blamed by the media on the women's movement. By now, legions of tireless essayists and op-ed columnists have dressed feminists down for making such a fuss about entering the professions and earning equal pay that everyone's attention has been distracted from the important contributions of mothers working at home. This judgment presumes, of course, that prior to the resurgence of feminism in the '70s, housewives and mothers enjoyed wide recognition and honor. This was not exactly the case.

Before feminists made it necessary for reporters to go into the heartlands and find Phyllis Schlafly to represent "the other side," the word "housewife" almost never made it into the daily news. (Quoting "both sides" has become such a routine substitute for objectivity in my profession that, if Schlafly didn't exist, the media would have had to invent her.) Except for Mother's Day once a year, when the job was romanticized beyond recognition, the women who produced the clean shirts and hot meals and good table manners in America every day did not much occupy the thoughts of newspaper editors. It was exceedingly difficult for housewives to get anyone's attention, in fact, doing the work all women were presumed born to do.

Every now and then, there would be a headline about the one who colossally screwed up—the wife of the Toledo minister, say, who in her haste to exit a motel parking lot was caught when she collided with a station wagon of conventioning Shriners on their way in. Or one who broke down—the attorney general's wife, who disappeared into a private sanatorium after calling a *Washington Post* reporter in the middle of the night, crying and incoherent. Or there would be an occasional, haunting story about the one who gave up—an anonymous mother in a quiet San Diego suburb, a lovely woman, according to neighbors, "never made any trouble"— who killed herself and her three small children on a rainy Wednesday afternoon. Long before feminists were accused of ignoring them, housewives, to make the news, had to be either missing or dead.

IN THE course of their day-to-day dealings back then, it was hard for most men to remember women and children existed at all. In the separate spheres of my parents' generation, fathers spent most of their time away from the home while mothers were assigned exclusively to its interior. Husbands and wives could get a vicarious sense of the other's world if they were good storytellers every night, at supper or in bed. But if they were too exhausted or frazzled for talk at the end of the day, their comprehension of each other's world was limited to the vagaries of rumor and myth.

The strict traditions that separated breadwinners from housewives were shaped by a generation yearning for symmetry, right angles, predictability. The impulse for order in the postwar years, appeared in every institution from commerce to the arts: By the early fifties, thirty-two million Protestants and Christians had organized into the National Council of the Churches of Christ; Senator Joseph McCarthy was vigorously weeding America of communists and sympathizers; and Esther Williams was thrilling audiences with the controlled synchronicity of water ballet.

Employers arranged work forces in unvarying nine-to-five blocks, and the early birds were rewarded with most of the worms. Developers and city planners met this hunger for order with suburban tract homes, which songwriter Malvina Reynolds later memorialized as "little boxes/on a hillside/little boxes/made of ticky-tacky"—all the same, all in neat rows. The family unit, the foundation on which all other institutions must invariably rest, had to be compatible with this boxed arrangement of civilization. Although strict social enforcement of a uniform breadwinner/housewife family unit guaranteed enough warm bodies to fill corporate time slots and suburban tract homes, it allowed little room for personal preferences or needs.

In my own family, small daily pleasures and individual talents were sacrificed in the crush of conformity: Except for Sundays when my father, whose wit and energy were irrepressible in the morning, marched his large brood to the kitchen table and persuaded even the nonbreakfast eaters among us to sample his waffles and sausages, we knew him mostly as the kind but subdued man who appeared at the end of the day, energy spent, camped out silently behind the pages of the *Chicago Daily News*. And except for those rare nights when we were not to disturb our mother at her typewriter, composing a quarterly den mother report for the church bulletin, her exuberant prose and infallible grammar found no expression outside the margins of our term papers.

If some of their affections and ambitions were thwarted, my parents were nevertheless among the luckiest citizens in the social dictatorship of the '50s. They were equipped with the essential dispositions to survive a long reign: They were deeply in love, respected each other, told good stories, worked hard, remained faithful to their vows, laughed a lot, and were completely nuts about their five kids. Being Irish Catholics, groomed in guilt, they thought it was almost a sin how happy and proud they were of their family—they regularly spared the praise in order not to spoil the child. But if they had had a genuine choice about whether to marry, have lots of kids, report for work every day, go to church, and serve their country, my mother and father might very well have chosen exactly the life they lived.

My parents faithfully followed the script issued to middle-class families after the war—its themes resonated with their own values—and genuinely believed that was the case all over America. For my family, "The Loretta Young Show" and "Father Knows Best" represented real life. A critic in the *New York Times Book Review* once accused me of "pulling punches" in a memoir about my family because, despite all the pain and suffering it frankly described, she could find no real villains in the story. She suspected a cover-up. Many New Yorkers I know can't believe there was ever any genuine innocence or goodness in traditional Midwestern families, along with our colossal naivete and ignorance. There was.

THE INTERIOR world my mother occupied back then was safe and cozy, and provided plenty of contact with other women. Kay became an active parishioner of Immaculate Conception Church and elementary school, an energetic volunteer with the Boy Scouts and Girl Scouts of America, as well as a devoted monthly attendee of Couples' Study Club. ("C'mon, Jer, put your tie back on—we're late and we promised to pick up Father Conleth at the monastery.") Each home and neighborhood we moved into was roomier than the last as the family expanded and my father, a self-educated banker, moved up from teller to officer at Pioneer Trust and Savings, the largest bank outside Chicago's Loop. My mother passed the yardage requirements and was invited to join the Norwood Park Garden Club, a socially striving group modeled on more established clubs in Evanston and Winnetka. Before dropping out a few seasons later, she received an honorable mention one summer in the peony competition.

My mother was also in weekly communication with my four aunts throughout the year in order to plan the huge buffets and backyard barbecues celebrating all the baptisms, birthdays, first communions, musical recitals, confirmations, graduations, bridal showers, weddings, and army homecomings among their twenty-three nieces and nephews. Many articles of used clothing passed through their tristate distributorship, with an efficiency that challenged Montgomery Ward's catalog division. Grandma Manney, when her senility made it impossible to live on her own, was gently rotated from home to home. Kids were exchanged for overnights and vacations. Recipes were traded. Money was lent.

In each of my mother's social networks, the organizing principle was family or children—except in one. A few afternoons each year, when it was her turn to hostess, I would come home from school to an altered environment in the living room. Card tables and chairs would be set up where the television console and octagonal coffee table used to be, and all the plastic slipcovers were stripped from the couch and chairs. The bare upholstery, seldom exposed, looked as pale and vulnerable as the tender new skin under a scab. On the dining room table, trays of Betty Crocker date bars on paper doilies surrounded a crystal punch bowl, filled with what looked like red Kool-Aid but was not—despite the melting scoop of orange sherbet floating in the center—for the consumption of children. Next to the spiked punch, a mound of chicken salad garnished with toasted almonds and green grapes sat weightily on a china platter, a sure sign that the spread was "not for family." Although Kay kept trying inventive new recipes, Jerry, a strictly meat-and-potatoes man, did not approve of fruit or nuts showing up anywhere but in dessert. In the half hour before the doorbell rang, my mother would dash around the kitchen in hair curlers and her famous chartreuse toreador pants, hurrying through last-minute details. After making sure no one had dumped any school bags or athletic socks on the couch, she would then disappear into her bedroom.

My mother spent little time in front of the mirror and actively discouraged the rest of us from "preening over yourself." And since her pedestrian rules of the road required her to avert her gaze from passersby on downtown sidewalks, she rarely saw the admiring glances her auburn hair and blue eyes, classic cheekbones and muscled calves attracted from strangers. But she did enjoy it when friends said she looked so much like Katharine Hepburn, "you could be her sister." (It's only a hunch, but I suspect my mother may have counted her pleasure in this frequent compliment among her sins of pride in the confessional. She was an ardent Hepburn fan.) The Kate persona emerged mostly on Saturday nights. When it appeared in the middle of the week, it usually meant Ladies' Bridge Club would be arriving momentarily.

I loved to hang around the fringes of Ladies' Bridge. The eight members were smart and competitive in their game, teasing and affectionate with each other. Great wits, to a woman. My brothers and I could hear them laughing even from the basement where, after saying hello and politely answering any questions, we were to busy ourselves with Ping-Pong or Scrabble until the Ladies departed. They always left faint fumes of smoke and liquor behind, nonexistent aromas in our house except when company came. After the party I helped empty ashtrays and fold card table chairs, and I could sometimes coax my mother into telling me what had been so screamingly funny. But sometimes not. Those times she would just remember something and smile to herself, shake her head, say only "that Ra*m*ona . . ." She often lost interest in feeding the family after Ladies' Bridge. She'd fry my father a hamburger, slap some leftover chicken salad onto a plate with a date bar for the rest of us, call it dinner.

THE "LORETTA Young Show," of course, had some rocky scenes off camera. There were periodic frictions in our close-circuited, passionately opinioned, seven-member household—some of which were greatly relieved when my father installed a second bathroom in the basement. A long series of emotional disturbances erupted in my mother's unified field when her children moved, en masse, into adolescence. I remember heated arguments in the early '60s, when my attire for dates slipped alarmingly below the modesty standards I was pledged to uphold as an SDS model. (Long before the acronym became synonymous with radical activists on college campuses, Catholic girls in Students for a Decent Society put on fashion shows downtown once a year, advancing virtue among

Chicagoans by demonstrating how beautiful knee-length hems and high-collared necklines could be.) During the same period, Kay and my younger brother went through some tough scrimmages after he joined a neighborhood softball team called the Moon Men, whose standard equipment at games included a twenty-gallon beer keg. (I'm not sure my mother understood what the Moon meant, nor do I think she was familiar with "pressed ham." She did know, however, that these boys were into "some kind of monkey business.") And there was a deeply troubling announcement at dinner one evening, when another brother declared he was not only leaving the seminary, but he wasn't going to Sunday Mass anymore.

Serious though these infractions and disappointments were, they were not unheard of within the deep interior my mother then occupied. Help was readily available: Father Conleth, a warm and gentle man whose deep eyes suggested he knew something of soul trouble, would talk with the son who'd lost his vocation; a garden club friend would produce the name of a military boarding school for the Moon Man, the very mention of which prompted a latent desire to do homework; and the problem of cleavage and knees would be tackled by the worldly members of Ladies' Bridge, who decided in their laughing, irreverent, smoky voices that if miniskirts were a sign of moral slippage, they were all in trouble. My mother would eventually regain her lost equilibrium.

My mother's social plenum was, from all evidence so far, dependable and complete. Although she and her friends were all white, married, Catholic, heterosexual, monogamous—as far as they knew—their curiosity about groups outside their daily circles was roughly equivalent to a newspaper editor's interest in housewives. The Kinsey Report and the Cicero race riots produced vague questions at Ladies Bridge about sexuality and justice, but the impact of these events in Norwood Park was ultimately no greater than a stray softball landing in the prize-winning peony bushes.

IN THE apartheid world of Mayor Daley's Chicago, I was nearly ten years old before I ever saw a black person in our middle-class north-western neighborhood. It alarmed me because, although the ebony woman waiting for the Higgins Avenue bus had smiled at me when I darted a fearful glance at her, I knew from discussions during the sale of my grandmother's house that this woman, by her very presence in my neighborhood, could make "the roof cave in on the housing market." At age ten, I did not know exactly where this housing market was—in which mall, Golf Mill or Oak Park—or why its roof caving in mattered so much since we already had a nice house, and so did everybody we knew. I only knew that this cave-in business was bad. My friend Casey, who lived in Morgan Park next door to my grandmother, was not allowed to play with me after my parents sold Manney's house to a black family. "They seemed like lovely people—and they have to live somewhere," I told Casey, quoting the family line.

"Then why not in Norwood Park?" Casey replied, quoting hers. After my sighting on Higgins Avenue, I came panting home to report the news: They're here. Many reassurances were immediately forthcoming. One woman alone could not make the roof cave in—it took a lot of people for that. Besides, she probably didn't live in the neighborhood; she probably worked for someone who lived here. Or "she might have just been lost." At any rate, I was always to be polite when I saw "a colored person" and not "show your prejudice."

"Nigger" was the operative word among most second-generation Irish immigrants in Chicago, but my parents were trying to inch our language toward a closer affinity with "those people." They forbid us "to use it or even to think it." Most of my lessons on race were a confetti of mixed messages, from outright prejudice to budding consciousness.

My conversation with my mother about the woman on Higgins Avenue made an enormous impression on me because, while my extended family was struggling between clan loyalties and social justice that year, I was memorizing the section in the Baltimore Catechism that described the three conditions necessary before bad behavior tipped over into actual sin. A mortal sin involved a strong temptation (you wanted to take something or kiss someone); a grievous matter (the thing belonged to someone else or the person you wanted to kiss hadn't promised to marry you yet); and "full consent of the will" (you recognize all the reasons why you can't do what you want and do it anyway). Given the spring-loaded tensions in Chicago during the '50s and '60s, diocesan pastors remained largely mute on how the lessons in the Baltimore Catechism applied to racism. Sexism wasn't even on the distant horizon. But the Church did offer this general rule for human behavior: Love other people as you would love God and yourself. One came under the jurisdiction of this law immediately upon recognition of "other people"—a category that, as defined by most Irish and Polish and Italian priests across the city, did not include either women or "niggers." Whenever you had to deal with these invisible people, you were okay just loving God and yourself.

The uneasiness I felt that summer, after we'd sold Manney's house and changed our language, was an unconscious discomfort over my family edging into moral greyness. With two of the three requirements met, the bases were loaded, as it were: We had a strong temptation to keep a sturdy roof over our heads in a volatile housing market, so condition number one was solidly present. We had adopted a language that forced recognition of "other people"— however we qualified them as "colored people" or "those people" or "lovely people"—and thus automatically came under the single most important law governing human behavior. So grievous matters were sliding rapidly into consciousness. Mortal sin was perilously close if the last condition, full consent of the will, was met. If we looked carefully around and comprehended the whole of our reality, it would be impossible to continue certain habits and traditions and still remain innocent of their devastating consequences. The choices we faced that summer were these: Stick with the going social program and relieve any guilt in the confessional; stick with individual conscience and pray that "doing unto others" would catch on in Norwood Park; or—avoiding the question of consent altogether—don't look around.

Catholics were routinely advised that when we felt our innocence shaky we should avoid "occasions of sin"—environments where gambling or sex or loan-sharking were common. But racism was rampant in Chicago the summer of my tenth year. A racist clergy and police department and media made it increasingly difficult to remain unconscious of Daley's apartheid policies, as well as the benefits of continuing collaboration. There was no escape from the third condition, full consent of the will, unless one kept one's blinders securely on at all times. That was what my mother and I generally did, especially whenever we ventured outside the protected interior.

It was hardest not to notice black women during our annual mother/daughter shopping excursions downtown, when I exchanged cash and parcels with them at department store counters. I was firmly instructed on those occasions "not to stare, not to touch." The same rules applied to handicapped people, Skid Row bums, and the scary, vacant-eyed men who wandered through the Loop, shouting insensible slogans with loud urgency to no one in particular. What did "Fuck you!" mean? Were they speaking to me? "It doesn't mean anything. Pay no attention." Walking along State Street in our knee-length, flower-printed, mother/daughter dresses and white gloves, palms grimy from the El ride, we kept our eyes trained straight ahead and did not break stride between Marshall Field's and Carson Pierre Scott's. For many years, my mother and I avoided occasions of sin through this tunnel vision.

Another reality lurked just below the seamless, uncracked surface of my mother's life, but the earth did not begin moving under her feet until Frank reached eighth grade, when he developed a case of scruples—a too literal interpretation of religious beliefs. By the time an administrator at the University of Illinois called eight years later to report that Frank had been placed in a psychiatric hospital after a series of "bizarre incidents" on campus, such calls had become depressingly familiar. Over the next decade and a half, the initial prognosis of a temporary "nervous breakdown" evolved into a prolonged nightmare of unremitting psychosis, shock treatments, public disgrace, and private grief.

As my brother's severe manic depression spun him through the revolving doors of state hospitals, seedy downtown neighborhoods, psychiatric institutions, unemployment offices, and locked isolation wards, it spun my mother with him. Kay, whose formal education was in a convent boarding school, was suddenly thrust from her cloistered world into a secular reality where male psychologists talked openly about breasts and penises, demanded detailed accounts of her weaning habits and potty training, and found her deep Catholic faith either quaint or pathological. The respect and authority my mother had established among family and friends were not transferable to the professional world.

When she took up too much time with her long list of questions, she was often shown the door before she'd finished. When she rejected an established psychological theory about what had gone wrong and offered her own insights into her son's childhood, she had no credentials to back up her twenty-year education in the private sector. When she disagreed with a drug therapy or a hospital transfer and the decision went before a judge, she learned that an "overprotective mother" stood no chance against expert medical opinion. When a public defender who'd spoken to Frank on the phone for fifteen minutes decided he sounded a bit eccentric but not at all "dangerous to himself or others," she knew the hospital administrator would release him to the streets rather than risk a costly court case, despite her own compelling evidence that a young man who can't resist wrapping his arms around pimps and hustlers on Rush Street, hollering "I love you! Come follow Me!" was indeed dangerous to himself, if not others.

Perceived as "just a housewife," she steeled herself for myriad negotiations with police officers, county judges, court reporters, public defenders, medical librarians, doctors and specialists, hospital chaplains, burned-out social workers, and testy nurses. A flowered stranger in a strange land, she kept losing track of the narrative line as her script began to unravel. The life story she had always imagined as pure Capra turned out to have strong Arthur Miller themes. The cast on this larger set wasn't all white. The men who asked her about her breasts weren't all married. The patients whose stories she heard on the wards weren't all heterosexual. The plot no longer followed any recognizable order.

Although some of the officials she met with managed to be polite, few looked her directly in the eye and understood who she was—a competent, hard-working, intelligent woman. Treated as if she didn't belong in their world, as if she were a simple domestic "just lost" in a psychological jungle, she felt stung by the ubiquitous contempt for her. Becoming aware that the wider reality she had entered was a universe apart from her own, she found herself speechless before the great divide, stupefied by their professional belief in the myths about bonding, nature, instinct.

How can one explain all the time and thought that goes into raising a child, all the opportunities for mistakes, all the chances to recover and try again? How does one break the news that nothing permanent can be formed in an instant—children are not weaned, potty trained, taught manners, introduced to civilization in one or two tries—as everyone seemed to imagine. The police officers who brought Frank home after a public disturbance, instead of taking him to the hospital where they could get hung up for hours of legal paperwork at the admitting desk, found her maternal instincts wanting when she refused to take him in and insisted they do their job. The professionals who had so much trouble managing Frank's behavior—despite their vast stores of tranquilizers, straightjackets, handcuffs, and their twenty-four hour support staffs—all seemed to think a mother should be able to handle the madness alone at home, if only she'd try harder to apply her magical maternal instincts. With almost no regard for the great distance between unconditional love and "neglect," the young police officers assigned my mother to the same psychological category where they held the mother of the Boston Strangler.

A woman in this situation may start to understand why a housewife would want to enter the professions in order to change her footing in these rigged negotiations. It would not be just for the equal pay—although that would be important—but for the chance to add her own critical two cents to laws and policies that directly affected women and children. She may begin to understand, too, why it would take hundreds of housewives inside the professions, perhaps a whole movement, before anything changed significantly. One woman cannot make a roof collapse.

AS THE script she had been given made less and less sense, my mother and I spent long hours at the kitchen table, sorting through all the provocative facts she brought home from her travels between spheres. On those nights when we were still going strong after midnight, my father would appear in the doorway, point to the clock, give me a scolding look: "You've got *school* tomorrow, young lady." My mother would straighten her back, signaling the shift from confidante back to mother, and agree with the boss. "He's right . . . you should be getting to bed." I would remind them both that I was now a high school senior, a fact I thought should firmly settle any questions about Who Knows Best. Jerry would disappear—he had banking tomorrow—and I could usually persuade Kay to resume her story. I'm sure now that the insights and empathy of an adolescent therapist must have been grossly inadequate to my mother's needs. But in terms of availability, I was it.

Where else could she to go with the shocking news and alarming events she now confronted almost daily? Neither the Garden Club, nor my emphatic aunts, nor even the savvy members of Ladies' Bridge were prepared to deal with a problem this bizarre. Outside of her private prayers, my mother had only one dependable source of help: the middle-aged women who worked the floors of the men's psychiatric wards.

The professionals who most clearly understood her hands-on experience and eventually taught her how to love her son in his altered condition were the uniformed matrons at Dunning State Hospital, the first of Frank's many public institutions. These compassionate women provided the most human moments in my mother's psychiatric nightmare. They couldn't cure Frank—nobody could—but they restored small dignities in an otherwise humiliating environment. My mother was grateful. She noticed how they called him by name from the day he arrived, and were soon using all of his aliases to get his attention as well—including Jesus Christ.

"You should hear how they talk to these patients," she said one night, openly admiring their fearlessness. "They even tease and joke with them." Working among the modern-day lepers of Chicago, living in virtual poverty on the wages the state paid them, "these women are just *saints*," my mother concluded. She described women braver than herself, and I could tell she wanted to get up to their speed. This new field of saints who so inspired my mother and revived her faith, she felt obliged to add, "are all colored women."

MY MOTHER went on most of her excursions alone, until I finally convinced her I was mature enough to handle any frightening scenes I would encounter on the wards. This self-delusion might have qualified me for Dunning myself. I remember my terror during my first visit there, when my mother disappeared down the hall and a small group of agitated men surrounded me in the TV lounge, hands flapping in the air, talking loudly in chants, "do-do-do you have any cigarettes/do-do-do youhaveanycigarettes/matches/gum/do-do-do—" I started shrieking my own hysterical chant, "Go away! Go-away-goaway-goaway!" Which only got them more excited, as if I'd started singing their song. An enormous woman in starched grey cotton walking down the hallway saw my distress and came to my rescue. She calmed the men down and settled them into a row of orange vinyl chairs, where they resumed their glazed attention to a horizontal pattern flickering across the black and white TV. With her troops situated securely, she returned to me, a frozen department store mannequin in a cranberry velveteen jumper.

"This is where they live, honey—where they gonna go?" she asked, eyeing my dainty attire for the combat zone and smiling, but not unkindly. "You don't have to be afraid of them. They just sick, girl. You just have to let them be."

Adopting a uniform of cutoff jeans and sweatshirts after that day, I became a regular visitor to the surreal landscape of my brother's new life. While my mother attended meetings with staff doctors and psychiatrists, I tried to hold up my end of many lunatic conversations with Frank, who was obsessed that year with his campaign for mayor. It was official—he'd filed candidacy papers with the Chicago Board of Elections and had already mailed his press releases. But how to reach voters from Dunning? Overhearing a loud, fragmented campaign speech outlining his platform of loaves and fishes for all, one of the matrons gave him the high sign and shouted, "Amen." She chuckled. "I tell you what, Jesus-Frank. You promise to change the water to wine there in Woodlawn, and you'll carry the whole district." Frank's manic smile lit up—Good idea! He made a note. I was amazed. She connected.

Perhaps because the aproned women working in psychiatric wards knew so much about being invisible themselves, they learned not only the names but also the tastes, temperaments, histories, and obsessions of the broken, sick men they cared for. They had to laugh to keep their own sanity but they stayed right with the hallucinating madmen, whenever possible, bending reality to meet their craziness instead of the other way around. These small accommodations eased tensions greatly. I watched them in the mess hall—appropriately named—removing the red Jell-O from one patient's tray, where bright colors caused too much internal disturbance, and putting it on another, where it could do no harm. Their complete familiarity with human brokenness and sickness gave them a kind of power over it. They moved through the wards without pity or fear.

Observing the matrons taught me what I most needed to know about loving my brother in his altered state. They understood how to look at and touch the handicapped, the Skid Row bum, the vagrants from the Loop. My mother and I had to pay attention now, for they were speaking to us. My brother had become one of "those people." Once we lost our tunnel vision, it was impossible to read all the stories in the newspaper about the mothers who got caught, broke down, who gave up, without seeing a close resemblance to our own lives. It was more than a little unnerving, especially for the woman who could have been Kate Hepburn's sister, to turn the page of the newspaper and realize she could also be the sister of the lovely woman in San Diego, the one who "never made any trouble," who broke down violently and anonymously on a rainy Wednesday afternoon.

MY MOTHER didn't break down, although she cried more in those years than she ever had before. I remember picking her up late one afternoon at Walter Reed Mental Health Center, one of the few community hospitals that was actually built with the funds Congress set aside after antiquated state facilities like Dunning were shut down. It was a sprawling one-story compound a few miles from our home, with long corridors connecting patient wards and doctors' offices. Waiting in a lounge at the mouth of one of these long tributaries, I heard a muffled outbreak of angry screams erupt in the locked ward at the other end. The hair at the back of my neck still stood up every time a patient reached the pitches of pure rage, no matter how many times I heard it. Keys clanked against the heavy iron door, and Sandra, who ran the evening shift in Ward B with the combined grace of Mother Teresa and Ma Rainey, ushered my mother out into the hall and locked the door behind them. They stood there talking a moment, in a cloud of disinfectant someone had just sprayed to mask the omnipresent odor of urine. I couldn't see my mother's face, but her normally straight back was slumped forward and her head drooped with deep exhaustion. She looked beaten.

It had been a long day of critical meetings with doctors and lawyers—it might have been one of the times Frank was suing her for freezing his savings account. It was also the winter—although it's hard to time these vague dawnings precisely—that she had begun to acknowledge it was futile to continue her search for a cure. The smart, quiet, beautiful son she had once loved extravagantly was gone forever, and it was time to accept the unkempt, often provocative, sometimes hauntingly familiar stranger who'd taken his place. Her shoulders slumped under the royal blue pattern on her crisp white blazer.

Sandra, whose arms were nearly twice the size of my mother's, grasped her sagging shoulders and began speaking softly, urgently, like a boxing manager to a cornered fighter woozy from battle. This spontaneous kindness undid my mother. She pulled a handkerchief from her purse and covered her face, her head dropping gently against Sandra's strong coffee arms. My mother seldom cried in front of anyone, and never in public.

"They don't really know 'bout these things . . . how they happen . . ." Sandra was saying to my mother's bowed head. "They think they do, but they just guessin' . . . You can't go blamin' yourself, now. You love that boy more than anybody—'cept maybe God . . . You go home, get some rest . . . You need a few days vacation from this nonsense here." Pursing her full lips into the familiar frown that marked the end of her sermons, Sandra asked, "You hearin' me?"

My mother nodded. She drew a long breath, filling her slump with some air. Then Sandra, whose tolerance for high seriousness was dependably short, slipped into jive: "And don't worry—I'll get our Jesus here back to his miracle business. I got some maps he asked for the other day in my purse—I'm gonna put him to work on the subway system tonight." My mother laughed in spite of herself. "That *San*dra . . . " she was always saying after her visits to Reed.

Sandra then patted my mother's royal blue shoulders, squaring them up for the next round, and let her go. She put her key back in the door and, with a swell of noise from inside Ward B, disappeared back into the chaos. My mother stood in the hall another moment composing herself, preparing for the transition back to "normal"—wherever that was in those unsteady years of shifting realities.

It occurred to me that afternoon, watching my mother reorient herself, that to fit this scene into her first forty-five years, she might be revising her script for the rest of her life. In her desperate search for meaning and compassion in the Windy City that Christmas, the only person in her universe who completely understood how she felt was a large black woman in the men's psychiatric ward of a state hospital. Where did a Norwood Park housewife put that saint in her plenum?

3
Becoming Outlaws

When a woman loses her innocence about the game of Let's Pretend, several barriers stand between her and any comfort friends may be able to offer: There is the initial embarrassment of giving those still living behind intact facades a tour of the ruins; there is the strong probability that they, no wiser than she a few years earlier, will think that she's done something terribly wrong; and there is the problem she dreads most—the fear that once the tears start flowing she'll never be able to stop them. My mother resolved to brave her new world with the same solo nerve as her immigrant mother had, keeping her chin up and toughing it out alone. She was incredibly disciplined in this regard.

Kay didn't leak any details of her private ordeal even to her close friend Mary, the unflappable matriarch of another outsized Irish Catholic family whom she admired greatly. They first met years ago at Parents' Club, recognizing each other by name because Mary's children and my mother's kept trading scholastic standing every year at Immaculate Conception elementary school. Their long friendship was cemented when they enlisted together as leaders of my second-grade Brownie troop. Mary's daughter Shelley was my classmate that year; she was as smart and pretty as her siblings and set a daunting pace for me with the multiplication tables. I was something of a laggard in these family academic competitions, much preferring the lively action on the playground to solitary hours of homework. I did my best to slow Shelley down. Since our older siblings had already broken achievement records and copped most of the school's top honors, my argument went, why not just play volleyball?

My mother and Mary soon discovered they had a lot in common beyond the joys and trials of raising large families. Mary also loved bridge, had a golfing husband, and like my mother—who frequently purloined her children's text books to teach herself Spanish or brush up on Latin—never had enough time to read. Mother Francesca Cabrini—the first canonized saint in the United States, who not only founded dozens of orphanages and schools around the world but so intimidated the crooked contractors she hired in Chicago that they completed Columbus Hospital under cost and four months ahead of schedule—was one of their more daunting female role models, just shy of the Virgin Mother. This rich mutual territory sustained them through the next long decade, when conversations about my brilliant oldest brother became more and more infrequent.

From my second-grade perspective, Mary was a tall, beautifully erect woman with thick, dark hair and quick, alert eyes, who presided over our weekly seven-year-old chaos with calm but towering authority. Unlike other high-rise adults who had an annoying habit of speaking down to anyone listening from a slightly lower altitude—as if children were dim-witted as well as short—Mary addressed the Brownies with the same elevated vocabulary she directed to my mother. We listened intently whenever this quiet woman spoke up. When she explained the most enduring technique for sewing on a button (". . . the trick is, you wind the thread *underneath* the button a few times to create a shank before stitching off—that little rascal will never come off again, and believe me, you don't want to spend your life sewing on buttons"), we believed. When we learned the history of American quilts (and how courageous women in the Old South sewed coded messages into certain patterns and hung them on clotheslines to signal conductors in the Underground Railroad), we sewed our entry for the Scout competition with more than mere bedding in mind. Neither a babbler nor a nag, Mary ushered our young troop painlessly through dozens of tedious merit badge activities, holding our rapt attention even on high-humidity afternoons. To this day, I cannot sew on a button without first remembering Mary's shank theory and then thinking about the Civil War seamstresses who cut up their wedding gowns to broadcast secrets through the laundry in their yards.

As a mother of seven who had heard just about every cute or wiseacre remark the Chatty Cathy crowd had to offer, Mary was no fool for the charmers and pranksters in our troop. Our best efforts were greeted with an amused half-smile that suggested she had been around our block a few times before. When we did surprise her with something out of the ordinary, we were rewarded with the purest, most genuine smile. Her laugh was a huge, affectionate hug that took in the room, and the Brownies knocked themselves out for it. "That Mary . . . ," my mother would say after their planning sessions together. "It takes time to know her—but it's worth every minute."

Mary and my mother had twelve children between them, with birthdays spanning almost twenty-five years. The youngest ones, always in tow, became adjunct members of our troop. A picture from that time shows my five-year-old brother dressed in a crepe-paper hula skirt, rehearsing his part as an understudy in one of our many theatrical productions. (Although Kevin, now a successful banker in Cleveland, appears thoroughly delighted in his hula skirt, this photo might have aroused suspicions of a twisted stage mother to the ISPI therapists, had things turned out otherwise.) Throughout the next punishing decade, Mary never broke into Kay's closet of "private family matters" because these two otherwise forthright and direct women had no vocabulary for discussing mental illness that was not drenched in a language of blame and guilt. Mary offered my mother what comfort she could in this vacuum of words with knowing glances and nods.

There were no consciousness-raising groups back then where women might gently peel back the multiple husks of guilt and shame that grow in the shadows of secrets. With no visible women's movement to expose the deep political roots of private family matters, with no evidence of other heretics who'd lost faith in the given script, women battled the madness invading their lives without allies. As the poet Muriel Rukeyser observed of those years, "If one woman told the truth about her life, the world would split open."

THE EARLY years of my own motherhood fortuitously coincided with more openly skeptical times. By the time my sons were born in 1974 and 1975, the truth had begun to leak out. If my mother's experiences had given me a vague, intuitive notion that "something's wrong here," the explosion of information from the women's movement in the early '70s provided specific details on what, how, why. The year Darren was born, I left my full-time job as dean of students at the high school and started teaching part-time at Indiana University/Purdue University's regional campus in Fort Wayne. My first Women's Studies course was called "Philosophic Theories of Feminism."

My classes often included several "displaced homemakers," a lively population of older mothers the administration had just discovered were not only not dead, but had done more reading and writing—without credentials—than most of their bright young professors. They constituted a lucrative but demanding market. Some of my male colleagues groaned when they found certain names on their lists, as if their mothers had enrolled in their classes. For one thing, these older women made flirting and posturing next to impossible, and they generally gave their professors about two weeks to say something interesting. If you couldn't move beyond that half-smile—the one that had been around the block—by the refund date, you were history. If they stayed for the semester, however, you were guaranteed some riveting stories and discussions.

Whether the topic was psychology, marriage, motherhood, economics, or religion, anyone who tried to romanticize women's position was immediately slapped upside the head with a stunning hit of reality. These older students were responsible for my first "radicalizing experiences," as we used to say. The younger students were fascinated by their stories, too, and got truthful answers without the usual obfuscations that creep in when a daughter asks her own mother, let's say: "Mom, were you a virgin when *you* got married?"

Our reading and discussions took critical aim at many famous misogynists as well as a few local politicians and chauvinist professors. Our class motto, if we'd had one, might have been: "Throw another hero on the fire." Psychologist Erich Fromm excited deep irritation in my older students with his theory that mothers were capable of "unconditional love" because of "an instinctive equipment to be found in animals as well as the human female," while fathers, rooted in "the real world" and having "little connection with the child in the first years of its life," provided the essential conditional love that brought about success in later life. They fairly smoked with indignation at being lumped together with animals, having their most difficult mental calculations mistaken for "instinct," and seeing all positive results of their work credited exclusively to fathers. What Fromm described as "the ease with which a mother can love her infant" they said wasn't easy at all, especially when fathers rarely helped with the daily grind and withheld love until their unreal expectations were met. He obviously knew nothing of the homicidal impulses a mother had to overcome in those treacherous first years, when a recalcitrant human-in-training could smear feces all over the bathroom wall and then call you in just in time to see a tennis shoe going down the toilet. No, my students thought, any woman in those circumstances whose natural instinct was "unconditional love" had to be on drugs.

The displaced homemakers were especially vehement in their objections to his prescription for a lifetime of "delayed gratification" for mothers, and reported that husbands and children did not have any instinctual equipment for gratitude, now or later. Even children who happened to think about why they were still alive could never truly appreciate a mother's sacrifice, viewing the lamb from the fire's point of view. There were certainly other compelling reasons for a mother to postpone some of her own wishes and dreams, they acknowledged, but not because there was a pot of gratification at the end of the rainbow. In their experience, as Gertrude Stein said, "There's no there there."

Instead of unconditional love, the class preferred the phrase my friend Cathryn used to describe what transpired between mothers and children: "nonreciprocal love." (The chairman of the Philosophy Department once cautioned me, after taking notes during a formal evaluation of my classes, not to rely so heavily on "quotes from your friends." Never mind that Cathryn had a Ph.D. in child psychology—he would have liked to hear a little more from John Stuart Mill. Neither Cathryn, nor my neighbor Alice, nor my friends Joan and Marti, were recognized philosophers in the department's literary canon.) Students wrote papers analyzing how use of the phrase "nonreciprocal love" still acknowledged the sacrifice involved but clued mothers in from the outset that their emotional payables, as it were, would exceed their receivables for many years. Those committed for the long haul would therefore be wise to pace themselves in the self-sacrifice department.

Since there could be no accrued debt, no obligation, no lien against the love of children—a gift that could only pass forward in time, batonlike, from one generation to the next—a mother had to balance her children's gratifications with her own every year if she wanted to avoid emotional bankruptcy in her retirement. The major problem with the martyrdom theory was the rarely acknowledged reality *after* the sacrifice: The theory worked only if a mother managed to stay dead. Everybody hated martyrs who hung around, sometimes for decades, reminding survivors of how painful it had been. When self-sacrificing mothers tried to resurrect their lives after their children left home, applied for jobs, or went back to school, the grown children of other sacrificing moms treated them as invisible nobodies. The real results of self-denial, according to those who had actually tried it, was delayed mortification.

Every myth about motherhood contained some element of truth, of course, but the language was slightly off: painless childbirth, unconditional love, delayed gratification. In truth, there were some pains, some conditions, some immediate needs to be met. Before we could think clearly, we needed more precise language. Although "maternal instinct" did not exactly describe it, I *did* sense a subtle but significant shift in my thinking after my sons were born. Being physically plural for nine months and then painfully singular again had a powerful psychological effect on me. With Ryan's birth and then Darren's—a violent division of cells not unlike an atomic chain reaction—I ceased to be a single person and became a group. After the explosive separation of birth, I became a kind of psychological plurality larger than one self—in my case, larger than one gender. Within months, I was thinking in a perpetual, lower-case editorial "we." The powerful reaction to a newborn that may have looked like "maternal bonding" to outsiders felt more like "maternal exploding" on the inside.

I began to see the world through this triple vision of my past and our present and my sons' future. Although it was more deliberate than instinctual, this habit of simultaneously thinking I/we, then/now, eventually became as unconscious and regular as a heart-beat. Ever since, it has been my hunch that when a woman startles a man with her uncanny "female intuition," she is merely tapping into this uncredentialed knowledge of what the human organism will do/has done under certain circumstances. Within nanoseconds, for example, she might see beyond the angry lawyer fuming at the dinner table, making a connection with the wounded boy who lost his truck in a sandbox wager that afternoon and then popped his teammate on the head with his plastic shovel. "I'm sure you can win your appeal," she might encourage her lawyer-husband, and then add, before he has mentioned the rest of the facts: "But you'd better rehire your secretary first thing tomorrow."

THIS "KNOWING" is not exclusively maternal, although mother-hood is certainly one route to human intuition. Many women with-out children have it. Men can get it too, although they tend to do so less often and more slowly. A few years ago Professor Erik Erik-son, the venerable psychologist who gave us the term *identity crisis* and spent his life defining seven of these crises from infancy through adulthood, elaborated on yet another one after his eightieth birthday. The final developmental tasks involved a kind of mental time travel, he said, in which a man acquires the ability to see future consequences for every action and accepts his responsibility for the next generation. The *New York Times* reported that Erikson named this final evolution of wisdom and compassion the "age of generativity," and estimated that it took most men fifty-some years to master it.

Except for the time allowed, this was precisely the same theory Professor Dorothy Dinnerstein had proposed nearly two decades earlier, when she tried to interest men in exploring their dormant paternal instincts. In *The Mermaid and the Minotaur* (1976), she described the extensive damage of separate spheres, which redlined mothers out of public life and fathers out of family life. She suggested that if men became more directly involved in the daily tasks of raising children, the lust for killing other people's children would lose most of its zing. Had she still been alive when Dr. Brazelton proposed his theory to Bill Moyers that faulty bonding was responsible for terrorism, she might have heartily agreed if he had been talking about paternal bonding. She believed, in fact, that unless men who ran businesses and governments and armies made the connection between what they did with their days and how it affected what their children would be able to do with theirs, the breakdown of civilization was more or less guaranteed. Although Professor Dinnerstein brought auditoriums of women to their feet and stirred readers from coast to coast throughout the early '70s, her work received the most prominent media attention on the obituary pages, after newspaper editors noticed she was dead.

Perhaps now that the *New York Times* has reported Erikson's "age of generativity," more men will start thinking about investing in children, however nonprofitable or nonreciprocal the relationship may be. Maybe this is the kind of news that has to come to men from another guy.

FEMINIST SCHOLARS were producing new studies and revelations at such an accelerated pace, I was lucky to stay a chapter ahead of my students. As the class discussed Betty Friedan's description of "the problem that had no name" in *The Feminine Mystique*, (1963), I was thinking incessantly of my mother. What a difference it would have made if she'd had the language, the names, the larger vision of *something's wrong here*.

AS SOON as it was published in 1976, we read *Of Woman Born* by Adrienne Rich, a poetic and passionate treatise on motherhood as a political institution. It had the same electrifying impact on mothers in my classes that Thomas Paine's *Common Sense* had on the colonists. *"Vous travailez vous pour l'armee, Madam?"*—"You are working for the army, madam?"—a Frenchwoman asked the poet, meeting her during a stroll with her three young sons. In this excruciatingly honest account of the price women paid for carrying out work orders in a culture they had no power to design, Rich questioned the wisdom of further compliance. At what cost to ourselves and our children did we follow traditions that kept us economically dependent, necessarily obedient, silent and invisible, until we were needed to cook a dinner or stop a bullet? Who did we work for? Why did we do what we do? What ends did our sacrifices serve? Could we really reduce terrorism by staying isolated at home and bonding more tightly with our children in a country where children were exposed to two hundred thousand episodes of televised violence by age eighteen and were taught in churches that women were "vessels of sin"?

OVER THE next five years, there were dozens of midwestern conferences and legislative hearings about family issues, but with two small toddlers at home I relied heavily on secondary reports. One time the kids stayed with their grandparents while I attended a weekend conference. (They loved visiting their grandmother's house, where a treasure trove of hula skirts and wigs awaited them in her basement.) Another time, I drove a van with six Fort Wayne friends to Chicago for a Women's Studies conference at Northeastern Illinois University, sans kids, and invited Kay to join us. It was only after seeing my mother in the rear-view mirror, sitting on a bench toward the back of the van, that I noticed how radically my friends departed from the norm in Norwood Park. There was a generally uncorseted feeling about the crowd, bouncing and bra-less in large cotton T-shirts with provocative slogans like "What Part of 'No' Don't You Understand?"

My friends' irreverent humor brought an expression to my mother's face that I hadn't seen for years, not since she put the punch bowl and ashtrays away after Ladies' Bridge. She laughed as much as the rest of us that weekend, inviting us in for coffee after the first long day of meetings. She was still with us after Jerry made his midnight appearance in the kitchen doorway and pointed to the clock. From the position of her eyebrows now and then, I suspected that she was wondering whether hanging out with this crowd might be an occasion of sin. Mostly, however, I remember her absorbed concentration as we sat next to each other during the last session in the auditorium the following day, listening to a panel of distinguished professors discuss Naomi Weisstein's classic essay, "Psychology Constructs the Female—Or, The Fantasy Life of the Male Psychologist." Riveted to the upholstery, she suddenly sat bolt upright, astonished to hear the same questions we had approached defensively in our bathrobes at the kitchen table years before. Our very own private family matter—and here were hundreds of women out in public with it. She turned to me, relief and rage and gratitude flashing through her eyes. Women were telling the truth; her world was splitting open. She gripped my arm and whispered incredulously: "Do you think we could get a *copy* of this?" We could. I pointed to the stacks of research material in the back of the hall, free for the taking.

MY MOTHER was off on her first European vacation when I heard that Dorothy Dinnerstein, Adrienne Rich, and Tillie Olsen would be breaking new ground at a conference called "Motherhood: Challenge and Option" at Ohio State University the next year. Several friends were going and had promised to take copious notes, but I was burning with pressing personal questions on this topic myself. It was not an auspicious time to leave home: Ryan was in the throes of the tantrums that afflict every human being when it's time to face life without pacifiers, and Darren was cutting new teeth that spring. Howard, not coincidentally, was recovering from outpatient surgery after a vasectomy. It was still unusual in 1977 for a mother to leave two babies in the care of their father for an entire weekend, unless she had an unarguable excuse—a brain aneurism, say, or a dead relative. My reasons sounded limp and self-indulgent, thanks to the old language problem. When Howard and his buddies left town to attend a weekend convention, it was called "professional development"; when a housewife left her family for a conference on motherhood, it was suspiciously regarded as "another one of those hen conventions." I went without anyone's blessing, wondering if Mr. Schlafly ever gave Phyllis any grief for not being home to make his dinner and tuck his children in bed.

I remember sitting unhappily in the campus auditorium, suppressing small waves of guilt, my eyebrows probably doing what Kay's did whenever she felt uneasy. After an unnecessarily lengthy introduction to the writer everyone in the audience already knew, Adrienne Rich stepped up to the podium. A roar of applause greeted her, and, like many writers and speakers who crested with the second wave of feminism, she smiled warmly and applauded us back. With everyone in those days distrustful of hierarchies, movement leaders were in an especially tricky position. Questioning authority was the theme of the day, and becoming an authority yourself, even an authority on feminism, was like wearing a bull's-eye on your forehead and inviting target practice from the crowd. Movement leaders generally encouraged a collective spirit, since we were all flying by the seats of our pants. The two-way applause meant that we would be speaking as peers; there would be no stepping back from the hard truths we had acknowledged so far, however much difficulty they were causing in our personal lives.

During the discussion that followed, Rich related a story I had highlighted in her book, about the summer she left the city to live with her three young sons in Vermont. It was a vacation from both her familial and work routines, and she described falling into "a delicious and sinful rhythm" with the boys, eating most meals out-doors, hand-to-mouth, staying up late to watch bats and stars and fireflies, reading stories until dawn, sleeping through breakfast, run-ning under sprinklers to cool off:

> I remember thinking: This is what living with children could be—without school hours, fixed routines, naps, the conflict of being both mother and wife with no room for being, simply, myself . . . (W)e had broken together all the rules, rules I myself thought I had to observe in the city or become a "bad mother." We were conspirators, outlaws from the institution of motherhood. I felt enormously in charge of my life.

Although I was already familiar with these words, I remember the intense shiver that ran through me when I listened to them again that afternoon in Ohio. I remembered having the same kind of delicious days with my sons when no one else was around— when the ubiquitous judgments (Were they polite/well-behaved/ smart enough?) and expectations (Should they be weaned/walk-ing/reading by now?) were absent. The difference between those stolen moments of being entirely who we were and those times we tried to pass for "normal"—being who everyone else wanted us to be—was becoming increasingly distressful to maintain. I, too, had thought of myself as a "bad mother" when I was most myself— most at ease with the physical pleasure of them, most amused by their quirky wit, most unconcerned about enforcing behavioral mandates that were not my own. The possibility that I could redefine those aberrant times as "normal"—I could be who I was without guilt—brought that same electrifying sensation my mother had in her auditorium seat the winter before. I felt the astonishing power of thought connecting with real life—it opened my collarbone, released deep sighs: Yes, *yes*. Perhaps because I had come fresh from a close encounter with "bad mother, bad wife," I instantly recognized myself as an outlaw. A deep shudder ran through my whole being.

My friends and I talked nonstop in Ohio that weekend; we talked in classrooms and in auditoriums; we talked in cars coming and going. We stayed up all night talking between twin beds in dormitories and hotel rooms. We kept talking on the phone after we came home. Whenever one of us had a "radicalizing experience," it always presented an immediate problem. How, in day-to-day terms, did one put the theory of outlawdom into practice? Becoming an outlaw did not mean living without rules, since children cannot be raised in a vacuum of moral thought. Leading an utterly examined life required constant thinking. We had to know exactly what we were doing and why. If a three-point mother faced punishing judgments when her kids proved imperfect, we knew that a deliberately unconventional mother could expect to be stoned from all directions. There was so much I needed to know about loving and raising my sons. My laggard academic soul finally woke up: forget about volleyball; I had urgent reading and thinking to do.

I had once believed that after the truth about motherhood was out, a period of energetic social change would naturally follow, but I'm much more familiar with the relativity of time now. It moves too slowly for people who want change and much too fast for the people whose job it is to resist it. Although the first stages of questioning authority had been scary but exhilarating— "strident and hysterical," in press language—the next stages of putting theory into practice were laborious and exhausting. The media heralded this less noisy period as a sign that the "postfeminist" era had arrived.

Why did it take us so long to remodel family structures in the interior? To alter her own role, a mother either had to win alliances with or be strong enough to do without the support of teachers, pediatricians, therapists, politicians, doctors, bosses, colleagues, relatives, fathers, and friends. There were toy manufacturers and television producers as well as food packagers and advertising executives to educate. These exasperating negotiations eventually made it clear that if we sought everybody's permission before making the changes we needed, we could die waiting. Wherever possible, we had to Just Do It. This approach required a nerve and conviction that it would be impossible to sustain alone. Luckily, I had not only become a familial "we" after my maternal exploding, but I also became a member of one of the oldest, if strangest, consciousness-raising groups in Indiana.

Shortly after Howard and I had moved from Chicago to Fort Wayne, Joan invited me to join a lively group of friends who'd begun meeting weekly. A good consciousness-raising (CR) group could be destroyed by a member who was too needy or whiny or defensive, and Joan didn't know me well in 1973. I was a risk—the invitation came from her intuitive hunch that I might be educable. I was then what she called a "baby feminist," just dipping my toe into the shallow end of women's rights, testing out such advanced thoughts as "I believe in equal pay for equal work, but I'm not into all the rest of that crazy stuff"—the crazy stuff being abortion rights and lesbian rights and divorce rights, ideas that a Catholic girl couldn't easily say out loud. By the end of the first year, I had joined the rest of the group congregated at the deep end, lining up for the high dive.

While Women's Studies classes educated a growing stream of displaced homemakers and energetic young recruits for community organizing, CR groups sprang up to provide the necessary on-the-job training. They formalized the coffee klatsch, as it were. The local media regarded these cells of talking heads as either completely meaningless or so threatening to the national triad of motherhood, apple pie, and the flag that decent Fort Wayne citizens had to wonder whether it was time to resurrect the House Un-American Activities Committee. Even female reporters could offer only thin support, since their objectivity was under constant suspicion.

"Save us from our 'secret pals,'" Joan said once, folding up a newspaper after reading a "balanced" interview by a reporter who said, off the record, that, although she was with us 100 percent she was obliged by journalism ethics to quote an antifeminist every time she quoted Joan. Once, setting up a television program about the Equal Rights Amendment, the producer asked her whom she could recommend to present "the other side." Nobody, she said.

"When you invited Vernon Jordan on your show, did you ask him who was good in the Klan?" Joan asked.

A female journalist in those days had to suppress any Thurgood Marshall tendencies in order to convince nervous overseers in news rooms that they could depend on an Uncle Tom numbness to the pain of her people. Although we understood Erica Jong's astute observation that "the best trained slave is the one who beats herself," our understanding did not reduce the sting when the trivialization of our issues came from a woman. Joan Didion, praised in The *Los Angeles Times* as the "quintessential essayist" of our day, offered this withering judgment of consciousness-raising activities in the early '70s: "Even the brightest movement women found themselves engaged in sullen public colloquies about the inequities of dishwashing and the intolerable humiliations of being observed by construction workers on Sixth Avenue." In exquisitely beautiful prose, Didion roundly mocked the concept that women could be oppressed by housework, or motherhood, or men, or that it mattered much if they were.

I'VE THOUGHT a lot about the nine years I spent in my CR group in Indiana. I thought about it most recently when I read about the Saudi Arabian women who were refused service at the new Burger King in Riyadh because Islamic law forbids grown women from ordering a hamburger without male accompaniment. The traditions in foreign countries are greeted with a certain incredulity here: It's impossible for my New York colleagues to imagine going along with laws prohibiting them from eating a hamburger in public—even though, under the social sanctions currently governing Manhattan, most of them do not ingest anything more caloric than a salad without dressing for lunch. Once the oddities of a given culture are normalized, it can take a good decade before a veiled mind can imagine another way of life.

The women in Riyadh probably know that if they removed their veils and boldly bit into a hamburger, roofs would cave in all around them. Relatives would be mortified, husbands would be upset, children would be ashamed. The quintessential essayists of Riyadh would wonder at the fuss—it's no big deal to wear a face mask, starve yourself. Women do it all the time. If a numb acquiescence does not finally dull the appetites, a woman yearning for more bears a life of constant hunger. Without a support group to validate her yearning and inspire her to brave the resistance, unconsciousness wins.

THE PUBLIC trivialization of women's issues, though a constant annoyance, was not something an American female would find at all unusual. What stunned me was the regular assertion that feminists were "anti-family" because we insisted on entering the professions. *Anti-family*? It was motherhood that got me into the movement in the first place. I became an activist after recognizing how excruciatingly personal the political was to me and my sons. It was the women's movement that put self-esteem back into "just a housewife," rescuing our intelligence from the junk pile of "instinct" and making it human, deliberate, powerful.

It was not on second thought that we noticed the need for child care, loving families, a place to call home—or, lacking those, at least a place to call for hot-line assistance and emergency shelter. These domestic issues were basic to our social agenda. The economic campaigns came later, when we realized that we could never be "enormously in charge" of our lives without money. Long before we attracted media attention by invading men's turf in the public sphere, we had been meeting in consciousness-raising groups, reclaiming our own territory in the interior.

These momentous changes on the home front went largely unreported because, although there was a lot of hoopla about unisex toilets, the media missed all the subtle aftershocks of our great maternal exploding, the vast ripple effect of our deep shudders. They heard we were "talking" but accepted Didion's view that talk was cheap. The libbers, as strident and hysterical as we were, had no impressive body counts or demolished cities to show for their bloodless revolution. The only thing that mattered to the press covering the "battle of the sexes" was the usual question: Which side won?

A media obsessed with sides, with winners and losers, completely missed the point. Stacking up evidence that mothers had suffered enough with the Supermom role model and were leaving the professions in droves, fathers weren't taking the paternity leaves we'd won, women were bumping their heads on glass ceilings, men weren't paying child support, the op-ed writers felt obliged to report: We're sorry, Ladies, you didn't win. The disparaging tone in these opinions implied that we were somehow wrong to have tried. There were endless analyses of how the feminist movement had collapsed because its leaders had failed to bridge the gap to the housewives of America, which struck a weird note with the leaders, since many of them *were* the housewives of America. Betty Friedan got her radical beginnings interviewing women in suburban tract homes.

As the battles were framed by the media, a case could certainly be made that we didn't "win." The culture has not yet become the peaceful and economically just society we imagined. But even if all our talking didn't entirely change the culture, it certainly changed the talkers. As Professor Mary Daly once suggested to a fellow theologian who tried to short-circuit an acrimonious debate by presenting scriptural evidence that Jesus might have been a feminist: "Fine. Wonderful. But even if he wasn't, I am."

The presumption seemed to be that because we didn't "win" women would return to life as they had known it—that is, the overnight tradition invented to suit Cold War values. Every time I read another headline announcing the women's movement was dead, I would remember again Sydney Harris's words: "Dominance makes a ruling group stupid." Or, watching a member of the Senate Judiciary Committee sweating through a press conference after the polls revealed how grossly he had miscalculated Anita Hill as no big deal, I'd remember a line from *Poltergeist* and think: "We're ba-a-ack."

Wherever the next generation takes us, as author Tillie Olsen reminded the audience at the Ohio conference, we are not to forget the history of our mothers. In *Silences,* (1978), a moving and brilliant collage of thoughts that took her nearly twenty years to assemble because she had children to raise and several wars to protest, Olsen wrote that being a survivor among so many casualties had obligations: "For myself, 'survivor' contains its other meaning; one who must bear witness for those who foundered; try to tell how and why it was that they, also worthy of life, did not survive. And pass on ways of surviving; and tell our chancy luck, our special circumstances."

It was my "chancy luck" to have an extraordinary mother who reflected intelligently on her life, who kept righting her course with new information. And it was my "special circumstance" to have my motherhood begin in a decade when women were splitting the world open with their truths, however unenthusiastically they were received. Ever since 1976, when I published my first essay on the myths of motherhood and announced my outlaw status in print, I have celebrated the anniversary of my dual passions by writing an essay for Mother's Day. I remember the one time in my life when I managed to finish an assignment before deadline, because I wanted time to discuss it with my mother before submitting it to my editor. It was the story of Kay's personal family matter, fragile in the telling, and it had to ring exactly true. I was then writing a monthly column on women's issues for *Vogue*, and it was a violation of house policy to let a subject read a story before publication. But I wanted her to know what was coming, since more than a million strangers would be in possession of her secret.

"It made me cry," she said, calling me from her retirement home in Florida. She described all the memories it brought back of the embattled years in psychiatric wards. "But if you think it would be useful to other mothers, well . . . go ahead." I couldn't guarantee the reaction of readers, I said. There were tireless scouts out there for Unnatural Moms, lots of people still deeply invested in the game of Let's Pretend. But I could guarantee her that if the truth were never told, there was no possibility her story could be useful to others. I told her that all those hours at the kitchen table with her, all those shivering epiphanies we'd had with psychiatric matrons, had been enormously helpful to me. They introduced me to truths I was grateful to know.

The month after it was published my former Brownie leader, who was not a *Vogue* subscriber, happened to have an appointment at a beauty parlor. Sitting under the hair dryer, Mary began leafing through the beat-up, curled copy, stopping short when she came across my byline. She read my mother's story and, once more, the same truths that once made me and my mother sit bolt upright now riveted Mary to the hot seat. She, too, cried when she read my mother's story. In the long letter she wrote that afternoon, she told my mother she had several friends who'd had similar trials. She wanted to share Kay's story with them, to let them know that they were not alone. "I have never done this before," Mary confessed, "but I ripped the pages out of the magazine."

The letters Mary and my mother exchanged that summer began the conversation Kay had been waiting fifteen years to have. I suppose if one tallied the letters-to-the-editor, counted up the winners and losers, and measured how much had changed as a result of those curled pages of *Vogue* that month, it would be hard to make a case that anybody "won." But if putting another piece of our oral history on record could turn my former Brownie leader into a beauty shop vandal, those pages had done their job. Like the coded quilts women used to hang in their yards for conductors of the Underground Railroad, Kay's story marked the trail for her friends. More deep shudders rippled through the interior; more outlaws slipped through the Hole in the Wall.

PART TWO

THE BOYS

Making the decision to have a child—It's momentous.
It is to decide forever to have your heart go walking
around outside your body.
—Elizabeth Stone

4

The Big McSmack

The notion that one wrong move and I might ruin my sons for life turned out, in retrospect, to be one of the most absurd fears I could have entertained. Since civilizing children takes the greater part of two decades—some twenty years of nonstop thinking, nurturing, teaching, coaxing, rewarding, forgiving, warning, punishing, sympathizing, apologizing, reminding, and repeating, not to mention deciding which to do when—I now understand that one wrong move is invariably followed by hundreds of opportunities to be wrong again. Even the simplest cognitive advancement—remembering to put the shower curtain *inside* the tub, let's say—took my sons half a year and dozens of mopping lessons to master. If there was one right moment, one right method for each developmental step, it was never obvious to me. My early angst about three-day potty training plans and other culturally imposed deadlines relaxed considerably once I began to understand that change takes time, especially for children.

I didn't exactly abandon my disciplinary duties, as the frequently arched eyebrows among more traditional relatives and friends implied. Considering the big picture, I just figured we had plenty of time. The uphill climb through Abraham Maslow's famous hierarchy of development takes an entire lifetime, but the beauty of this slow human evolution is that one never runs out of material for more "learning experiences."

After nearly twenty years, for example, my sons and I are still working on the concept of personal organization. While they'd made marginal progress on planning ahead and picking-up-after-yourself before they left home, their recidivism into primitive habits was immediate. On return visits, they made plans from phone call to phone call and crammed their days with a ceaseless round of activities: reunions with friends, impromptu soccer games, brief library stops, pickup basketball at the local gym, and marathon video nights at home with a half-dozen other raucous Eddie Murphy fans. Completely oblivious to the soda cans, research notes, and sweaty jerseys that accumulated in their frenetic wake, they were house-blind to litter habitually strewn around the quasi-anarchist dormitory environments they now occupied. Waiting until the last possible minute to collect their far-flung matter, they'd inevitably leave something essential behind. I'd wait for the long-distance calls later that night, the panicked inquiries about lost wallets or term papers.

They would sigh with relief after I reported my findings and then, their long-distance voices mellow with gratitude and fatigue, we'd extend the visit a little longer, recapping highlights and remembering jokes. I savored this last hour with them. I'd notice their homesickness, recognize love. These late-night calls, I sometimes think, are as close as I'll ever come to what theists experience during prayers.

Finally, it would be time to say goodbye and hang up. "Oh, and Mom . . . would you mind sending my wallet right away—maybe overnight mail?" No, I wouldn't mind.

And I never would—until the next day when I was standing in the long lines at the post office, wondering whether I should. Since we appear to be moving backward through Maslow's hierarchy—not only am I still picking up after my grown sons, but I am wrapping, addressing, and mailing their big shoes and shin guards to them—I had to wonder whether it served their best interests to rescue them from the consequences of disorganization. A lifelong second-guesser of all things maternal, I wondered whether I should have packed that tin of chocolate chip cookies in with the gloves and calendars they forgot. Would my anti-homesick remedy be received as a reward for incompetence? Should I have enclosed a sermonizing note instead? Or should I perhaps just have sent the note, letting the frostbite of a gloveless winter teach them to keep better track of their stuff? I've spent a fair amount of time in post office lobbies these days, assulted by "the shoulds," watching the crowd and contemplating the yin and yang of motherhood.

When to support and when to withhold, how to educate without cruelty, and which philosophy to embrace—the Irish-American tradition of "spare the rod and spoil the child" or the ISPI therapists' belief that coddling children, even boy children, can hardly happen too often or too much—these questions about discipline, and all the harrowing issues they raise about who's out of control, have preoccupied me since the day Ryan was born. In motherhood, where seemingly opposite realities can be simultaneously true, the role of nurturer invariably conflicts with the role of socializer. When trouble came, as it surely must, was I the good cop who understood, the bad cop who terrorized, or both? Which role—ally or aggressor—served the greater good, and when? Since wrong moves were a given in this ever-changing, twenty-year endeavor, was it least harmful to err as a spoiler or a spanker?

While Benjamin Spock and a few other forward-thinking experts had begun to rethink the punitive advice that dominated the childrearing practices of the '50s, most of the training manuals I consulted in 1974 proved exceptionally useless, squaring mothers off against children in a kind of Cold War deterrence. Questioning authority was never encouraged as a desirable American trait, particularly among women and children, and maintaining control—by whatever means necessary—was the dominant American value. Mothers raised children to be seen but not heard, to fit in compatibly and move with the herd. We were to be, above all else, consistent: Say "no" once, and it's "no" from then on. Obedience was the primary goal, and corporal punishment the swiftest route. The pediatric experts advising the mothers of my generation could have been trained by the Pentagon: they had a proprietary attitude toward developing countries and shared a fondness for big sticks.

It's hard to believe that parents who genuinely liked children went along with such punitive attitudes, but in the culture of separate spheres, fathers hardly knew their kids and mothers had precious few options. The social pressure was intense, since the mandate from neighbors and teachers and shoe salesmen for obedient, unwhining children ran counter to their natural dispositions. All human beings are born narcissists, wholly self-absorbed in the first few years of life: Babies eat, sleep, play with their toes, pee when they feel like it, cry when they want to. Converting these raw talents into thoughtful and intelligent behavior involves many unpleasant and frustrating scenes, even in the most benign environments. Under a rigid family structure where fathers were strangers to their families, mothers were taken for granted, and children felt guilty for being who they were, corporal punishment offered a therapeutic release for everyone involved.

It was clear from the start that I wasn't temperamentally suited for the role of spanker, and I never achieved any consistency. Corporal punishment posed the same ethical problems for me that capital punishment presents to the executioner: There is no room for error in judgment, and the motives for inflicting pain on powerless people must be pure. Spankings could never be executed in anger, and whenever my sons exhibited aggravating or obstinate behavior, it almost always inspired an element of heat. Since I possessed neither the infallibility nor the purity to be a reliable punisher, I relied on the less dramatic tactics of reason and persuasion. When that failed, I tried simply to outwit them.

Changing behavior by changing minds, of course, proceeded at a much slower pace. The standard juvenile response to all verbal requests for more reasonable behavior was the tedious refrain children learn right after No! and Me too!: "But *why*, Mom?/But why?/But why?/But *why*?" (This incessant refrain, in fact, could explain the genesis of corporal punishment: Why don't I just smack some sense into this kid?) Although a firm swat could bring a recalcitrant child swiftly into line, the changes were usually external, lasting only as long as the swatter remained in view. Permanent transformation had to be internal: Once my sons finally understood why running into the street was not a good idea, they weren't tempted to do it again even when I wasn't looking. The habits of self-discipline, as laborious and frustrating as they were to achieve, offered the only real possibility of keeping children safe from their own excesses as well as the omnipresent dangers of society.

IRONICALLY, THE same year I was struggling to develop a coherent philosophy on crime and punishment at home, I became a professional disciplinarian at work. At the end of my first year as a high school English teacher, the principal asked me to stop by his office "to discuss your theories on handling behavior problems." Since I didn't yet have any—theories or problems—I naturally assumed the invitation sprang from an incident the day before. The academic dean, who preferred more sedate environments than the one I maintained, had dropped by my classroom for an unannounced observation. I figured I had some explaining to do.

Keeping a roomful of hyperactive adolescents interested in the nuances of grammar for a full hour requires a great deal of comedy and sometimes, especially on high-humidity days in late June, outright slapstick. My students were never out of control, though they often appeared to be, particularly to anyone who didn't recognize teaching composition as performance art. When my freshman class had trouble identifying parts of speech, I borrowed an effective technique from family therapy called "body sculpting," where clients formed a physical model of their relationships—hanging on, leaning against, lording over, hiding under, turning away—allowing them to see the invisible tensions and pressures they put on one another. I would line up my composition students in a long sentence and instruct them to act out the function of nouns and verbs and prepositions and modifiers, so they could see the relationships between words. My youthful conjunctions, straining to hold hands between the hopping, jumpy action words, lost their balance and the whole line went down like a row of dominoes. The kids laughed but immediately saw the pitfalls of run-on sentences. It was during this giggling body heap that Father Michael suddenly appeared.

As if caught doing something illegal, the kids, without a word from me, quickly scrambled back into their seats, and hardly spoke for the rest of the class. They thought I was in trouble because they had been rowdy. Adopting the bored, obedient persona they thought the dean would admire, they clammed up on me, trying to save me from a negative evaluation. It was the most labored discussion we'd ever conducted. I reported to the principal's office the next day, prepared to explain that while it probably looked like we were only goofing around in Room 111, there was a method to my madness. I rehearsed my theory that, like potty training, drilling good grammar into adolescents' heads had to contain an element of fun.

Fun between faculty and students was in desperately short supply because most high schools in the early '70s were organized around the same Cold War principles that dominated every other American institution. Since there were only about fifty of "us" and more than a thousand of "them," the threat of rebellion was a constant fear. The two deans of students, one male and one female, were responsible for containing this threat. Joan occupied this office—with brilliance and ingenuity—when I joined the faculty but had given notice after winning a political campaign for county auditor. The principal, a huge, quiet man who rarely ventured outside his office (despite his towering height, he seemed terrified of the natives), announced that Joan had recommended me as her replacement. Was I interested in the job? It was the last thing I expected.

He eyed me skeptically, noting my obvious flaws: I was young, inexperienced, and, at five feet five inches and 115 pounds, I could pose no physical threat to juvenile delinquents twice my size. My single qualification for the job was that "for some reason," as he put it, "you have the kids' loyalty." We briefly discussed my flimsy theories on discipline which, like the mystery of transubstantiation, he accepted on pure faith. His own theory was quite straightforward: Keep the problems out of his office. Since there were no other candidates for the position, it became my job to run interference and secure peace between a tense faculty and a potentially explosive student body.

Because the threat of force was never an option for me, I had to rely exclusively on my wits. In 1974 guns and knives were not so much of a problem as Krazy Glue and water pistols. The band director was a frequent target of adolescent ennui. I spent half my time asking my young criminals the famous question: "But why? Why did you glue Father Fred's chair to the top of his desk?" I spent the other half trying to answer theirs: "But why? Why do I have to 'show more respect' to an English teacher who wears the same dress every day, smells like a brewery, and is never prepared for class?"

In a population of a thousand kids, there was the usual statistical representation of thieves, bullies, vandals, cut-ups, hysterics, kleptomaniacs, drinkers, drug abusers, incest victims, battered children, dropouts, and unwanted pregnancies. I heard a thousand stories in the confessional of the dean's office, losing another layer of my innocence almost every day. When the kids agreed to level with me—and they had plenty of reasons not to trust adults—they frequently revealed more pain and confusion than I could relieve. It wasn't my job to counsel them (there was a guidance office for that) but to keep them in line. This I did, except I kept redrawing the lines. To keep my own sanity amid the craziness I encountered every day, I adopted the philosophy of the matrons at Dunning, bending the institutional rules wherever possible to fit the special needs of the inmates. My experiences on psychiatric wards provided the most useful training for my job in the dean's office.

The rules I had to enforce were often dumber than the kids. One afternoon, a senior honor student was hauled in for taking an unauthorized leave in the middle of the day—an offense that earned him a three-day suspension. Depositing incriminating evidence from Burger King on my desk, the friar who apprehended him smiled triumphantly over an airtight case and left me to do the dirty work. The truant boy, a terrific kid who'd been a student of mine, had exceptionally sensible answers to all of my whys. Since he had two consecutive study periods with no school work to do, he explained, he decided to get the prescription his mother asked him to pick up on his way home. (He had a mandatory play practice so he wouldn't get home until late afternoon, and his mother had been in obvious pain that morning.) As for why he hadn't secured the necessary pass from me, he said that there was a long line outside my office, and he would have missed his only free period to run the errand.

And what about the half-eaten hamburger on my desk?

"Hell, I was hungry. I pulled into the drive-thru on my way back," he said. "If you had a choice between Burger King and the school cafeteria, what would you do?"

Kids often lie—"powerlessness corrupts"—but I knew he wasn't lying. There was always a long line outside my office, especially in June, when body temperatures rose and tempers grew short. I handed him his cold hamburger, and while he finished off the evidence I made a few quick calls, confirming that his mother was indeed sick and he had gone exactly where he said he did. I didn't suspend him; in fact, I might even have congratulated him for using his head. The friar who'd turned him in, who had a running argument with me about being "soft" on the kids, complained to the principal that, once more, I had undermined faculty authority. By then, there was mounting evidence of my inconsistency with the rules. I was summoned to headquarters.

"You can't make an exception for this student," the principal said, "or you'll have to make an exception for everyone."

"Okay," I said. "I'll make exceptions for everyone. For everyone who has a story as legitimate as his." This was an unimaginable attitude to my Franciscan principal, for without blind obedience we would have to think about everything we did, over and over and over again. With a thousand kids, all of whom were exceptions to one rule or another, he didn't want to open any cracks in the dikes.

"You can't do that—we'd have chaos in no time." He reminded

me that it was my job to uphold faculty authority. Where would we be if I made them look like fools?

"I can't *not* do that, if you want me in this job." I reminded him it was also my job to maintain "the kids' loyalty." How could I betray them by deliberately doing the wrong thing for the sake of some arbitrary consistency? They would know it, I would know it, and my credibility would amount to doodley-squat. I was certainly sorry if the friar felt like a fool, but I had nothing to do with it— he did it all on his own. This student had been both compassionate and wise—was the goal of education to teach critical thinking or blind obedience? With the battle line perpetually drawn between "us" and "them," no wonder it takes fifty years to reach Erikson's age of generativity and the recognition of a universal "we."

I didn't get fired, though I sorely tried the faith of my principal, who sometimes regarded me as a bigger discipline problem than the ones I solved. Neither, however, did I succeed in changing the system. After I resigned to become a self-employed writer, my successor quickly reversed the peace initiatives Joan and I had begun. ("If you want to see what difference we made," Joan once said in an uncharacteristic moment of despair, "put your elbow in a bucket of water, take it out, and study the impression you've left.") The high school, like the country after Ronald Reagan took office, made a U-turn back to Cold War attitudes and military solutions.

"If your only tool is a hammer, you see the whole world as a nail," a medical writer once summarized the relentless use of invasive surgery in Western medicine. So, too, with the habit of declaring war on social problems—the War on Poverty, the War on Drugs, the War on Crime. It's heartbreaking to think that children must be frisked before they can study composition, but like the innocent shoppers who were once offended by having their bags stapled shut or airline passengers who were once outraged about having their luggage searched, children will no doubt adapt to the humiliations. In time, ordinary citizens come to regard being treated like shoplifters and terrorists as normal. There are myriad alternatives to surrendering our dignity, but they all begin by asking, But *why?*

Why is there so much crime and violence today . . . and who should surrender their guns first?

Although my job in the dean's office raised tough questions about the multiple causes of bad behavior, the answers came readily enough in the early '70s, thanks to the popular bonding theory. When I did have to suspend or expel a student, I would discuss the case with the administration before calling a parent conference. At some point during our analysis of a delinquency problem, I could depend on being asked: Is the mother at home, or does she work? Translated, the question meant: Are we dealing here with a good mom or a bad mom? Never mind that the students were fifteen, sixteen, seventeen, eighteen years old, that a mother, whether she worked at home or outside it, could hardly be responsible for what her kids did in school all day. And never mind that I, like the majority of the female faculty, was a working mom myself, having taken two pregnancy leaves from this very institution. Could the friars be unaware that a full-term pregnancy resulted in actual children? To compose myself during moments such as these, I would silently recite the Serenity Prayer. An adapted version, from my friend Marti: "Lord, grant me the serenity to accept the things I cannot change, the courage to change the things I can, and the wisdom to hide the bodies of people who pissed me off."

THE PRACTICE of hammering disobedient kids into shape was bad policy, as numerous studies on the cyclical nature of domestic violence would later prove. It was also unlikely to produce "the kind of sons our daughters, born and unborn, would be pleased to live among," as the poet Audre Lorde named the major task of motherhood. To accomplish that end, mothers had to reject prevailing practices and invent their own. If the goal was to raise sons who were good negotiators, empathizers, listeners, and thinkers whenever a problem came up, that had to be their experience. "You cannot dismantle the master's house using the master's tools," Lorde warned. I was happy to abandon the hammer method with my sons, since I wasn't any good at it anyway.

I'd already learned from my work in the dean's office that using my wits was more effective than force, that loyalty and respect guaranteed more cooperation than fear and loathing. I had yet to discover, however, that to be a spoiler in a spanker society one needed a healthy sense of self-esteem. It was a challenge for mothers, given the dim view of our work in the *Psychological Abstracts*. I vividly remember the day I permanently retired from the corporal ranks. Mine was not an honorable discharge.

After I resigned from the dean's office and began writing, I worked at home so I could take care of the kids, then aged two and three. Being an unpublished writer and a full-time mother had a shrinking effect on my confidence, largely because I was the only adult in my work environment who could supply any feedback. Compounding my personal vulnerability, family tensions had been mounting on all fronts the during winter of 1977.

That year a series of financial setbacks obliterated all our savings and left us in debt. Howard had good reason to believe he would be among the City Planning Department layoffs after the first of the year, and the double-digit unemployment rate in the Midwest was climbing. Money was exceedingly tight as we approached the strenuous expenses of our second unmerry Christmas. I'd begun moonlighting as a waitress to help make ends meet, feeling the exhaustion of daily double-shifts deep in my bones.

My right arm began to stiffen painfully that November, which the specialist whom I consulted initially diagnosed as "frozen shoulder." He prescribed a "muscle relaxer," which had the general effect of relaxing my entire brain. For two weeks, I cried nonstop. While the tranquilizers melted my psychological defenses, they didn't unfreeze my shoulder. By the end of the month, I returned to the doctor with stiffened fingers, wrists, elbows, ankles, and knees; every joint in my body was swollen and inflamed.

"Rheumatoid arthritis," he concluded, describing my affliction as an autoimmune disorder in which the body attacks itself. My overwrought nervous system had apparently responded to my multiple S.O.S. alerts by sending out aggressive platoons of antibodies, which vigorously attacked all the wrong cells. I got out of bed slowly each morning, rocked by waves of pain as I stood up, and moved my stiff body down fourteen stairs, taking almost as many minutes. I remember the exact number because whenever I ushered the kids to bed, their little legs taking one step at a time, we always went slow and counted. They learned their numbers on that stairway.

My strength was so impaired that winter that I couldn't lift either of the boys without sending jolts of pain through every limb. Both in public and at home, I was totally dependent on the voluntary cooperation of a two and three year old. Issuing my orders—please come with me, put on your coat, hold very still while I zip you in, get in the car, get out of the car, put that candy bar back . . . please, honey, we have to keep moving—I then had to wait until they were ready to come, to put, to go, to hold very still. I lived on toddler time in a world geared for high speeds. In retrospect, it's something of a miracle that our handicapped trio functioned as well as it did. I was always terrified they could disregard my orders at any moment, maybe endanger themselves, and I wouldn't be able to stop or help them. I feared losing control of them, which translated unconsciously into losing them completely. Obedience, the quality I had so far disregarded as an inferior virtue, became my singular goal. Irony was becoming my middle name.

It was during this frozen/inflamed period that Ryan and Darren ganged up on me one afternoon. I don't remember the details of their campaign—maybe they wanted some expensive toy they'd seen on television, or maybe they just wanted a popsicle before supper. I had to say no a lot that winter, explaining the limits of our new financial reality, but young children are not remotely interested in theories on downward mobility and delayed gratification. Whatever it was they wanted, my refusal incited a rebellion. They started yelling and screaming, and in no time at all, so was I.

My sudden shrieking terrified them, and they both dove for the kitchen floor. I was terrified myself, convinced that this was It, the ultimate test of my control, my right to remain their mother. I

grabbed Darren's wrist as hard as I could, my arthritic arm siz-
zling with heat, his two-year-old face contorting with fear, and
hauled him up the fourteen stairs. He kicked and screamed as I
dragged him into the nursery, every jolt sending a charge
through my swollen limbs. Tears were already stinging my
cheeks as I heaved him clumsily over my knee. Insensible to his
frightened screams, I began hitting him with all my might. I felt
sharp axes slicing through my shoulders and wrists as my
pathetic, limp whacks thudded down on the thick padding of his
diaper. I hit him harder, savagely, trying to kill something, convinced something was killing me. Both of us cried hysterically,
my tears soaking the back of his T-shirt, his running down the
knee of my jeans.

"Mommy!" he bawled, full of despair and abandon, the way he
did whenever he lost sight of me in foreign territories. "Mommy!
. . . Mommy!"

"Mom, stop!" Ryan shouted frantically from behind. I turned
around and saw him standing in the doorway, shock and horror
marbling his blanched, livid face. My hand froze in midair as I suddenly saw myself. My rage exploded in a piercing shriek as a riveting jolt penetrated every fiber of my being: *Something's terribly
wrong here . . . this isn't who I want to be*. My arm dropped uselessly,
and my head, sinking to my chest, was throbbing with pain. For a
few minutes or hours—time had lost its borders—I heaved for air,
quaking in a prolonged wake of dispersing sobs.

With enormous effort I lifted the baby, his taut little muscles
shivering as they unjelled, and stood him between my knees. I
wrapped my limp arms around him, burying my wet cheeks in his
hair and kissing his head. Still shivering, he stood silently between
my legs, neither returning my hug nor pulling away.

"Oh honey," I said softly, straightening up. I brushed his damp
hair away from his forehead and cupped his cheeks with my
inflamed hands. Swollen pink patches covered his face as he stared
at me with open-mouthed, shattered innocence.

"Mommy?" he asked, his voice coming from a deep cavern somewhere far below him. What could I say? It's okay, sweetheart, I'm here?

"Oh honey," I repeated softly, heavy sorrow thudding like sandbags against my chest. "I'm so sorry. This won't ever happen again."

It never did. One bad mother day can change you forever.

WITH NEW respect for the force of my own maternal violence, I became a committed pacifist on the discipline war after that uncontained explosion in the nursery. I've often thought about the painful ironies that became clear during those six months of my frozen period. Instead of the enormous power I thought I'd feel if I ever deployed my most threatening weapon, I had only a sense of utter helplessness. Darren says he doesn't remember that day. Layered over with sixteen more years of small and large hurts, those shrieking voices are now buried deep in a canyon of his unconscious. He might hear them again sometime in the future—that's what unconscious memory is for, storing the stuff that's too difficult or terrifying to remember until it's safe or necessary to examine.

Like most of the black days in my life, it took several years to discover the silver lining. Establishing talk as the central feature of our future negotiations had this advantage: It's still useful once your children outsize you. According to the growth chart inside the door of the broom closet, Ryan and Darren started overtaking me about halfway through their childhood. I became the Incredible Shrinking Mother the year they started junior high. If our relationship today depended on physical clout, I would have about the same influence with them that the republic of Liechtenstein has on world politics.

Certainly, words can be as abusive as any blow—maybe even more so, since wounding words live on in the mind, gaining weight and coloring attitudes, while most surface bruises eventually heal and disappear. Nor did using language eliminate the need to recognize power imbalances. When a three year old yells, "You're so stupid! What a dummy!" it doesn't carry the same weight as when a mother yells those words to a child. And the risk of becoming a nag is constant, since it takes so many words to work those subtle, internal changes in immature behavior. Even if you don't physically abuse young children, you can still drive them nuts with your words.

Spoilers like myself were routinely despised in the '70s, because it was virtually a crime in the Midwest to be different from anybody else. You had to move with the herd. I had to ignore a lot of arched eyebrows when I didn't respond with threats or swats to the boys' unseemly behavior in public. Sometimes I even had to ignore the raised eyebrows across my own kitchen table. Here I was, a spoiler mother, a word person striving for self-disciplined sons, co-piloting the socialization process with a spanker father, a corporal person aiming for obedient sons. All measure of consistency was doomed to failure. The issue of discipline caused steady friction between Howard and me.

During the years I worked at home, dinner became the most fractious hour of family time together. Exhausted after eight hours in Fort Wayne's Department of City Planning, Howard came home ready to relax and relish the gratitude a breadwinner in such circumstances might expect. Instead, his two distinctly untelegenic sons sometimes noticed his arrival home and sometimes didn't, depending on the preoccupation of the moment. What is more, his wife didn't seem to care when they played on his newly seeded lawn—sometimes "running under the sprinkler in their *underwear*, for heavensakes." His domestic crew seemed to have no enthusiasm about being like the Brady Bunch.

From day one, Howard had been an affectionate father, spending a lot of time with the boys on evenings and weekends. He'd successfully quelled a mini-riot among playmates in the family room, and he was delighted when he taught Ryan to identify all the vowels on a cereal box one Saturday morning. Because he was far more involved with parenting than most fathers of his generation, he assumed parity with me and imagined he understood the content of my days. He thought raising kids was amusing and fun and wished he could do more of it himself. He simply couldn't comprehend my exhaustion at dinner time. Unaware of the mental strain that sets in after reading *The Sneetches on Beaches* for the hundredth time, let alone weathering seasons of temper tantrums, he did not think it was too much to ask that I teach the kids proper table manners by age four.

The high expectations were his, but it was my job to achieve them. One evening, when Ryan dropped his peas into the moat of his mashed potatoes, Howard shot his Look across the table at me. The Look was prompted by any number of lapses in civilized behavior the boys exhibited almost daily that year, and I understood it to mean, "What are you doing with these kids all day?" I didn't say anything. Ryan dropped another pea. Howard reprimanded him. Then again. His father drew the line, promising a stint of solitary confinement in his room if it happened again. Then Howard looked at me, his eyes demanding backup support. The war now escalated into a confrontation over whose will would prevail—who would lose face, and who would be accused of desertion? Would I be part of a unified front, or not?

"Please, Howie," I said. "We're talking *peas* here."

The Pea Incident proved a major turning point for me because it was the first time I recognized why I felt so overwhelmed during those years. In the range of things toddlers have to learn and endlessly review—why you can't put bottles with certain labels in your mouth, why you have to sit on the potty, why you can't take whatever you want in the store, why you don't hit your friends—by the time we got to why you can't drop your peas, well, I was dropping a few myself. I was unable to work up any alarm for behavior that was not life threatening, especially by dinner time.

Howard's smoldering disapproval across the table that night came at the end of a long day: already our neighbor had asked me to teach them that her impatiens bed was not to be considered the "safety crash zone" when their Big Wheels spun out of control; the cashier at Kroger wanted me to keep them from whining in the Candyland at the checkout lane; the salesman in the shoe store did not want them running around his carefully arranged display racks;

Darren's preschool teacher wanted me to tell him to stop drawing when she said so. And now Howard wanted Ryan to turn in a better performance with his fork. All of these people, when their wishes for more mature behavior were not met, aimed their disappointment at me—as if I could control all Big Wheel traffic or contain all excitement over new shoes.

Although most of the behavior so important to other people was nowhere near the top of my list, I would nevertheless go to work on everyone's behalf: translate into memorable three-year-old language why it's important to honor an elderly neighbor's attachment to her flower garden, why their daddy gets bothered by peas, why we all have our own peculiar reality but should nevertheless respect other people's. A mother who takes on everybody else's socialization agenda becomes the perpetual bearer of bad news—do this, don't do that, stop coloring, stand still. Much of what I said to them was not welcome news. Ryan liked watching his peas plop into his mashed potatoes; Darren wanted to keep drawing after his teacher said "Stop now."

Running interference between their inexperience and other people's expectations was having a dampening effect on my own relationship with them. The nature of the bond we were forming during those first five years was heavily laden with prohibition and punishment. I felt overwhelmed by the excessive demands and was fairly sure they did, too. The peas that so annoyed Howard that night led to a startling revelation: I didn't have to carry on crusades against behavior I could live with. If their father and teachers and neighbors had further expectations and demands, *they* were free to explain it to them.

IRRITATED BY my failure to support him, Howard and I argued that night about our conflicting views on the kids' behavior. We were hopelessly divided over what constituted a crime and appropriate punishments, communicating across an unbridgeable gap in experience. Months of heated debates produced no winners and then, seemingly overnight, everything changed.

When I returned from the Ohio conference after leaving the boys with Howard that weekend, I was greeted by a dazed and deeply subdued man. There were none of the usual recriminations or subtle extortions of guilt a mother in my deserter role could expect. He regarded me, in fact, as if Joan of Arc had just marched in to save him. The family room was strewn with toys, both boys were smeared with something that looked like peanut butter, and Howard showed no sign of having showered for two days. Watching me take in these facts, he shrugged. "Hey, they're still alive," he said, quoting my familiar line.

While I had been taking notes on Dinnerstein's theory about the critical evolution of "paternal instincts," Howard was having a hands-on radicalizing experience of his own. It had an immediate effect on the atmosphere at the dinner table the next evening. When Ryan's vegetables dropped off his fork, as usual, I braced myself for the impatient reprimand and smoldering look. Instead, Howard shot me a knowing glance and said to Ryan, trading a spoon for his fork, "Here, Kiddo, this will get those peas where you want them a little easier." It was a miracle.

Living my life for three days had given Howard a new understanding of the reality in the interior. A man who planned whole cities—how the traffic should flow, where the river dams should be, which neighborhoods should have parks—had spent two days entreating a three year old to take a nap with no success. He realized that his beautiful, funny young sons could be monsters and could reduce him to pleading. He'd intended to impress me by accomplishing in a weekend the manners I had not managed to introduce in a year. Instead, he shook his head, saying I wouldn't *believe* what they'd gotten into when he tried to take a little nap himself. I did believe. Now we had two believers.

The vague beginnings of something else stirred Howard that weekend. Merely keeping them alive, paying attention to the triumphs and casualties of their days, affected his intuitive faculties. The insider knowledge you can attain only by being there—learning what children can do and what they cannot do yet—changed his vision of the outside world. This double vision of things marked a subtle shift, but it felt important to him. Everything that was familiar to him— his traffic and dams and parks—looked slightly different in light of this other reality. Knowledge from his private world leaked into his professional judgments, leading to the perception that maybe the traffic, not the children, should be slowed down here; maybe fences around the reservoir, not warning signs, should be raised over there. When looked at from this new perspective, there were innumerable adjustments to make in the world. Our dinner conversations evolved into far more digestible talks after that weekend I took notes on "Motherhood: Challenge and Choice" in Ohio, the same weekend Howard started traversing realities at home.

SINCE THOSE first punishing years of do-right insecurity when I thought that I alone was responsible for my sons' socialization, I've delegated some of the work to fathers, teachers, even strangers. Those early, proprietary feelings about a baby's behavior— "You don't want a *stranger* to watch your son take his first step, do you?"—had given way completely by the time my teenagers were ready to drive their first car. By then, I knew strangers could do a better job with some learning experiences than I could. After many long lectures to my sons—to no avail—about why aggressive, hot-dog driving was hard on passengers, a New York cabbie successfully drove this lesson home during a memorable, white-knuckle trip through Manhattan without uttering a word.

AS I stood in the post office line, it occurred to me that I might not be the most qualified instructor for their current disorganization problem either. After all, I had to ask American Airlines to find my eye glasses and mail them to me—three times, no less; any sermons on disorganization would be pretty hypocritical coming from me. Not that I regard this picking-up-after-yourself as a trivial issue. If my sons are to become the kind of men our daughters would be pleased to live among, attention to domestic details is critical. The hostilities that arise over housework, like the wars that can escalate from peas, are crushing the daughters of my generation even as I write. Change takes time, but men's continued obliviousness to home responsibilities is causing women everywhere to expire of trivialities. I've sent this message to my sons a thousand times, but perhaps it will be a stranger who finally gets the point across. Maybe they'll gain some insights about getting organized from the straightforward personnel at American Airlines, who can take them through the panic of lost and found without burdening the facts with cookies or sermons.

I had plenty of time to contemplate the many ironies of our ongoing trek through Maslow's hierarchy as I stood in line at the post office, since it had stopped moving altogether. The same customer had been occupying one of the windows far too long, fraying everyone's nerves. As people shifted weight from foot to foot, a young mother behind me had been impatiently calling her daughter—a lively three-year-old red-head whose green eyes were familiar with mischief—to return to the line. These entreaties had an imperceptible effect on young Catherine—everyone knew her name after a dozen futile pleas, "Catherine, come here and stand *still.*" She now had her back to her mother, cutting off contact with the control tower, and was playfully flipping the metal lid on the out-of-town mail slot.

By all public standards, Catherine appeared to be a spoiled child. She seemed to have a hefty sense of entitlement, insisted on being seen and heard, and wasn't buying into obedience for the sake of obedience. Her mother's repeated orders to stand still, stop jiggling the velvet rope, and come away from the display case had so far offered no convincing answers to "But why?" In a new place, with a lot of curious things and a bunch of boring people, Catherine was making her own fun, quite harmlessly except for the rising level of annoyance in the packed lobby. Faces were arranged in expressions of blank neutrality, but the air was growing thick with contemptuous sighs.

"Catherine!" her mother yelled, "Honey, *please* . . . stop that." If you knew what to listen for, you could hear the good cop competing with the bad cop in the dropping volume of her voice. You would know, too, that these not quite firm reprimands were not coming from her but from "the shoulds" of the crowd. Sometimes total strangers can be a mother's most useful ally, and sometimes they can divide you from your own agenda. A grey-haired gentleman in expensive new casual wear, perhaps recently retired and certainly a newcomer to the lines at the post office, sighed heavily and then said to his wife, "Outrageous." He did not specify whether he meant the slow service or the time-consuming customer or the noisy mother and child.

When he first came in, he looked curiously around the lobby, observing the largely female population as if he were thinking, "So, this is where Ethel comes with the Christmas packages and Harriet brings the certified mail." He did not appear to be a line-stander himself. His boredom set in shortly before young Catherine's. He left his wife to stand in line and leaned against a nearby counter, reading the newspaper. As he reviewed the national news, glancing up occasionally to look at the pleading mother, there was nothing in his expression that suggested he'd ever spent an afternoon waiting in a pediatrician's office with a cranky toddler. It was even possible, at sixty-something and counting, that life in the interior was still completely invisible to him.

Taking his outrageous remark personally and absorbing some of the heat aimed at Catherine and her mother, I was gripped with an urge to do something, to protest somehow. But what? And how? Instantly, I was riveted by a sudden flashback. I remembered a steamy July afternoon fifteen years ago, when this very same scenario played out in a Fort Wayne McDonald's, to disastrous results.

It had been unreasonably hot in the long lines that day—it was the peak of lunch-hour rush, everyone standing with a pre-hamburger impatience. We stood five lines across and six people deep, with the same enthusiasm and alertness as a busload of reluctant draftees. I was searching the crowd for my two small companions, who'd departed earlier to check out the condiments table, when my attention was abruptly diverted by the distressed look of the woman coming through the door.

She was carrying a writhing toddler in one arm and holding the hand of another child, slightly older, walking with the tragic gloom of a boy who'd been without french fries for too long. An unmistakable look of panic crossed her face as she took in the lines, measuring them against the weight of her children. For an indecisive moment, she wavered on the threshold. Then, with an audible intake of breath, she plunged into the pool of people. It was the reverse of a sigh—a little gasp for air, like the breathy gulp of a swimmer reaching for the edge of the pool. This was not, judging from the weariness in her expression, her first lap of the day.

I easily imagined her fatigue. I had once walked through a large department store when the boys were still babes, pushing Ryan in a stroller and balancing six-month-old Darren on my hip. The store had just opened, but to me, it felt like the middle of the day. We'd been up since daybreak, and intermittently through the night, for feedings and diaper changes, for laundry and baths. I was not actually shopping that morning; I was just being Out. It was one of those days when infancy seemed a permanent condition. As I strolled down the aisle, smiling at the babies who had actually become children, I saw a woman coming toward me, pushing a toddler in a stroller and balancing an infant on her hip. Total strangers to each other, we clicked with instant recognition and laughed as she said, "My God! How were you able to wash your face this morning!" That was all we said, but it was a whole conversation.

"Hush now, Sarah, hush," the woman in McDonald's said into the child's neck, feigning patience. "I'll let you down in just a minute." It was clear that just a minute was far longer than Sarah was willing to wait, because she responded with several swift pushes. The woman held her tightly, stoically reading the menu overhead while her body absorbed the thrusts and jolts of the writhing limbs. Then Sarah, with the expression of a born heller, revealed a hearty lung capacity by issuing a loud, reverberating wail.

"Do you believe it?" the man behind me asked, addressing no one in particular. "She shoulda left those kids at home." The eyes in my section of the line reflected total agreement: She shoulda left those kids at home. I, too, would have been willing to listen to almost anything other than Sarah's wailing, even Muzak. But I was struck by the readiness of the crowd to assume a mother has no business doing her job in public. Almost no other laborers experience the intolerance for their work that mothers do. Most people have found themselves snarled in a traffic jam, inconvenienced by some construction work, but it would be weeks before anyone would roll down a car window and yell, "Hey! Can't you guys do that stuff at home?!" Moreover, they would probably admire the construction workers for their skill and endurance in performing such a strenuous, difficult job. The general public tolerates the irritating delays and upsetting vibrations because the work is valued. Not so with mothers.

"What a way to spend a lunch hour," the man behind me said, now the self-appointed spokesman for the crowd. A few nods of agreement came from other people who wanted a lunch hour of peace and quiet. Lunch hours are especially valued by mothers because we don't have one. Anywhere a mother goes, she has to take her work with her. I wish mothers with small children could have an express lane, like the special counter truckers have at truck stops. But nowhere do mothers have top priority because there's little recognition that we're working under pressure and strain.

The woman obviously regretted the distraction she caused and surely felt the condemnation of the people who were on "real" lunch hours. She heard the unspoken message to silence her child. With hesitation, she let Sarah down, instructing her young son, "Take care of her, Billy." The boy accepted the order with a sense of doom. There wasn't a person in sight who could have taken care of Sarah in her current tempestuous condition. Her feet hit the ground like a pair of wound-up propellers, and she shot off through the lines, her brother following after like a nervous David looking for Goliath.

Just then Ryan and Darren returned, fists full of napkins and straws and packages of salt. We entertained ourselves by reading all the posters on the walls, identifying vowels, reviewing the special offers—the Sippy Dippy straws, the "Great Muppet Caper" glasses, the Happy Meal prizes. Suddenly, a loud but now familiar wail sounded from the opposite side of the counter. It was Sarah. Her brother was trying to take this whirling propeller of a sister back to mom. Sarah was holding a french fry, obviously purloined. I don't know whether it was the french fry, or the hollering children, or the weight of public opinion, but Mom snapped.

She swooped down on the boy's backside with a powerful swing, nearly knocking him over. She exploded with hysterical shrieks, shaking the children violently. Clearly, she had crossed the boundaries of reasonable discipline into a minefield of uncontrolled anger. The two children froze, stunned by her fury.

The crowd stiffened at once, watching fearfully as the woman teetered on the brink of child abuse. There was absolute silence for a moment. Then the woman fixed her eyes again on the overhead menu, her face flushed with emotion, her body shaking with the aftermath of rage. Everyone then looked up at the menu, as if we had suddenly forgotten our orders. There had been a wretchedness in her voice that sent chills up my spine, a wretchedness I recognized in myself once, the voice of maternal violence I could never forget. Everyone who had wanted Sarah to be quiet went from anger to a vague sense of shame. We stood in our shared discomfort.

"I hate to see a mother treating her kids like that," the spokesman said self-righteously. The woman looked at no one, an outcast among the ranks demanding perfect motherhood.

Finally, it was my turn to order. I followed instructions to ask for two Sippy Dippy straws, when I felt a tug at my sleeve. Since the straws were free, could we have one for our friend Meagan? Another tug. And two Muppet Caper glasses? I was extremely patient with all their questions, acutely aware in that moment of the shortcomings of all mothers to all children. While I translated their messages to the clerk, I heard the man behind me shuffle his feet, signaling his heavy impatience.

The spokesman for the general public didn't like mothers shrieking at their children, but neither, apparently, did he like it when they spent so much time on them. He didn't understand the great influence a Sippy Dippy straw could have on his peace and quiet. It seemed that any mother who appeared in public ran a high risk of becoming an outlaw. A mother, I'd decided that afternoon, had nothing to lose by following her own judgment, since the public judgment often comes from people who know nothing about raising children, how the peas drop, how much hopping and jiggling and crying it takes before very young human beings understand that life isn't fair.

The final, violent scene with Sarah's mother was foreshadowed from her first look of panic in the doorway. Surely, had she been operating from reason instead of distress, she would have left or resolved to ignore the irritation with her jackhammer children. But maybe a dark source inside told her that being isolated at home was much more dangerous that day. Maybe she was Out that afternoon because she needed people around as a safety valve. Maybe alone she would not have been able to control the rage. Any mother who's been in that position has felt the powerful frustration, the frightening anger. I promised myself that the next time I recognized a mother under the strain of two difficult children, I wouldn't leave her stranded at the end of the line. Because this time, the safety valve of the general public had turned into a pressure cooker.

THE DRAMA in McDonald's had lingered in my mind for a long time, compelling me to search for a better ending. I imagined a nervy mother, one who trusted her own instincts and experiences, using the scene to educate the public. Perhaps she might say, in a strong voice intended to be overheard:

> Children, listen up. I want you to look at the faces of the
> people here . . . See their narrowed eyes? The way their lips are

all pinched up? Well, that expression means they are pissed off about something. I have a hunch it is you. My guess—it is only a guess, because no one has spoken directly to us—my guess is that you are being too loud and rambunctious for tastes here. No one knows Sarah has been up since four o'clock this morning, after a nightmare scared the wits out of her, or that Billy ate hardly any breakfast because his Cheerios "drowned in the milk" again, and he has a rule about eating only the floaters. They don't remember the odd laws governing food, or what it's like to be tired and hungry at your age. They probably *could* remember if they thought about it at all. But as things stand, we have to assume they won't. I would prefer a little less noise myself—I'm hot and tired and crabby too—but I am going to ignore that for the moment and concentrate on getting you some french fries. But it's my duty to tell you that if you don't quiet down, these people here will think you are brats.

Those speeches happen only in the movies, of course, or in front of the bathroom mirror two days later, when you finally think of what you wished you had said. But here I was in the post office, fifteen years after my solemn promise in McDonald's, reliving the scene.

"Catherine! Stop that right now!" the desperate voice behind me yelled again. Flashbacks are not without purpose. I quickly assessed the situation. The retired gentleman and his patient wife were now at the window, and I was next in line. The clerk motioned to me. On cue, I turned to the crowd and announced:

"Why don't we move Catherine and her mother to the front of the line—create an express lane for them . . ." My voice sounded slightly rusty, not nearly as strong and nervy as the mother I imagined in my movie. I forgot the rest of my lines. Looking directly at the young mother, I motioned for her to come forward. She looked at me, stunned, then looked uncertainly at the crowd, as if this invitation could be some kind of test.

"Please, come to the window," I said. "You deserve a break today . . ." I caught myself before the rest of McDonald's old advertising jingle popped out of my mouth; that was not part of my script. I motioned again and sent a look to the crowd, trying to mean, "Help me out here, folks."

"Sure," someone else said, "go on ahead." The motion seconded, everyone took a small step aside and opened an aisle for Catherine and her mother to pass through. The whole damn line. With this one tiny gesture, one little exception to the rules, the atmosphere in the post office lobby changed. Blank neutrality on the faces relaxed into the empathetic grins of strangers having a bonding experience. I was so happy and proud of everybody, I could feel my own grin reaching into my ears. You don't often get to play movie scenes in real life, but when it happens, it's even more thrilling than you imagined.

While Catherine's mother took care of business at the window, I invited her daughter back to the glass display case she'd been ordered to abandon earlier. In one of her several crimes, she had entertained herself by mimicking the hands in a chart of the manual alphabet, illustrating a new line of stamps commemorating the deaf. I'd noticed Catherine was quite dexterous with her fingers. I pointed to the poster of a mother holding an infant in one arm and signing a message with her free hand.

"She's talking to her baby," I said. "Did you know you can speak with your hands?" Catherine shook her head shyly. Now that she had everybody's attention, she wasn't talking. But her bright green eyes took in every word as I briefly explained deafness and sign language.

"Want to know the secret message?" I asked, pointing to the stamp mother's hand. She nodded. I crouched down to her level, my knees cracking audibly. As it turned out, the stamp mother's message was the only sign language I knew. I raised my pinkie and said "I," then my index finger, "love," then unfolded my thumb, "you." Strictly nonverbal now, Catherine opened her green eyes in mute wonder, as if asking, "Really?" I nodded, and pointed again to the mother's hand in the poster. She compared the position with her own, confirmed "really," then smiled with satisfaction. We did it again—pinkie, index, thumb—then again and again. Catherine silently mouthed the words each time she mimicked my gestures.

"That's it," I said. "You've got it." I stood up slowly, unbending stiff knees, while she hopped energetically back to her mother just as she concluded her transaction at the window.

"Mommy, look!" she said excitedly, her speech miraculously returned. Beaming with the pleasure of unlocked secrets, she held up her three fingers, one by one. I–love–you. Her mother looked mildly confused.

"It's when you're deafness," Catherine said, fracturing the translation slightly. She did it again, trying to help her mother understand by mouthing the words. But her mother didn't read lips— though I was sure she'd get the message somewhere on the way home. Catherine wasn't the type to hang onto a good secret for long. They left the lobby, her mother smiling gratefully at everyone as Catherine flashed us the fingers. I smiled and flashed back.

I then went to the window and mailed the boxes containing my sons' shin guards and cookies, full of mixed messages about responsibility and love. There are hundreds of forgettable wrong moves in my history by now, as well as a few permanently imprinted, deeply regrettable ones. Change takes time, it's true, sometimes as much as fifteen years. But then the same scene rolls around again, giving you another chance to make it turn out just right.

5

Adjusting to Reality

"I *know*, Mom," Darren said, holding up a hand to stop the speech he thought was coming. Slumped deeply into the couch pillows, he looked up from the TV screen, his features striving for cool composure but his cheeks a bit too highly colored to quite succeed. A few minutes earlier, I'd shown up unexpectedly in the living room. He had reached instinctively for the remote when I paused to see what was so absorbing on TV, then apparently decided that switching channels would invite suspicions of guilt—and why should he feel guilty? A newly eligible voter with certain inalienable rights, he elected to stick with his First Amendment freedoms. Together, but from wildly different points of view, we watched a succession of gorgeous, nearly naked models arrange themselves provocatively before the camera in a news documentary about the making of the *Sports Illustrated* swimsuit issue.

We each had the same uncomfortable feeling that ocurred when we sat next to each other in movie theaters during a sexually explicit scene, causing an awkward moment of paralysis when nobody is sure who should say what. We both erased our faces of any clues about what we were thinking, or trying not to think, faking nonplussed expressions to suggest, "I know you think you know what I'm thinking, but you don't." These telepathic messages had to do for the moment, as we both scanned our separate confusions for something appropriate to say. I knew my lines didn't begin, "After all I've tried to teach you . . . " He knew his didn't start, "Hey, no big deal . . . "

It wouldn't have been a big deal in millions of homes, but it bordered on one under my roof. Since I am annually incensed over the *Sports Illustrated* swimsuit issue, a gross misconduct of journalism that nets the magazine more revenue than it earns from any other issue, Darren fully "knew" what my thoughts on it were by now. He would know I thought it was a form of sexual harassment to make sport of women in a magazine obliged to take female athletes seriously the rest of the year. He would know how my eyes roll at the bone-headed defenses from Time Warner every year, when the same public controversies erupt again and again. And he would know, too, that I find the pervasive cheesecake images of women as disturbing as the violent and degrading ones, since they saturate every cell of our consumer society, making sexism as unexceptional and American as sales tax and junk mail. Because it's my job as a cultural reporter to pay attention to gender issues, my sons have heard many more facts about women and money and sex than they've known where to file.

Darren closed his eyes and, guessing which sound track might be playing in my mind, elevated his voice slightly to impersonate me: "'Did you know that after the Dow Chemical scandal, the media reported that the majority of today's fashion models have had breast implant surgery? Isn't it tragic how the singular image of female beauty, beginning with Barbie, has maimed so many women? Can you imagine men having to . . .'" His voice trailed off as his hand, still aloft, motioned the ongoing cadence in his head. Opening his eyes, he looked at me for a few entreating seconds, then offered a slow shrug. I understood it to mean: "Look . . . have mercy. Silicone wasn't *my* idea." He then returned to the program with blank enjoyment. Recognizing my exit lines, I left the room without comment.

I couldn't help wishing he would turn to less exploitative entertainment, but in truth, a young man with a keen interest in human sexuality would face a long search before finding any erotica that offered a more balanced point of view. At any given moment on MTV, the channel that regularly celebrates arrested male development, the subtitle could be "Just Discovered His Schwang." But by the time my sons' were in their senior year of high school, only months before leaving home, we all understood their program selections were largely their own business. Although I still felt the urge to influence their choices, we were well beyond the age when censorship was an option—futile though it always was.

The current debate over the sexist and violent content on TV has placed the country's big thinkers in the quandary of having to defend freedom of speech without appearing to support the moronic argument that such images have no influence on reality. Recently, an essayist in *The Nation* chastised the narrow-minded prudes and righteous moralists who keep trying to pass laws that might have a "chilling effect" on First Amendment freedoms and then acknowledged that more than two hundred studies have proven such images have a profoundly chilling effect on children. It's a knotty problem but fortunately, because of our wonderful free market economy, neither producers nor advertisers nor government regulators are responsible for containing this damage. Who is responsible? Who should be the narrow-minded prudes and righteous moralists we love to loathe? Whom did *The Nation* essay blame when a five year old in Ohio, inspired by an animated episode of MTV's "Beavis and Butthead," set fire to his family's home? His mommy, of course. If mothers would do their duty and change the channel, then the arson—and presumably all the homicides, murders, rapes, and assaults—would never have happened.

Imagine how much fun motherhood could be if the culture actually reinforced the values we're obliged to teach. Then the mother's job would be to say yes, yes, yes instead of no, no, no. Even if mothers could sustain the hated role of censor without incurring the contempt of children, our influence is limited. Even if I had managed to prevent my sons' exposure to sexist or violent images at home, I could not have prevented encounters everywhere else: the locker rooms where they regularly hung out, the movies they now paid to see with their own money, the newsstands that displayed women as cheesecake every day. The question was not whether they should be exposed—that was a cultural given—but rather how they would react whenever they were.

Especially during their last months at home, my interest in further discussion of these issues was often halted by an upraised hand or a long-suffering look. Pleading for mercy, my sons short-circuited any urges to have another go at them because, as they frequently pointed out, I'd been pitching the same family values for nearly twenty years. Since change takes time and resistance takes even longer, I had introduced them early on to the pressing social issues of our times. For most of their lives they've been navigating two worlds—the one I encouraged them to see and the one they had to live in.

BORN INTO an activist family in the mid-'70s, they attended their first civil rights marches in Snuglis and strollers. They met most of the other toddlers in our neighborhood, some of whom eventually became their friends, when we canvassed the precinct together during Joan's campaign for county auditor. For many years, they thought friendship began by ringing someone's doorbell and asking, "Are you registered to vote?" Their vocabularies and seasonal activities revolved around grass-roots politics the way children in farming families learned to view spring in terms of planting crops and fall as harvest season.

Growing up in Fort Wayne provided an exceptionally rich medium to observe how social movements grow or wither in the heartland. Our demographic profile attracted regular attention from political analysts and market researchers who believed residents in our little microcosm could speak for the vast, silent majority in middle America. The natives referred to the city as "Test-Market, U.S.A.," since we were endlessly polled and probed for opinions on everything from toothpaste to nuclear weapons. Children were drafted into focus groups before they were out of diapers. Every trial product, from McDonald's new sandwiches to Procter and Gamble's new detergent, had to pass muster with us before qualifying for national distribution. If we liked it, you got it; if we didn't, you never saw it.

As factories kept closing, unemployment kept rising, and racial disputes kept erupting in Gary and Detroit, Hoosiers became increasingly edgy and upset throughout the '70s. In November 1980, predictions of a reactionary swing to the right were confirmed during the presidential election. Indiana was the first state to go blue on Walter Cronkite's map, several hours before the polls closed. In a stunning upset, a widely respected incumbent senator was defeated by a dim-witted Republican party boy who was swept into office on Reagan's coattails. Editorial writers across the country mourned when Indiana voters retired Senator Birch Bayh, who'd given some of the most impassioned and intelligent speeches of his career that November, opting instead for the blue-eyed simplicity and pledge-of-allegiance solutions of Danny Quayle. Pundits on both coasts interpreted this political regression as proof that hayseeds in the Midwest were hopelessly behind the times, although history would eventually prove we were quite a few years ahead. When Hoosiers were hurting we made Danny a U.S. senator. But when the whole country had its collective nervous breakdown eight years later, he became vice president of the United States. Just like the toothpaste we preapproved, the politicians we elected became national favorites. We liked Danny, but the country went mad for him.

Despite outward appearances of a unified right-wing allegiance, Fort Wayne had a thriving community that actively resisted the backlash. A strong coalition of labor, women, minorities, and homosexuals—the usual suspects for "special interests"—prepared for a long siege. It was our luck to be stationed in an exceptionally lively division of the resistance. My sons and I saw a lot of action in Fort Wayne, and traveled in crowded car pools and buses when battles called for support elsewhere.

Since their first days as baby activists, we have tied a ribbon around the Pentagon, contributed a patch to the AIDS quilt, served as foot soldiers in ERA marches, escorted clients through picketers at abortion clinics. We joined the outraged Coalition for Justice on the steps of the Allen County courthouse to demand the impeachment of Judge Herman Busse, whom the local press described as a "salty fisherman" after he declared during a rape trial that a woman "out trolling bars until 3 A.M." deserved what she got. And in the sobering years before we left Fort Wayne, we stood shivering together in silent protest on a downtown curb in Waynedale watching a river of hooded white robes flood through the street—my sons' first encounter with the ominous chants of the Ku Klux Klan.

IF I sometimes felt like an outsider in my sons' world of male sports and soap box derbies, they were foreigners in my world of feminist rallies and political demonstrations. Although we participated together in the tumultuous social revolutions of our day—the civil rights movement, the antiwar movement, the women's movement, and the green movement—our memories differ considerably. This became obvious during a household organizing project I began last winter, when I dumped the contents of several cardboard boxes on the kitchen table and we sifted through hundreds of family photographs.

Studying a dark, blurry scene from the first Take Back the Night march in Fort Wayne, I remembered holding Ryan's hand and guiding Darren's stroller through the throng, hoping the grim testimonials from the podium would not cause nightmares; they remembered the thrill of being allowed to hold their very own lighted candles. In mittens and stocking caps in front of the telephone company another year, they numbly held picket signs to support the Fighting Grannies of Essex Wire. I get goose bumps remembering the jitters before my first public speech; they recall their impatience with how long it took the grannies to get around to the hot chocolate they were promised for "being good."

"Who's this?" one of them asked, picking up a curled photo of a distinguished young black man surrounded by a small group of admiring white people, making a toast with plastic cups at a living room reception.

"Vernon Jordan," I said.

"Really? I didn't know we were friends with Vernon Jordan."

"You were only a baby when you were introduced," I said. "He wasn't in Fort Wayne long enough to actually become friends. It was a brief meeting, as I recall—only long enough for you to spit up on him."

Someone had handed Mr. Jordan a handkerchief and he had smiled, graciously, as he wiped his expensive sleeve. That same night, nurses in a local emergency room would be frantically wiping blood from his gunshot wound, trying to keep him alive. When Jordan was shot leaving the house of a female friend two blocks from our home, the response among the citizens in Judge Busse's realm was this: "Well, what was he *doing* there in the first place?" Wasn't he asking for it? The police chief determined that the would-be assassin couldn't have been a local guy. He was a lousy marksman, and besides, "the good people of Fort Wayne were not racist." If we were, then so was everybody in the country, since we had a mountain of data proving we were the most typical Americans you could find anywhere.

"I doubt Mr. Jordan remembers you or the sleeve," I assured my son. "You were seriously upstaged that night."

RYAN AND Darren, of course, didn't feel the same urgency I did about the political issues we addressed in those years, nor did we laugh for exactly the same reasons at an old photo of eight Fort Wayne friends in bizarre costumes—eight hefty, overly made-up women in a chorus line of nuns, jailbirds, cocktail waitresses, and hairdressers. When the Fort Wayne Feminists' lesbian dance troupe needed to practice their number for the Bloomington Women's Music Festival, we cleared the couch and chairs out of our roomy living room once a week to provide rehearsal space. Ryan and Darren, then three and four, invariably won their case to stay up past bedtime on rehearsal nights, on the reasonable grounds that they couldn't sleep anyway.

Perched on the staircase in their sleeper pajamas, they laughed and clapped all evening; they were appreciative fans even though the humor was quite over their heads. They responded to the sheer fun of grown women acting like nuts, most of whom they recognized—their baby-sitter Sheryl, their friend Travis's mother, the volunteer at Sisterspace Bookstore who read their favorite stories during Children's Hour. Although we held these fond recollections in common, I also remembered that their Irish Catholic grandparents came for a visit a few weeks later and asked, "What's new?" They don't remember flawlessly executing a choreographed performance of "The Leaping Lesbians," the "ha-ha-ha-ha-haaaaaaa's" and all.

Wading my baby activists into the strong currents of political controversies in Fort Wayne, I deliberately let them get in over their heads at times. Their world was swamped with painful realities, but, like the sandbags we threw when the Maumee River flooded its banks, there were meaningful things to do that could relieve the feeling of helplessness. Howard and I both wanted them to know that, by organizing with like-minded people, it was possible not only to raise barns but also to collapse roofs in redlined housing markets. Not that we taught them what it felt like to win. As John Kenneth Galbraith said, I have passionately supported "all the great losing causes of my day." During our Indiana years, we mostly learned how it felt to persevere.

DID MY sons' early involvement in the women's movement—all the marches and rallies they attended—mean they would become "feminist men"? Not recognizably so. They listened again and again to the songs on "Free to Be You and Me," and they could sing all the verses to "William Has a Doll," a song encouraging young boys to think of nurturing not as sissy behavior but as fatherly behavior. But what were the first dolls they bought with their own birthday money from Gramma? GI Joe and Masters of the Universe. "Question authority," I had insisted from the start; so, of course, the first authority they questioned was me. It had to be. Since "you cannot dismantle the master's house using the master's tools," I couldn't force pacifism on my sons without giving them a lesson in passive aggression.

Raising sons at the same time that I was questioning patriarchal values, I used to worry that I might alienate them from their culture and perhaps stifle their opportunities for later success. I had to worry then because I was applying what were regarded as radical feminist theories to actual human lives. I worry less now, of course. For one thing, in any contest between a woman and the culture for the allegiance of her sons, the culture has every advantage. For another, if I were serious about bringing up sons who had a chance of becoming such men as our daughters would be pleased to live among, they would have to drop the charade of superiority anyway. So why handicap them with it in the first place?

Even if I had wanted to keep my motherhood separate from my political beliefs, however, it wouldn't have been possible. Through no fault of their own, my sons were born to a mother who made speeches. In 1976, shortly after Darren was born, my journalism career was launched, quite accidentally, in the women's pages of the local press. A friend working at the *Journal Gazette* heard a university lecture I delivered on "The Myths of Motherhood" and asked if I would contribute an essay for the paper's Mother's Day issue.

"Do you want that greeting card fluff, or do you want the truth?" I asked.

"The truth," she said.

Adapting my speech about how far the myths departed from reality, I published as much of the truth as I knew in 1976. It ignited an impassioned, three-month debate in the letters-to-the-editor column. One Fort Wayne reader felt my education had ruined me for the job, citing a brief reference I had made to William Faulkner as the damning evidence. Another suggested I was a communist because I had referred to Howard as my "comrade in parenting." One kindly grandmother sent me a list of psalms she thought would be helpful on oatmeal-splattered, tantrum-driven days like the one I'd described, suggesting that I "offer it up to God." As for the young mothers—at least those who found time to write—they invariably expressed relief and gratitude to find their own unspeakable feelings expressed in mine.

The deep resistance to the outlaw philosophy of motherhood—which collided with cherished assumptions about women's capacity for self-sacrifice and martyrdom—was evident when the newspaper photographer read my essay before coming to shoot me and the boys. He was confused. What kind of Mother's Day photo could possibly go with this? The usual madonna-and-child shots he took every year would seem a parody next to a story about the real life of moms. He asked the editor: "Do you want candids, like, of her beating her kids?"

Beating her kids? Using the same either/or dichotomy that governed female sexuality (if a woman wasn't a virgin she was automatically a whore), the photographer thought since I didn't seem to be a madonna, I must be a child abuser. In the mid-'70s, many Fort Wayne residents held the same view, expressed by Christian Coalition leader Pat Robertson much later in Iowa, that feminists "leave their husbands, kill their children, practice witchcraft, destroy capitalism and become lesbians." Both in Fort Wayne and elsewhere, mothers who encouraged egalitarian ideas in sons were regarded as part of a dangerous plot to emasculate men. Back then, plenty of people were convinced that female equality led to male impotence.

I can hardly exaggerate the hostility aroused by "women's lib"—"women's lip," according to some readers—in the state where both the Ku Klux Klan and the John Birch Society were deeply entrenched, not to mention heavily armed. After my sons learned to read, they would see the phrase "man-hater" regularly attached to my name in the letters-to-the-editor column—this, about the person who was supposed to love them unconditionally for life.

My public feminism aroused strong feelings of agreement or anger but rarely ambivalence. These attitudes were extended to my sons by association. Ryan was only in kindergarten when he was accosted by a teacher's aide in the hall at school, still fresh with indignation on a steamy Monday morning after one of my columns had run. She dumped her contempt for me and "all those crazy libbers your mother likes so much" on his five-year-old head. It took me a few moments to unscramble his breathless account when he came running home from school that afternoon. He thought the aide had objected to his mother's crazy "livers," pictured the appetizer we often served guests, and begged me to give them up. I could still save the bacon—just take out the livers he said, looking at me with the wide-eyed, beautiful innocence of young children who have said more than they know.

I wrote the teacher's aide, sending a copy of my letter to the administration, and requested that all further explosions of spleen be directed to me or the newspaper. I observed a moratorium on chicken livers for a while, until they could be served again without causing alarm. In the subsequent months, I noticed how often other adults assumed that, because Ryan and Darren were my sons, they shared my opinions and beliefs. When they gave their last name to the school nurse or the coach at soccer tryouts, they were usually greeted with more enthusiasm or contempt than they themselves merited.

They felt guilty when they couldn't defend me—it was hard, at four and five, to understand people's hatred of chicken livers. They felt ashamed and disloyal when they didn't try, even though they didn't remotely qualify for a fair fight with angry adults. Still little guys, they were already branded as outlaws before they could defend themselves. In 1979, before my first book was published, I filed papers in the Allen County courthouse legally changing my name back to my birth name. The newspaper editor used a hyphenated byline for a few months to help readers make the transition, which drew a few sniper shots in letters from Eagle Forum regulars who accused me of a fuzzy identity. But it did provide the boys with a measure of anonymity in future schools and cities. Under their father's name, they now had a choice about when to acknowledge their relationship to me. And when to take cover.

I MAY have stumbled into freelance journalism by accident, but it soon became obvious that was exactly where I wanted to be. Although the lack of monetary rewards would guarantee further downward mobility and my approach to deadlines would forever be one of sweating panic, writing about social issues proved to be exceptionally compatible with motherhood. My job as a cultural reporter was to study the meaning public events had for private lives—in brief, to pay attention. Both lines of work, mother and writer, required the same habits of mind, the same criteria Virginia Woolf named as essential to independent thinking: A room of one's own, an independent income, and a willingness to live by your wits.

Although the stress of managing the "dual careers" of work and family has been well documented by now, the hardest part of being a working mom for me was handling the enormous information load. Commuting daily between these separate spheres—writing about the most alarming social issues and then bringing them home to my own private family—I was in a state of constant mind-shock. For anyone with passionate commitments to both worlds, any hesitancy about questioning authority instantly evaporates. I have no doubt that my professional work served as a catalyst for my speedy evolution into Unnatural Mom. Once certain truths about the culture were acknowledged, you either became an outlaw from the going program or a fraud about everything you knew.

The truths I've been stalking for the past twenty years have cost me most of my innocence (despite a seemingly inexhaustible Midwestern supply). I still have a poster in my office that I bought years ago, a one-sentence summary of my life as a writer: "The truth will make you free, but first it will make you miserable." Naturally, I've shared most of my miserable truths with my sons. Although it was my job to introduce unwelcome facts, I didn't expect people to accept them. I expected people to change them.

"Accepting reality is the first step to insanity," I used to tell Ryan and Darren, quoting an early outlaw theory. Because violence and sexism had become so normalized by the time they were born, I wanted them to feel comfortable being odd, to question the given reality. Throughout their childhood in Testmarket U.S.A., we often found ourselves in the margins of public approval. I particularly remember a period of disorientation in 1981 when we moved and the boys transferred from their small alternative school in Fort Wayne to a large public elementary school in Ann Arbor, Michigan.

The school they came from was a courageous experiment in education, founded in the early '70s by a handful of parents who dreamed of launching a program where children might learn the value of peace and tolerance. While we were at it, we dreamed that they might learn self-government and how to live in a democracy. The laws and customs, therefore, came from the kids' own experiences. Their statutes included such items as: "Nobody can spit on you," and "You can't give someone a 'noogie' in car pool," and "Don't hassle kids who have a Twinkie in their lunch."

When my sons moved from an alternative to a regular school, I expected some confusion. The subject of how to mainstream our kids after their experimental education had been a constant topic among the parents, as we agonized over whether we were advancing consciousness or retarding their successful participation in the greater world. About two weeks after the move, the boys detected the first signs that their lives had changed considerably. One morning Ryan received the news that without any conscious effort on his part, he had earned three "tardy" marks. One more, he learned, would win him a trip to the principal's office. From the reaction of the other third-graders, he quickly determined that the principal's office was not a place a boy with three tardy marks was likely to enjoy.

What he didn't know, and what filled him with anxiety, was how he got marked that way. Tardy was a concept that had not yet been introduced to his eight-year-old life. That morning at recess, he pressed one of his buddies for the lowdown on tardy. What was it, he wanted to know, and how do you get marked that way? He learned that tardy was a state of being, a condition that existed any time you were not in your seat when the second bell rang. This changed his perspective significantly. He had thought the 9:00 bell was like a musical invitation, a charming suggestion to enter the building. The way most people go to church, Ryan went to school.

On the morning of his third offense, Ryan had stayed in the parking lot a few extra minutes to perform a corporal act of mercy, unlocking his younger brother from the bike rack where Darren had accidentally chained himself through his back belt loop. At dinner that night, he announced to Darren that the next time he got locked to the bike rack, he'd have to stay there until recess. For a boy only one small slipup away from a visit to the principal, mornings became highly anxious times.

My son's crisis was similar to the alienation my Women's Studies students reported after they left the supportive environment of their university classes and attempted to live their new ideas in the professions. Since women were newcomers to nearly all careers besides teaching and nursing, there was a deep suspicion that women would screw up corporate organization—a suspicion used to justify why women were paid so much less. Women worked in an atmosphere of anticipated tardiness. Even if you were never late—never so snarled in a life jammed with responsibilities that "tardy" was a given—you couldn't escape that atmosphere. And then the day would come when you would have to choose between leaving the baby strapped into the high chair until the sitter arrived or be half an hour late for work. There was a cure for tardy and for anxious mornings, but flex-time was not a concept that American business had yet absorbed. After nearly twenty years of employee campaigns, companies today have finally granted more flexible hours, but usually without benefits and at even more unequal pay. And so the national waltz continues: one step forward, two steps back.

Darren also had a rude surprise during that first disorienting autumn in Ann Arbor. Usually a lively second grader, he walked in the door one afternoon with the shuffle of an eighty-year-old man.

"What's the matter, Darren?" I asked him. He looked up solemnly, seemingly weighted down with an unspeakable tragedy.

"You can't call me that anymore, Mom," he announced heavily. "They took my name in the hall today."

Apparently, he had been one of the dominoes standing in line for the drinking fountain that afternoon when a strong shove rippled up from the rear. A harried teacher's aide whipped around the corner and took down everyone's name on a piece of paper.

"What happens when they take your name?" he'd asked one of the other dominoes.

"They just take it, that's all," he'd said.

Darren thought that having your name taken was the same as "losing your voice," which is what happened to kids at his other school who violated a peer-approved rule. They couldn't vote or have any influence until they'd made up the transgression. He was convinced he couldn't use his name until he'd made things right with the teacher's aide, who had it on a piece of paper. It was a week before the aide came back and cleared up the misunderstanding. In the meantime, we had to call him "Rocky."

I'm sure my Women's Studies students hardly imagined losing their names, having them evaporate into thin air. Indeed, they could see their names printed boldly on diplomas, attached to the solids of honors and achievements. Nevertheless, millions of women as thoughtful and deliberate as they had lost theirs. Look, for example, in the telephone book of any city, and count the number of women's names. There are hardly any Sandra's or Nancy's or Gertrude's; they are mostly men's names and initials. The women have cleverly disguised themselves to throw off obscene callers and rapists. When the consultant at Michigan Bell advised me against using my full name for that reason, I asked her if the obscene callers and rapists hadn't figured out by now that the initials are the women.

"Yes," she said, "I suppose they have."

Some women's names are lost because it's unsafe to use them, and others are subsumed in the interests of money and power. I remember reading all the names on the "Women's Board" during a long intermission at the Goodman Theatre in Chicago. The officers called themselves "Mrs. Thomas V. O'Neill, Mrs. William McKittrick, Mrs. Thomas Gowenlock III, Mrs. Anthony Antoniou, Mrs. Richard Strubel, Mrs. Richard Tourville, and Mrs. Donald Bowey." It was possible my former students would be listed in phone books and on who's who lists under names like Bill and Tony and Frank. It was even possible one of them could be identified as Rocky for awhile.

The worst shock during that difficult transition year came when Ryan arrived home an hour late, after serving the first detention in a week-long sentence for "talking to his neighbor."

"*Mom*," he said, with rising incredulity, "Why don't they want you to talk to your *neighbor*?" Neighbors, in his opinion, were what talking was *for*.

"Well, Bugs," I said, reaching for an explanation, "It's generally considered a good thing to love your neighbors, but not necessarily to talk to them . . . at least in school." I suggested that he save his talking for recess and lunch time.

"But what about art, Mom? What if you get a good idea in *art*?" His eyebrows were raised to his hairline at the thought of stifled art. Maybe in art, I told him, he could whisper—at his own risk.

I could hardly persuade my sons to adjust to reality when I completely identified with their position. The penalties against women for "talking to your neighbors" were even more rigid than the sanctions against tardiness. After the free-flowing discussions in classrooms and CR groups, the enforced silence felt particularly punishing. Out there in the professions, talking to your neighbors is one of the most feared and damned acts you can perform. Not long ago, four nuns in a New England parochial school were fired by their bishop without cause, and the sisters had to press a civil suit to find out why. The bishop said they were guilty of "being cliquish." The courts determined that this was just cause.

This fear permeates all professions. Congresswoman Patricia Schroeder, for one, observed it in government. "It's really funny if two women stand on the House floor," she said. "There are usually at least two men who go by and say, 'What is this, a coup?' They're almost afraid to see us in public together." The congressmen and bishops and judges aren't being paranoid: When women get together, it does often lead to a coup, of sorts: They complain about the pressures of their dual careers and their feelings of invisibility.

Every painful learning experience provides a nugget of truth, of course, and these periods of alienation taught my students that there was always a penalty for those who broke from the herd. Rather than encouraging them to adjust to the status quo, I hoped that they would suffer being tardy whenever their personal commitments were inseparably connected to their professional ones; that they would never become reconciled to being called Ralph; that they would risk talking to their neighbors—whispering, if necessary—in klatsches and cliques and coups. I hoped, most keenly, that they would continue to dream about alternatives. What was the point of raising one's consciousness, inch by agonizing inch, if you couldn't live what you learned?

It wasn't my mission then, and it's not my mission now, to help anybody adjust to reality. My sons eventually understood that their survival, too, depended on learning the public agenda, although the rules weren't always comprehensible to them. Their logic and reason were useless in breaking the code of behavior; the rules weren't logical and the customs not reasonable. Much like two mice in a blind maze, their thoughts ran this way and that, and they tried to memorize what seemed like a random pattern. They struggled hard to adapt. Interested in learning why they didn't give up, I asked them why they kept trying. Because they liked the way things were with their old teachers, they said. "School is nice when they like you." They wanted to live that way again.

My sons now seem to have a touch-and-go relationship with the ruling social order. Perhaps because I learned so many important lessons about motherhood from the matrons in an insane asylum, I never felt particularly alarmed when they exhibited signs of disorientation. I can't hope for their complete adjustment—or that the current social order will ever become reasonable, or easy, for them. I'm interested mostly in keeping the idea of alternatives alive, in remembering the days when being flexible and keeping your name and talking to your neighbors were considered honorable.

I suspect my sons probably have multiple reactions by now to the dual worlds they have been navigating for nearly two decades. I doubt Darren was thinking about Dow Chemical and its critical behind-the-scenes role on MTV before I arrived, uninvited, to prompt his memory. My role is largely a silent one now, dependent on telepathic insights, and most of their future ideas about sexual politics will come from other sources. It grieves me that the culture provides so little reinforcement for what they have learned so far, and I naturally wonder how the lessons of their youth will hold up in the challenging years ahead. The pressures for conformity will be enormous. Although God knows, if their peculiar childhood has given them nothing else, they have plenty of experience being the odd men out.

6

The Holistic Divorce

The boys and I have wildly divergent memories of our political history, and the photo project at our kitchen table revealed profoundly different takes on our personal history as well. It's said that "pictures never lie," but ours sometimes did. A candid shot taken in the park across from our house in Fort Wayne, circa 1977, shows a young family romping playfully in the fall leaves, looking like the insanely happy foursome we desperately wanted to be that year. The boys, dressed in miniature tie-dyed T-shirts and overalls, are still tots, I am a writer in my late twenties, and Howard a professional city planner in his early thirties. The faint shadows under Howard's and my eyes are the only traces of the argument we had the night before, the usual one about money and job prospects and who was more irresponsible, the unpublished writer or the unemployed planner?

Ryan, miserable on general principle at two and a half, had been crying when the photographer arrived, and we spent the first hour of expensive time bribing him with treats to cheer him up. After his red eyes and blotchy face cleared up sufficiently for the camera, we went across the street to the park where, no doubt flying on an overdose of sugar, he tripped on his shoelace and we started all over again. The photo shoot took hours—the photographer wanted to pose our spontaneous fun just right. In the last shot, I'm lying on my stomach in the leaves, propped up on my elbows and looking over my shoulder at the kids, who are seated on my back and supported from behind by Howard. He is smiling through clenched teeth, since we can hardly afford this professional photographer we've hired. I'm straining to hold my grin but thinking, "C'mon, *c'mon* . . . , click the shutter. My back is *killing* me."

We kept trying to hold position through our excruciating discomfort that year. We thought we had just hit a rough patch, as every family does sooner or later. We didn't know we were on a long, dangerous downgrade that would demolish our brakes. Not long after I'd resigned from my position as dean of students, Howard lost his job. The boys now had two full-time parents but no one to pay the bills. It was a prescient sign of things to come. "For Sale" signs cropped up on lawns all over our tree-lined street after International Harvester closed its Fort Wayne plant. Mortgage defaults and foreclosures were common, and the only "help wanted" ads in the newspapers were from collection agencies.

The brief period of unemployment we were marginally prepared for stretched into one merciless year after another. To make ends meet, Howard and I patched together an ever-changing crazy quilt of part-time jobs (he painted houses for friends trying to attract buyers in a flooded market, while I wrote jingles for a local advertising firm at a dollar a word), or temporary teaching jobs (without benefits or health insurance). We alternated shifts as single parents to save on child care.

I still feel a vague ache in my back whenever I look at those old photographs, an echo of the acute strain I felt playing Let's Pretend in the park that autumn. I now see the body sculpture of a woman in deep trouble, her body twisted into a position the human form was never meant to hold. Ryan, too, fell into a meditative silence when he studied those photos last winter, although he couldn't have been feeling the same tension in his spine.

Without the facts that were swirling over his head at age two and a half—facts of family history that are still cloudy to him fifteen years later—he has no explanation for those faint shadows under our eyes, if he notices them at all. He wouldn't have known about the argument the night before; we were careful not to argue in front of the boys. He might not even remember his own crying that afternoon, or the day before—that whole autumn, as it turned out—a plaintive wail that railed against the natural frustration of the Terrible Twos, or maybe against a premonition that his parents were cracking up. Who knows what hurts when a baby cries for months and months? When Ryan saw that idyllic image of our faked happiness last winter, I supposed he couldn't help wishing we'd kept playing Let's Pretend. From his point of view, it must have looked like infinitely more fun than the real life he's known since we became a postnuclear family.

"Each divorce is the death of a small civilization," novelist Pat Conroy once wrote. I may spend the rest of my life trying to figure out why we could not mend our small civilization after the first symptoms of serious disorder appeared. God knows, we tried desperately to fend off that death. Night after night at the kitchen table, Howard and I argued about money and responsibility, about which of us needed professional help, lowering our voices when the kids woke up.

Whenever I read the cold facts about unemployment in newspapers today, I immediately flash back to my own long sentence under that statistic. I automatically imagine the private stories behind the anonymous numbers, the personal grief and desperation the media mention only in passing. Once you have lived within those marginal asides about "tensions at home," you know there is nothing abstract about numbers. The unemployment rate, if it happens to apply to you, can become intensely particular in a hundred mundane details, from anxious moments in the grocery checkout to angry outbursts at dinner to silent, brooding nights in front of the TV. When certain facts attach themselves to you, they infiltrate every hour of your day. For us, the pathology that began with the germ of unemployment spread rapidly into guilt, depression, paralysis, poverty, denial, hostility, and emotional abuse.

Yes, we would co-sign another loan. Yes, we would both begin therapy. Yes, after five happy years of "for better" we would honor our vows through five long years of "for worse." And yes, as Mary

McCarthy once wrote in *How I Grew,* we would eventually discover "it really happens that someone you love could exhaust your capacity for suffering." After Howard and I agreed to separate, he left Fort Wayne to resurrect his life as a graduate student at the University of Michigan and I remained in Fort Wayne with the kids. I worked at home and supported us on my erratic income as a writer, which sometimes meant drafting fictional checks at Kroger.

The decision to divorce was made slowly and painfully, coming only after trips down every other avenue turned into blind alleys. In the end, whether the autopsy report establishes poverty or depression or emotional paralysis as the cause of death, the survivors face a prolonged period of mourning when their little civilization finally collapses. Three years after our posed joy in the park, the Colonial Mortgage Company began foreclosure proceedings on the beautiful house in the background. When the leaves fell again in the autumn of '81, the wooden stake of a For Sale sign was driven into our front lawn. The kids and I quickly discovered that neighborhood friendships were among the first casualties in the tense atmosphere of a postnuclear family.

In our depressed Midwestern community, the For Sale signs in front of homes struck by divorce were like the black Xs on the doors of quarantined families during the bubonic plague. Neighbors who felt safely insulated from the alarming statistics on unemployment or divorce or bankruptcy regarded us with pity; those who felt our tragedy could be contagious reacted with fear. Since marriages were fragile everywhere in Fort Wayne, where breadwinners were without work and housewives were working overtime, we became a frightening reminder that love cannot conquer all.

AFTER IT became clear that my ten-year marriage was unsalvageable, I prepared for the long negotiations ahead by reading everything I could find on divorce. I knew we weren't destined to have a "clean break," if there really was such a thing, because Howard and I both had a mutual passion for the children. I had assumed we'd be parents together for the rest of our lives. The other reason

I couldn't imagine letting go of love altogether was that more than a decade of my own history was spent with this man, my best friend and main enthusiast during those first rocky years of adulthood. I wanted to honor the tenderness of those years, hoping we could eventually salvage the friendship that once sustained us.

It was alarming, then, to read Judith Wallerstein's and Joan Berlin Kelly's prognosis for our recovery in *Surviving the Breakup* (1980). Most of the couples they studied spent an average of five years in an icy emotional white winter after divorce. Five years seemed an enormous wasteland to me. I became obsessed with beating the odds. Underlining the relevant passages, I added marginal comments with triple exclamation points and sent the book to Howard. I wrote countless letters urging him to help me create a "good divorce." I might as well have asked him to swallow a nice cup of Kool-Aid laced with cyanide. From his point of view, there was no such thing as a good divorce.

As it turned out, ours was to be as bitter and punishing as the national average. We didn't exempt ourselves from a single one of the casualty years: It would take us exactly five years to regenerate trust, the slowest growing human emotion. Divorce is the psychological equivalent of a triple coronary bypass. After such a monumental assault on the heart, it can take a whole decade to amend all the habits and attitudes that led up to it. Although the courts had invented the category of "no-fault" divorce by then, it didn't govern the opinions of the participants. Howard and I spent the last year of our marriage assigning blame and listing grievances.

After he moved and began his doctoral program in Ann Arbor in 1981, we communicated mainly by mail because all personal contact had become emotionally risky. On the phone, one or the other of us would start crying. Face to face, smoldering looks that were frighteningly close to hatred filled eyes that had once reflected love. Despite noble efforts at civility when we met to collect or deliver the kids on weekends, surprise attacks of anger and guilt ambushed us regularly. Those bursts of rage were necessary, I suppose, serving as the noisy booster rockets lifting us out of a depressed marriage. Sustained righteousness was the fuel that launched our separate lives, but for a while it obliterated all affection.

"He's in a freefall after ten years of security, and he's terrified," a friend remarked about the stomach-dropping jump into singleness again. In the grip of that terror, people are in no shape to negotiate the tough legal questions of divorce. Yet that's generally the stage when the attorneys are called in, jackhammers in hand, to chisel settlement terms into cement. Behind the clinical phrases and seemingly impartial laws, however, it's clear that anger and madness are writing the rules: A woman's standard of living drops 73 percent after divorce, while a man gains 42 percent; more than 60 percent of the fathers pay no child support after five years, and the majority exercise visitation rights erratically, if at all.

Once the courts reduced fatherhood to a monthly check to the clerk of the circuit court and two hours each week for a ball game, it wasn't amazing that so many fathers lost track of their children—their sizes, their ages, their passions. (What *was* amazing was that at the time fathers' rights groups blamed women for the tragedy. Did they really think that mothers designed this grand arrangement, plunging themselves into poverty and utterly single motherhood?) When, after a year of separation, it was finally time to negotiate our divorce, I didn't rush to the courts for help.

My friends had urged me to hire a "hard-ass attorney" to protect my interests, anticipating the financial strains ahead. Thinking hard-ass attorneys were largely responsible for much of the pain people suffered during divorce, I found a kind of holistic attorney to serve as a mediator for a settlement we could write ourselves. He called the document we created a "Dissolution Agreement." Before it was written down, I thought he was saying "Disillusion Agreement," and I was impressed with his poetic sensibility. The disillusion is overwhelming when love is broken down into its myriad, complicated parts. Like most couples who are crazy in love when they recite the standard vows to "love and honor," we never fully understood those fuzzy promises until we had to take them apart during our divorce negotiations.

The vague assumptions about sharing money and children were then written down in excruciatingly detailed, unromantic terms. Divorce exposes absolutely every buried assumption about marriage—what we mean by motherhood and fatherhood, who actually owns the joint bank accounts, how a husband's sense of entitlement and a wife's sense of duty turned the principle of "our money, our kids" into the reality of "his money, her kids." It had taken Howard and me only about ten minutes to pronounce the "I do's" at the altar, but we would spend the next ten years trying to figure out who, exactly, was supposed to do what: Who was responsible for providing child care, finding baby-sitters and tutors, driving car pools, for which periods and where? Who would pay for the kids' clothing/medical bills/music lessons/college tuitions?

Because we had made certain amendments to the traditions of marriage—I had retrieved my own name, Howard shared the care of the children—we were under the illusion that we had achieved a marriage of equals. In fact, we were like the hybrid produce being tested in the grocery stores of Testmarket U.S.A. that year. Bright red hothouse tomatoes and dyed orange citrus fruit heightened your temptation to buy, but when you brought the altered produce home and took a bite, you discovered the grainy, juiceless pulp of the "concept tomato." Although Howard and I had customized our marriage to suit the times, the fundamental attitudes we inherited were still firmly and invisibly in place. We talked a good game but achieved only concept equality.

Still, since we had been striving for a "nontraditional" marriage, it made sense to end it with a nontraditional divorce. Given the statistics governing the traditional ones, we had nothing to lose. The agreement we wrote was designed to expire periodically. I imagined we might need five or six divorces before we were through with the commitments we'd initiated by having babies. The first round of negotiations was the hardest, having to be conducted in the icy cold absence of trust and affection.

Because both of our careers were in a state of flux at the time, making it difficult to anticipate future incomes, our financial agreement didn't specify exact amounts of child support and due dates. Instead, I wrote a sort of essay-divorce, outlining the tenets of my faith: I would support the kids while Howard was in graduate school; he would resume his financial share when he became gainfully employed at a university—if possible, one that provided tuition benefits for the kids' college education; and we would renegotiate each time one of us had a change in income to keep monetary obligations fairly balanced against resources. Our financial settlement had the teeth of a newborn baby—all gums—and left us mutually dependent on each other's goodwill.

Leaving the specifics about dental bills and reading tutors to "the parent who could best afford them," I assumed that after ten years of love and friendship we would not be tempted to screw each other. We promised instead "to be fair and honest in all the future negotiations." The judge in Allen County who had to approve this document took off his glasses after reading it and studied us curiously, as if we had arrived in his courtroom directly from Mars. He commended us for "the most humane divorce" he'd ever granted.

"God bless you," he said, then put on his glasses again and shook his head. "I hope to hell it works for you."

IT SOON became obvious that the "best interests of the children"—which included a close connection to both parents—were strained by the 140 miles between us. After a year of infrequent weekend visits, Howard was feeling estranged and alienated from the sons he'd nurtured since birth, especially during the years of unemployment. And Ryan and Darren were cheerful but inept travelers, losing their baseball mitts or homework assignments when we transferred their kid things from car trunk to car trunk.

Since my work as a writer was portable and their father's doctoral program at the University of Michigan was not, I agreed to set up a home in Ann Arbor for two years and postpone my move to New York, where my career had moved the year before without me. On a tree-lined street a bike ride away from their father's cramped student quarters, I rented a large three-bedroom apartment. The kids lived there all the time, and each month, when I commuted to New York City for a week of meetings with editors and publishers, their father moved in. Howard resumed the lunch-making, laundering, and cleaning tasks of parenthood, and often at the end of those weeks, he was too tired for a game of baseball. But he knew what shirt belonged to whom, remembered to hold the onions on one of the hot dogs, and became privy to the inside chatter of his sons again.

My friends thought I was crazy when I moved to Ann Arbor, directly into the furnace of the long smoldering anger of an ex-husband. What was I doing in Ann Arbor when my own work was in New York and the man I'd begun keeping company with lived in Washington, D.C.? I went there, I suppose, to shed the last of my guilt for opting out of the death clause. "Til death do us part" had lost its romantic appeal once it threatened to become an imminent possibility for me. But I also hoped that by becoming a solid ally to Howard's fatherhood, we would eventually rebuild our friendship. It mattered enormously to me, for personal as well as familial reasons. We had at least another decade of close contact ahead of us if we both remained firmly committed to our sons—and I didn't want to spend the next ten years engaged in combat.

Did my decision to postpone my own career move to accommodate Howard inspire gratitude in our family? Certainly not. Gratitude never even occurred to the kids; children expect to be loved extravagantly, as they should. They were unaware that any extraordinary efforts were being made on their behalf because, while their parents had been acting oddly for two years, their essential needs for food, clothing, shelter, soccer balls, and boy scout uniforms were being met. Like all young children, they didn't think too much about how these things happened. And Howard, still nursing his wounds from the divorce, couldn't acknowledge any generosity from me. In his ledger, my move to Ann Arbor to facilitate his fatherhood didn't balance against my desertion as his wife.

Each month, renewed hostilities broke out during the changing of the guard. I would stock the kitchen with food and stack clean laundry in the kids' rooms before I left for New York each month in order to give Howard a running start on his week as a single parent. In the subtle sabotage between divorce opponents, he would forget to do the same for me. The Ann Arbor arrangement returned us to the same financial and household strains that ended our marriage, and I, too, wrestled with old rages. Divorce had changed the structure of our family relationship, but it didn't change who we were.

THE KIDS were not involved in any of the fractious negotiations Howard and I conducted through those hostile years—at least, not directly. Although they missed their Dad the year he moved out, they didn't appear to be any more traumatized than children whose fathers went away on long business trips. After I established our revolving household in Ann Arbor the following year, Howard often joined us for dinner in his off weeks, attended all their soccer games, and met us in the auditorium for school plays. My own demeanor was aggressively cheerful in the kids' presence, despite my financial strains supporting them alone. One month, when a paycheck from New York was late, our electricity and phone were shut off. I acted as if everybody lived in the dark once in a while; the kids, given their strong need to pass for normal, readily accepted my performance. Young children's capacity for denial is enormous.

They noticed, of course, that other parents lived together. But when the rhythm of their days was sufficiently smooth again, they no longer questioned our oddness. After two years of careful planning, I thought I had eased them as painlessly as possible into the reality of divorce. I remember the night I told Ryan and Darren that our life in Camelot, such as it was, had officially come to an end. I imagined they would accept the divorce itself as I did, a mere formality that simply named the life we were already living. I imagined too—because divorced mothers also have a huge capacity for denial—that they would adjust to the news without much grief.

That night, we were on our way back home from a brief vacation in Washington, D.C., with my friend Larry. The kids had been asleep for some time in the back seat of my old Dodge Dart, engine knocking and muffler rumbling. They woke up when I pulled under the bright lights of the toll booth as I exited the Ohio turnpike. They had once been such sound sleepers; they even slept through the cyclonic winds when a tornado touched down in the esplanade across from our Fort Wayne house. But they had both become light sleepers that year, prone to nightmares as unconscious fears repressed by day arose with a vengeance in dreams. It was well past midnight as we headed north on U.S. 23. Wide awake, they crossed their arms and rested their chins on the back seat, assuming their talking heads position in my rear-view mirror.

We had some of our most meaningful conversations in the car during those transition years, since we spent so much time on the road. That night we talked about our memorable adventures in Washington, the trip to the zoo, whether Pandas could have babies in captivity, the crabs we bought at the fish market on the Potomac, whether crustaceans felt any pain in boiling water. Larry had urged us to come back soon—there was still the Air and Space Museum to see, the Mad Hatter shop in Georgetown, and kites to fly on the river banks. This friend in Washington was doing his best to win their affections, and they undoubtedly noticed that his interest in Mom was being returned. Ryan, the main champion for his Dad's best interests that autumn, suggested that we invite Howard along on our next visit to Larry. Darren, who supported all of his older brother's campaigns that year, seconded the idea. It seemed like the right time to introduce them to the further ramifications of our new reality.

Family dinners with their Dad would continue, I explained, but family vacations would not. I told them, briefly: "We filed for divorce this month. It will be official in a few days." They had known for some time it might happen, for both Howard and I had discussed the D-word with them by then to help them imagine life after death. But this was the night they had to believe it. The impact was immediate and dramatic.

Both began wailing loudly, as if they'd taken a bullet in the heart. They flung themselves backwards into the back seat, vanishing from the rear-view mirror. Hearing their sobs between gasps for air, I felt a dam breaking inside my chest.

As I drove the Dodge into the night, I promised them the moon: They would still see as much of their Dad as ever; *they* weren't getting divorced from him—*I* was; we would both remain as committed to them as we had always been; we would both make sure they had everything they needed to be happy. I reminded them that the family had already been restructured for almost two years; that we were managing pretty well; and that divorce wouldn't change that. I reminded them, too, that they had already made most of the hardest changes—moving to a new city, learning to navigate new schools, making new friends.

In language as close to their youthful comprehension as I could get, I told them that change was the one constant in life and almost never without an element of pain. The best method of dealing with it, I said, was the one they had been using. Then I quoted the message Darren had received in a fortune cookie during our last dinner in Fort Wayne, a mantra he recited whenever he felt the heebie-jeebies coming on that year: "Work hard and you shall be rewarded." I said it with the same reverence he did, since the doctrine of fortune cookies was as close as my sons ever came to a catechism.

I made these midnight promises in good faith, but as it turned out I was wrong about almost everything. Life would not be almost the same. They would not have the financial support of both parents. They would not see as much of their Dad in the years ahead. The boys intuitively knew how the phantom pains of a missing parent, one or the other, would accompany them for the rest of their childhood. The wounds they sustained in the Dodge that night would reopen again and again before they healed, and expressions of pain too deep for their young faces would sink my heart. The days of passing for normal were over for good.

7

A Postnuclear Family

In our first postnuclear winter, Ryan and Darren developed a zero tolerance for family frictions of any kind. Living with them was like being under the surveillance of two miniature CIA agents, their eyes narrowing at the first hint of parental treachery. Ryan, then eight, was especially alert to any signs of disloyalty toward his father, whom he regarded as the needier, more vulnerable parent. He reacted with instant suspicion when he overheard me say to a friend on the phone one morning, "Sure, I'll drive—the Dodge is in the shop again, but Howard was nice enough to lend me his car today."

"What do you mean, 'nice enough'?" Ryan asked, unearthing what he judged to be an insult. "Dad is *real* nice, *all* the time," he said. I tried to explain that was what the expression meant, but his antennae for insulting remarks were turned way up and I didn't get through. He cast me a sideways glance from under his baseball beak that said: Just don't let it happen again. I was frankly jealous of the large empathy both boys had for their father. I also admired it.

Their insistence on parental civility was neither subtle nor negotiable. Even Darren's Halloween costume that October became a kind of political statement against aggression. He made a large cardboard triangle, painted it yellow, and became a walking YIELD sign. Given our enormous blind spots that year, neither Howard nor I knew what gave him the idea. Secretive, sometimes furtive, the boys allowed no information to leak between parents that would further damage allegiances. Questions like "How was your time with Dad?" or "What did you think of Washington, D.C.?" were answered in a monosyllable: "Fine" or "Nice." Under the boys' guarded scrutiny, Howard and I were both obliged to act in a more mature and generous fashion than we really felt. Eventually, we achieved a serviceable politeness toward each other.

Even the usual sibling rivalries between the boys disappeared in the fragile accords established that year. When Ryan eyed his brother's copious loot on Halloween night and artfully suggested they combine the booty and share everything, Darren yielded instantly, with an easy-come-easy-go kind of shrug. Without an invigorating fight, Ryan found little pleasure in snookering Darren out of his candy. He gave it back, inflicted with a baffling new urge to protect his younger brother, his former competitor and rival. They became an inseparable twosome, each other's constant companion as their unpredictable parents kept moving in and out.

I OCCUPIED the witch role that autumn—alternately, the evil witch who caused their father to disappear and the good witch who was "nice enough" to invite him back for dinners and birthday parties. But whatever I did, I could never conjure up enough magic to relieve all the aches divorce brought into their childhood. No mother can shield her kids entirely from pain, of course, but a mother recovering from large bouts of pain herself has an urge to keep trying. So I directed my attention to the kids, while they directed their attention to their father. Most of the attention given to me during these rocky transition years came from outside sources.

My period as Divorced Mom unfortunately coincided with the rise of a new breed of motherhood professionals: the family values evangelists. When these folks organized a witch-hunt, it wasn't hard to form a posse—especially in the Midwest, where the rising divorce rate went hand in hand with a sinking economy. The same way psychiatrists once blamed our mothers for the genetic tragedies of schizophrenia and manic depression, now the family values evangelists were blaming the mothers of my generation for the socially manufactured disaster of adolescents with guns and bad attitudes. Pat Buchanan's rhetoric reached fever pitch at the 1992 Houston Convention damning single, divorced, and working mothers for neglecting their children and loosing "barbarians from public schools" on society. Since we are all frightened by the barbarians among us, I imagine Mr. Buchanan felt better after venting his outrage from the pulpit. But here in the pews we know that motherhood, as currently framed by the culture, has nowhere near the power he imagines. Mothers are more or less in the janitorial position of the culture's power hierarchy.

My sister Regina recognized the futility of powerless responsibility after spending four years teaching the young barbarians in a high school in Massachusetts, the same four years our "education president" George Bush was in office. As Reg began her last term, six of her students did not have desks (not a problem, she was advised, once the dropout rate kicks in); there were no lights in her classroom for four months (a problem, especially on cloudy days, when she had to move her rowdy tribe in senior English to the cafeteria without losing any along the way); and she had to buy her own mimeograph paper that year (big problem, since it coincided with a teacher pay cut). Despite the contemptuous policies and attitudes surrounding public education—or maybe because of them— my sister was deeply moved by the daily courage of teachers who still cared and students who kept striving. Regina didn't know whether to laugh or cry when she read the description that Maria, one of the most determined seniors, wrote on her college application under Honors and Awards: "I have never been arrested."

A clean rap sheet *was* an outstanding achievement for a teenager in Maria's economically depressed and crime-ridden community, but would the admissions dean at Harvard, only a few miles away, recognize it? It was clear to Regina that even if every mother quit work and went on welfare so she could be home with her kids, or got off welfare and went to work so she could earn more money for her kids (or whatever else an individual mother could do so Mr.

Buchanan would like her better), she still needed desks and paper and dedicated teachers for her children. The education president, reluctant to "throw taxpayer dollars" at these needs, suggested instead that the problems could be solved with voluntary school prayer. Dear God, could we please have some *lights*?

THE FAMILY values evangelists made converts of frightened citizens right and left. Even the intellectual editors at the *Atlantic* abandoned all reason and joined the witch-hunt. In a cover story called "Dan Quayle Was Right," sociologist Barbara Dafoe Whitehead reviewed the theory that the Los Angeles riots could be traced to Murphy Brown—the weekly situation comedy that exposed television viewers to the dangerous image of a happy single mother. According to our former vice president, this positive portrayal of an independent, unmarried mother was the reason why the American family had broken down. Whitehead amassed scientific proof that poverty, urban violence, lousy SAT scores, and the bleak economy can be directly linked to the selfishness of divorced and single mothers: "The family has weakened because, quite simply, many Americans have changed their minds. They changed their minds about staying together for the sake of the children; about the necessity of putting children's needs before their own; about marriage as a lifelong commitment," she concluded. Since three-quarters of all divorces are filed by women, we can assume that these negligent Americans are mostly mothers. Having personally contributed to the high divorce rate, I'm constantly astonished by the notion of the flip, loose-living, self-centered single mother who's having more fun than anyone else.

Whitehead cites numerous studies to prove that children living with two biological parents are better off in every way than children in households headed by a single parent: they inherit more money, they live in nicer homes, they have superior medical care, they get better educations, and they tend to marry earlier. Undisturbed by the possibility that divorce might be the *result* rather than the *cause* of economic instability, she concludes that all children could live like Wally and Beaver if their parents would just stay married. The solution to the steady downward mobility of the United States' working classes, to drug abuse/decaying schools/overcrowded jails, Whitehead suggested, was to "restigmatize divorce." We can only be grateful she wasn't among the social scientists in Chicago studying urban violence in the early '60s, when rocks and flames accompanied black families into white neighborhoods. She might have suggested that the solution to racism was to bring back segregation.

"Stigmatization is a powerful means of regulating behavior, as any smoker or overeater will testify," she noted, as if the need for divorce were in the same category with cravings for a hot fudge sundae. Few of us who have actually been through the ordeal see ourselves as addicted—quite the contrary in fact. Most of the displaced homemakers in my classes were determined not to remarry, lest they risk the 50 percent chance of another dissolution. Trust me: The experts can relax about divorced moms feeling too good about themselves.

The more responsible family experts acknowledge that there might be "other factors" besides women's selfishness for the alarming deterioration of family life: The overwhelming violence in movies and on television; domestic battery and sexual abuse; rising unemployment; institutionalized wage discrimination; the disappearance of jobs that can support a family; the redistribution of wealth in the last decade that shifted 60 percent of all earnings to the top 1 percent of the population; increasing homelessness among the poor and mentally ill; the AIDS epidemic; the number of guns in U.S. homes; and the disintegration of good public education. Never mentioned in the same paragraph with "the rising divorce rate" is this factor, which is directly responsible for the death of thousands of small civilizations: 3.5 million men of my generation were enlisted during the Vietnam War—more than 1.5 million of them in combat, spending critical years of their youth under fire in a jungle in one of the most violent and dehumanizing conflicts in history.

The Vietnam veterans, the youngest and poorest soldiers in any

American war, were reabsorbed into mostly urban families. For the past two decades, a continuing flood of stories has revealed their persistent trouble reentering civilian life. These millions of physically and psychologically scarred men, *concentrated in one generation*, have sons who are coming of age today. Since the cyclical nature of domestic violence is so well documented by now, couldn't the scary, embattled, emotionally numb, and dangerously armed teenagers be the inevitable results of that foreign war coming home? Before we re-stigmatize divorce, which would imperil women and children living with tragically damaged men, shouldn't we first raise at least one generation of sons among whom our daughters can live safely? I long to read something from a family values expert who argues passionately that until we stop sending young men, future fathers, into the unfixable ruin of modern war, there is no possibility of bringing psychologically healthy, nonviolent, civilized children into this world. These urgent social issues are not "other factors," just as the symptoms listed in fine print on the warning labels of powerful medications are not "side effects." These are real effects; these are *the* factors.

Hardly anyone is more alarmed by the urban violence and poverty than the mothers of children most vulnerable to them. Nowhere, however, do the family values preachers acknowledge that my heart might be breaking, too, raising sons in a society where they must pass through metal detectors before they can study the multiplication tables, where it's easier and cheaper for a ten year old to buy a handgun than a pair of sneakers. Aiming howitzers of loaded facts at single mothers, the family values experts have bravely taken on an enemy that poses about the same threat the United States Army faced when they invaded terrified natives on the Island of Grenada.

For a brief moment, I felt an old urge to defend my group, to write the *Atlantic* editors and inform them they were holding the wrong hostages here. But the impulse passed quickly. For one thing, a divorced mom has about as much credibility in these social debates as a housewife had twenty years ago in psychiatric hierarchies. For another, the truth about real life in the interior has been out for more than two decades now. The startling gap between what I know from experience and what social critics conclude from their studies no longer inspires me to engage in lively intellectual debate.

It's not that I don't believe the grim statistics about female-headed households; indeed, I do. I've lived the facts and figures of single motherhood every day for the last thirteen years. The mathematics of my life, translated into a word problem:

Place me in a society where I am encouraged to marry young, have 2.5 children (two sons, one miscarriage); give us a few adjustment problems, because we are human; begin a recession that costs Howard his job; watch him devastated by guilt for not being a "breadwinner"; send me to work but apply a 35 percent discount to my wages because I am female; grant me a no-fault divorce after five years and make me dependent on child support, understanding there is less than a 40 percent chance the father will pay; make the odds even slimmer if he's angry, which he is; provide no day care or health insurance; watch me slide below the poverty line, where the vast majority of other residents are women and children; permit public education—the only kind I can afford—to deteriorate so severely that inner-city schools must put armed guards on the regular payroll; acknowledge the fatality of AIDS and the impulsiveness of children, but deny them access to condoms and sex education; declare a "war on drugs," offer a moronic slogan that blames the victim, and arrest the children of the poor. Be mystified when reports of "female voter outrage" start showing up in the *Times*. Decide it must be because of Anita Hill. Blame urban riots on working mothers and the absence of school prayer. Now calculate: If the only recommended solution is to couple every poor mother with a wealthy breadwinner who espouses family values, how many wives would Mr. Schlafly have to marry?

SINCE DIVORCE has never really been fully destigmatized, the family values evangelists shouldn't have too much trouble restigmatizing it. Maybe I missed some amnesty period, but it seems that my sons and I have had to live under labels like "broken home" or "dysfunctional family" for most of their childhood. If I'd had the time, I probably would have felt guilty about adding one more hardship to the already hard work of growing up. But guilt was another little maternal luxury that didn't make the transition to our postnuclear family.

When I visited with my friend Alice shortly after her divorce, a few years after my own, I was reminded of what an enormous number of woman-hours it takes to run these small civilizations. Alice moved nonstop from the moment I arrived—making a pot roast, washing dishes, doing laundry, solving her younger daughter's problems at the word processor, answering her older daughter's numerous phone calls, making arrangements for car repairs, ushering the child-women to bed, being patient, patient, patient. I watched her tight control all evening, seeing myself after my life had gone completely to hell, performing the same routines of faked competence. It's essential, in times of domestic disasters, to have clean laundry. Thus, making a great pot roast meant, "See? Look at that. I can make a whole meal." Doing the work of two people for the income of half a person, Alice and I needed every crumb of affirmation a day could yield.

After the girls were asleep, we opened a bottle of Cabernet and talked long into the night. We cried, we figured, we laughed, we indulged in the hysterical black humor that springs from the wells of deepest grief. How hard it was to lose "the companion of my youth," Alice lamented, the husband she had loved for almost twenty years. She regretted not being "more emotionally available" to her daughters, having been preoccupied with her dissertation last year and her divorce this year. The opportunities for guilt are legion for mothers, whether they are full-time, working, single, married, or divorced.

By 2:30 A.M. Alice and I were standing on opposite sides of the bed in the guest room, waving sheets across a queen-size mattress. I'd tried to convince her that I would have no trouble sleeping on the sheets already on the bed, sure that the last thing she needed was another load of laundry. But she couldn't bear the idea. Since we had been weeping on and off all night, it didn't surprise Alice when I suddenly burst into tears as we made the hospital corners. She assigned my tears to fatigue, while I said it was the Cabernet. Actually, they sprang from that absurd need for clean sheets, that doomed wish to be everything to everyone.

I remembered my own absurd conduct when I was trying to retain some claims as the Good Mother. Two months before, still recovering from major surgery, I'd gotten out of bed to bake my share of chocolate chip cookies for the cub scout bazaar. Another time, with a pulmonary tube wheezing between by ribs, I had walked three miles back and forth to town after the Dodge had broken down to get two new shirts for the boys' school pictures the next day. My behavior was completely crazy and dangerously self-destructive, but the self I once was had been so obliterated after the hostilities of divorce, it was hardly recognizable.

After Alice left for work the next morning, I meditated alone through two cups of coffee, still wrestling with despair. Watching my friend, I saw for the first time the overwhelming physical and psychological load we labored under, the strain of doing everything we could while knowing it was never enough. The night before we had said that there could be no more awful pain than being forced to leave someone you've loved. But the aftermath of shattered love in an unforgiving culture was punishing beyond belief. When Professor Whitehead looked at our lives through her statistics, she came up with "selfish." If she could have come into Alice's kitchen and witnessed the actual story, saw the grief and felt the love and heard the deep, dark wit, she might have come to another conclusion.

IF WE could set statistics aside for a moment and just listen to some of the stories, we would soon see that restigmatizing divorce would further handicap single mothers like Alice and me, and have a devastating effect on our married peers as well. Forcing every parent to stay married won't strengthen the family and secure the safety of children. Actually, it will do exactly the reverse. Marriage and divorce are parallel institutions, based on the same cultural assumptions about sex, children, and money. The condition of one has a direct effect on the other. If the practice of divorce were to become fair and just, if the life of single women and of children were to rise to a more humane standard, then life for married women and children would also become more fair and just. Likewise, the more miserable divorce becomes, the more miserable marriages will be as well.

Incest and sexual abuse, for example, are among the "other factors" Whitehead lists for the rising divorce rate, but she considers them less a factor than the central problem of women's selfishness. According to her statistics, incest accounts for only a small percentage of divorces. But this does not in any way reduce the horror of it for those who do file for that reason. Sociologist Diana Russell has confirmed that the incidence of sexual abuse is far greater than the meager divorce percentage suggests. Either women are disguising their motives under "no-fault" to get out of a bad marriage as fast as they can, or they are *not* divorcing when they should.

In a society where mothers cannot support their families—where we have to work double time to make up for discounted wages, where there is no system of dependable child care, flexible hours, or medical care—a dependent woman with children cannot leave her marriage, even if the safety of children is the very reason why she *must*. Faced with social ostracism and almost certain poverty, mothers trapped in abusive marriages are understandably frightened by the odds of independent survival. Perhaps "power corrupts," but powerlessness corrupts as well.

Increasing the sanctions against divorce would further endanger the mothers in this statistical minority, even if most experts would undoubtedly state that they meant only to punish the selfish mothers. By restigmatizing divorce, the message that goes out to abusive husbands and fathers is this: Be mean, be brutal, do whatever

you want—your wife can't leave you. In a culture where independent mothers were visibly thriving, however, the message would
be this: Better talk, better listen, better not take her for granted—
she knows as well as you do she could survive perfectly well without you.

The family values folks are so adamant about keeping marriages
together "for the sake of the children" that love doesn't seem to be
a key factor in deciding who should live with whom. Love is not
even expected to inform divorce. Friends who tried to imagine
themselves in my circumstances often said: "I couldn't do it—I'd
never let him see his kids again until he paid support." Withholding visitation rights to punish "deadbeat dads" is the divorced couples' version of Let's Pretend: We try righteously to believe that
what we are doing is "for the sake of the children," when the object
is really spousal revenge. Perhaps love is too high a goal for human
interactions. Perhaps we should "forget about love," as Kurt Vonnegut once wrote, "and just bring back common decency."

The contemptuous label "deadbeat dad" wasn't yet coined when
the issue of child support came up in our family; and that's not the
way Ryan and Darren have ever thought of their father. Howard
was chronically poor those years—his failure to pay support was-
n't motivated by revenge or abandonment, as it was for the fathers
who inspired the label "deadbeat." He wasn't withholding money—
he didn't have it. My sons didn't care about money and were completely irresponsible about it themselves. But they cared enormously about their dad's attention and affection. To have sabotaged
that filial relationship would have thwarted everybody's best interest, including my own. At the heart of my decision to be an unnatural mom and share custody with Howard was this self-interest:
The happier and more loved my sons felt, the more affectionate
and peaceful my own relationship with them would be.

Interestingly enough, the advice that I keep the children exclusively to myself invariably came from my married friends. They
urged me to "do something about Howard"—subpoena him, jail
him, make him pay—before sharing the kids. Not a single divorced

friend made this recommendation. Did married women feel more vulnerable somehow in the "her kids/his money" equation, causing them to cling more obsessively to their half of the assets? Did divorced moms tend to yield because they discovered exclusive rights to "her kids" was not only bad policy for children, but punitive to women as well? It meant we were perpetually grounded ourselves. With no weekend leaves, no furloughs, *and* no money, how could a woman be "enormously in charge of her life?"

The tighter a woman holds onto "her kids," of course, the tighter a man holds onto "his money." Keeping fathers at a distance almost never leads to a greater appreciation of the drain children cause on checkbook balances, whereas spending a lot of time with them will bring that point dramatically home. It's far easier to ignore kids' needs from a distance; it's much harder not to buy them dinner when they're sitting at your own kitchen table. Denying visitation is a dubious punishment for fathers anyway, given the depressing percentage who spend no time with their children even when they have ready access.

Social scientists generally attribute this emotional neglect to the alienation fathers feel from mothers. In truth, this tragedy more probably reflects the poor quality of the relationship they had with their kids before the divorce. Studies show that the practice of joint custody works only when a pattern of shared child care has already been established. If married men had to arrange regular visitation hours with their children, many would initially feel as awkward as their divorced peers. I couldn't agree more that kids benefit from the involvement of two biological parents, but marriage doesn't guarantee that. My friend Marge, a married mother of eight who worked in the Auditor's Office, once said, "Every mother is a single mother."

THE PROBLEM with the evangelists who are promoting "traditional family values" is that they are not interested in learning about anybody else's religion. The habit of either/or thinking—either you have a "good" (i.e., nuclear) family or you don't count as a family at all—prohibits recognition that some parts of marriage are bad and some parts of divorce are good. Despite the multiple hazards we face, single mothers often successfully restructure the old hierarchical pattern into a more consensual arrangement. Family therapist Thelma Jean Goodrich found that in many of these evolved families, "conflict is low, closeness is habitual, mothers feel competent and children are responsible, both in tasks and in decision-making." If divorce were destigmatized, all families could experiment with structures that would suit their needs.

Changing the institution of the family to fit the people is hardly a radical new idea. Suffragist and civil rights leader Crystal Eastman excited public discussion in 1923 with an essay in *Cosmopolitan* called "Marriage Under Two Roofs," in which she described how she kept her marriage intact by moving herself and the children into a separate apartment. After she eliminated her husband from the breakfast table, an immediate and dramatic improvement in family relationships took place. He was not a morning person and so reacted to the children's early rising energy about the same way Howard reacted to dropping peas in the evening. Longevity *requires* some adjustment to the rigid assumption that all families must live the same way, day after day, year after year. How many more divorces might there have been in the nineteenth century if a husband or wife had not managed to die before their small civilization did?

Since today's family experts seem to be in the grip of the same fanatical need for order and conformity that saturated the '50s, they might consider advocating universal divorce instead of forced marriage. Married couples in trouble might actually save their relationship if they had to distribute assets equally and establish joint custody. Even those lucky couples in great and happy unions might gain some insights into their relationship if they reviewed the myriad, minute details behind their vows to love and honor.

Besides creating a more humane environment "for the sake of the children," there is an even more compelling reason to stop stigmatizing working or single mothers. Because most of our work is invisible to the family values crowd, they're probably unaware of how valuable single mothers are in this society. Take us out, and you need four people to replace each one of us. The overseers never get it: If you whip the slaves nearly to death, who's going to bring in the crop?

TO HELP me move beyond the indignities of Divorced Mom, I spent two years visiting the Ann Arbor Center for the Family, where I paid a therapist $50 every week to use her Kleenex. She helped me imagine life on the other side of the wasteland, pointing out that in the postnuclear families who finally survive there is usually one person who plays the role of "connector," who keeps projecting everyone into a better future. The connector keeps children in touch with their grandparents, suggests treaties between fathers and stepfathers, tries to keep former in-laws from feeling like shutouts, and so on. The single qualification for the job is an unshakable belief in everyone's ability to change, despite damning evidence to the contrary.

I was a natural for the position, having been a believer in so many other impossible causes. My style as connector was summed up by one of my relatives, aptly I think, who said: "You praise a lot and yell a lot." Most of the yelling sprang from my triple-exclamation fear that we were running out of time and contained some version of the message, "Shape up!!!" The praise came from my enormous awe at the sheer, stupid bravery of human love. The boys were particularly gifted in this area, willing to keep loving parents who regularly slipped into anger or depression.

By the winter of our third year, I began to doubt my usefulness as the connector. Exhausted by the bimonthly commutes to my work in New York, strained by an overload of responsibilities, I felt this fatigue daily in my weakening body. Strange symptoms of undiagnosable illnesses had sent me to the hospital twice. The second time, exploratory surgery had left me with an untreatable staph infection in my lungs, and a pulmonary drainage tube had been inserted between my ribs. With each passing month, as the tube whistled its low moan after every deep sigh, I grew increasingly depressed over the shattered condition of my life and body.

I remember staying up late one night to watch a movie called *Tribes*, in which a peace-loving young man had to be reprogrammed to become a thoughtlessly obedient marine. Head shaved and uniformed in olive drab, he submits to the indignities of boot camp. Part of his training involved standing in a field for a long period of time, holding two full buckets of water in outstretched arms. The point of the exercise was to "break" the new recruits, melting their own will in order to establish blind obedience to authority.

I felt the weight of those buckets in my own arms and wanted desperately to drop them. As the pain penetrated the young man's limbs, he closed his eyes and dreamed himself into another world. In his mind, he was running through an open field, laughing and holding hands with a young woman from a former lifetime. He took pleasure in remembering her energy and affection. As all the recruits around him dropped their buckets in exhaustion, he held on, eyes closed and smiling. His drill sergeant was enraged, unable to break him as he dreamed his way out of boot camp. The movie made an enormous impression on me. Could a person really *dream* her way out of a crushing reality?

8

Approaching Ground Zero

Under the grinding obligations of being the sole wage earner, I began having second thoughts about the wisdom of my holistic divorce. After I absorbed Howard's share of the boys' expenses while he was in graduate school, the three years of double duty I'd anticipated was threatening to become our permanent arrangement. Since he no longer saw the kids' bills or paid any himself, I wrote countless letters and memos to keep him in touch with this reality. He responded to my urgent financial alerts essentially the same way my composition students did when I tried to drill them in the rudiments of grammar: He did not see how this information was useful to him.

Concerned about the obvious deterioration in my health, my friends alternately regarded me as a saint and a fool for not going back to court for a real divorce. Periodically, I contemplated hiring the hard-ass attorney they kept recommending but never made the call. I knew a contentious court battle would destroy the delicate familial treaties the kids were desperate to maintain. What's more, I was fairly sure a court order wouldn't make any difference anyway, since more than 60 percent of divorced fathers ignored them without consequences. I recognized a number that applied to me when I saw it. This man, who had treasured his wife and children and home more than anything in this world, did not accomplish the needed changes in the five years he had to save his marriage. He was hardly motivated to get it together for a "good divorce."

Although news about single moms and deadbeat dads began appearing regularly in the press, Howard and I perceived no part of this reality the same way. Whenever I came across the gross national default on child support I would think, "Here is why so many single mothers have nervous breakdowns—I'm lucky to be making ends meet at all." But I would imagine that a father encountering the same fact might think, "I belong to the majority—there's nothing unusual about me." When the kids' health coverage through the university expired, Howard tried to deflect my worries by noting, "Well, 35 million Americans are in exactly the same boat we are." It was a deeply ingrained Midwestern attitude that you did not put yourself above good people everywhere. From birth everyone who grew up in the heartland was familiar with the question: "Why should you be different from everybody else?"

THE ACTOR president we had in 1984 was fond of saying how the poverty of his childhood inspired him to become one of the wealthiest and most powerful men in the country. To Ronald Reagan, being poor was like eating a can of spinach. It didn't have that kind of invigorating effect on me. Every time I looked at the balance in my checkbook that year it prompted this thought: "Thirty days left to live."

While poverty is undeniably hard on everyone, children usually have someone looking out for their best interests. Their parents, however, have to jump without a net. Although Ryan and Darren had to face life without new dirt bikes and baseball mitts, and envied neighborhood pals who could take such presents for granted, they didn't have to stay up all night worrying about how to pay the electric bill, where to find the money for groceries or rent, and what could happen without money for the basics. It's easy to romanticize the character-building aspects of poverty for kids; but the erosive effects are devastating on the character of their parents. When my paychecks from New York were late, I kited checks at Kroger. When Larry lent me money to ease my strangled cash flow, I mistook my gratitude for love.

By the time the Ann Arbor phase of our marital dissolution was scheduled to end in the summer of '84, I felt like a marathon runner straining to make it through the twenty-sixth mile. The next phase, as outlined, would finally offer a more level terrain and a much saner pace: The kids were supposed to move east with me, where I would be closer to my work and colleagues; Howard was supposed to complete his dissertation and focus his job search near the kids' new home, where we would continue our joint custody agreement. By March of 1984, Larry had succeeded in moving his career from Washington to New York City. We had agreed to share a house in a small Connecticut town with excellent public schools for the boys, a reasonable daily commute for Larry, and a home office for me. We were all supposed to live happily ever after.

The plan to move three careers between three cities, two young boys with friends in two states, a mother, a father, and a significant-other father seemed so civilized and mature. In reality, the plan worked like "hell," as the Allen County judge who'd granted our divorce thought it might. We did not exactly achieve the textbook dignity of the blended family. We were puréed.

Almost immediately, a few complications became obvious. Howard resented Larry mightily. He saw a new "stepfather" not as a parenting ally but as a potential competitor. Now solidly reconnected to his sons after the Ann Arbor years, he seemed to think: "my kids, her monied boyfriend." Larry did not actually have any money, but he did earn a regular paycheck, which made him exotic among the group he was joining. Nor was there anything in Larry's history as an only child that prepared him for living with two young jocks, then approaching ages eight and ten. While he'd enjoyed many Washington weekends with Ryan and Darren—they flew kites and caught frisbees and paddled the Potomac—playing father once a month was hardly a realistic introduction to the actual job. He was still innocent about how completely a man could come undone when, say, he discovered his brand new electric razor in the driveway after being used to buzz-cut a mohawk on the neighbor's poodle.

The boys, too, wrestled with adjustment problems. Though long accustomed to odd family structures, they were unsure how to approach this new configuration. How should they explain it to friends? Larry wasn't their "dad," he wasn't exactly their "stepfather," and calling him "our mother's significant other" was a mouthful. What should they call him, and what would people in a small Connecticut town think about significant others? Good questions.

"How about calling him 'Larry,'" I suggested. "Say he's 'our friend' and just let it settle in. Your new friends will probably think of him the same way you do." It was my hope they would think well of him, but sons tend to take their time approving their mother's lover.

And finally my parents, still reeling from the shock of the first divorce in our Irish Catholic family, had not yet been informed that they would soon have to cope with the concept of my "living in sin." I wasn't remotely ready to consider another marriage. However marginal my existence, single mothers tend to remarry unenthusiastically, if at all. If Larry and I succeeded in living the terms of a "good divorce" for a few years, balancing work and family obligations better than either of us ever had before, there would be plenty of time to have a big celebration later.

AS FOR me, the architect of this plan, I would soon discover that beyond a working mother's "dual careers" there is a rarely acknowledged third role, the most exhausting and draining of all. Before I could live the life I longed for, I had to conduct a tremendous amount of negotiating first: I needed the cooperation of a still angry husband, an inexperienced stepfather, two oblivious young boys, and dozens of colleagues, none of whom felt the same urgency I did about changing traditional habits and expectations. As a critic in the *Washington Post* defined our third career, it is the job of every wife and mother "to pull off what anthropologists believe is a critical task for any civilized society—to harness the male into the role of husband and father."

One can only wish that the anthropologists had decided the crit-

ical task was for men to grow up before they married or repro-
duced, instead of assigning wives the job of raising an adult child
as well as a family. Once more, the social script calls for women to
be the foil, the narrow-minded prude, the nag, and the naysayer.
For a clear picture of how draining it is for women to socialize and
educate the fathers and bosses and husbands of America, imagine
a lone black woman trying to enlighten the nine white guys on the
Senate Judiciary Committee, each asking in turn, "Professor Hill,
surely you can't expect us to believe *that*?"

Maybe the rodeo theory of male/female relationships, where
guys are expected to behave primitively and girls to tame and
domesticate them, is more fun for the wild man than it is for the
harnessing woman. For me, this anthropological model was neither amusing nor especially efficient in advancing civilization. If it's
indeed true that men cannot be responsible without women,
shouldn't the *Post* be urging huge numbers of women to infiltrate
the Pentagon and Wall Street and the National Rifle Association—
and quick? In a culture that gives men irresponsible power and
women powerless responsibility, the advancement of civilization
cannot be a serious goal.

This belief that women are somehow responsible for men's
behavior has been with us forever, of course. During my Catholic
girlhood some thirty years ago, the message that women were in
charge of men's sexual behavior came through on all frequencies:
from priests, from nuns, from the *Lives of the Saints*, even from the
mother of a young man I was dating, who happened to interrupt
a "study session" at the very moment her son had slipped his hand
up my sweater. Embarrassed, she looked directly at me.

"Shame on you," she said. "You shouldn't let him get away with
that." She then hastily left the room without saying a word to her
son, as if the whole subject were slightly over his head. Although he
was a college sophomore at the time, skilled in English as well as
several foreign languages, none of us found this interchange extraordinary.

The nearly universal judgments from my friends and family that

I wasn't doing enough to change Howard's behavior—love him less, love him more, be tougher, be kinder, forgive him nothing, forgive him everything—were all variations on this theme that his fatherhood was somehow my job. Aside from being annoying, these were futile suggestions. If marriage counselors and lawyers and judges could not affect the desired behavior modification with all their court orders and lawsuits and jail threats, what chance did a wife, especially an ex-wife, possibly have? Whenever friends concerned about my deteriorating health insisted I "do something" about Howard, I would remember my mother trying to explain to the Chicago police why her maternal instincts could not restrain my wild-man brother.

THE STRESS and exhaustion of my triple career showed up everywhere—in my checkbook, in my overcrowded calendar, and eventually on my chest X rays. My doctors at the University of Michigan, puzzled by the mysterious shadows and inconclusive diagnostic tests, conferred with specialists in New Haven and Washington, D.C. Most baffling of all, none of the damage so visible on the X rays had any exterior symptoms. Whenever I was introduced to a new specialist who had first met me through my voluminous medical history, there was always a moment of blatant shock at my physical appearance: strong, upright, ambulatory, breathing regularly and even looking, on good hair days, like I could be a distant relative of Katharine Hepburn.

"I'm sorry," an embarrassed specialist from Yale Medical School said once, raising his dropped jaw. "I just expected you would be . . ."

" . . . dragging yourself around like a gut-shot bear," I said, helping him find the right words. "Everybody does."

My own doctor would put my X rays up on the lighted screen every month, observe the shadows growing wider and darker each time, and then look in complete amazement at me, blooming with color and provocative questions. We would both shrug our shoulders. He would order more tests and document more circumferences on more reports. I would look at the cloudy masses spreading across the X-ray screen and think to myself, "The Portrait of Dorian Gray."

Soul trouble is not easily discussed with medical men. I missed my regular heart talks with my Fort Wayne friends. I'm sure it's no coincidence that those three years I became so sick in Ann Arbor were the same ones in which I had to invent my life without the help of my laughing, screeching, weeping, loving friends. My therapist helped me grieve the loss of my small civilization, but nowhere in the American Psychological Association's diagnostic manual was the attendant depression even listed: acute withdrawal from female friends. My six CR war buddies, now scattered from coast to coast, called frequently with moral support and practical advice. ("Don't bounce checks at the *grocery* store," Mary Ann warned. "When you have to write bad paper, give it to the doctors who are convinced you're dying.") We still laughed long distance, but I missed the hugs.

BOARDING A plane for New York City on a chilly afternoon in March of '84, I felt weighted down by an enormous fatigue. In addition to the usual business meetings with my agent and editors, a million personal details awaited me: Larry and I had to meet with realtors and school officials, rent moving vans and settle on dates, negotiate a budget, and pay security deposits. As the pulmonary tube between my ribs wheezed its sickly tune, waves of nausea unsettled my stomach. I suspected I'd caught the kids' flu. A virulent strain of influenza had been leveling vulnerable members of the third and fourth grade that week, and Ryan and Darren were among its victims. Or maybe it was the weight of those buckets.

In either case, I collapsed in exhaustion the day after my arrival and spent nine unconscious days in the intensive care unit of St. Vincent's Hospital. The emergency room doctors diagnosed my comatose condition as "adult respiratory distress syndrome and ketone acidosis," although it could have been an extreme case of "disillusion." Although I can't recommend a coma as the cure for depression, it did solve innumerable problems for me. With their connector completely shut down, the members of my extended family had to do their own emotional negotiations. It took the combined efforts of half a dozen people to fill in the child care, breadwinning, connecting, and socializing duties I'd abruptly abandoned.

Howard inherited total responsibility for the kids. For the past three years, he had taken care of the boys during the weeks I worked in New York, but this visitation lasted more than a month, with grave doubts about whether I would be coming back at all. That March, he had to field calls from coaches asking for uniform fees, den mothers wanting money for field trips, and teachers who needed checks before the kids could see how their new shirts looked in their school pictures. It was shocking to see all the bills and day-to-day expenses his sons accumulated in a month.

According to our holistic agreement, the party responsible for these bills was "the parent who could best afford them." Since I was comatose, he knew where the bucks had to stop. Even if I survived without permanent brain damage—and neurological tests did not provide much hope—it would hardly speed my recovery to send these bills to the intensive care unit along with my get-well mail. After three years of futile communications, Howard finally understood my urgency during my nine days of profound silence. I no longer had to translate my life to him, for he was now living it.

Larry ran all my errands during the six weeks I was hospitalized, signed our new lease, and obtained all the school forms. My parents met the man I loved and, without much difficulty, accepted the "sin" if I would only get on with the "living." Joan and my Fort Wayne friends organized a fund-raiser—as feminists do in any emergency—and sent a large check to ensure a long recovery period. Ryan and Darren didn't wholly understand the gravity of "coma" at first. After three hospitalizations in Ann Arbor—a bike accident, a exploratory surgery, and a disastrous postsurgery infection—"going to the hospital" was just something their mom did.

I had always come back, though sometimes I was strangely

altered, as when I had tubes protruding from my abdomen and odd instruments of torture in my suitcase. Our bathroom had taken on a kind of hospital motif, with large quantities of saline solution, syringes, hypodermic needles, and sterilized gauze pads. Despite these ominous signs, I managed to convince them that they had nothing to fear, and produced the chocolate chip cookies and new shirts to prove it. Then suddenly, at the ripe old ages of eight and ten, they had to confront the fact of human mortality.

Talk about an unnatural mother: For nine days, my sons had a completely surreal mother, and for three months afterward, a semi-vegetative mother. Several layers of their innocence were molted in that anxious spring of '84. Again, they were without specifics. Howard tried not to worry them with the medical reports he gathered daily from Larry and Regina in New York. But they understood from his hushed conversations—and because their father was talking in an earnest, in-it-together way to their mother's lover—that something was seriously wrong. They knew from Howard's guarded expression that there was plenty to fear this time. My coma ended the habit all children have of taking their mother for granted. Whether I was good or bad, my sons wanted their own witch back. Now that I was missing, maybe dead, I became exceedingly visible to everyone who loved me.

I HAVE by now written extensively about my coma, the death that didn't take, and all the life-altering lessons it forced on me. When I desperately needed help in the B.C. years—Before Coma—I made little headway, getting only myriad excuses from every direction that "change takes time." Despite a decade of public petitions, employers still didn't take the need for flex-time and day care and equal pay seriously. And despite a decade of private campaigns, husbands and fathers still perceive requests for change as nitpicking or nagging. If I had expired of exhaustion in 1984—which my body actually did for a few terrifying minutes—my epitaph could have been: "She died of trivialities."

I finally understood that even if other people couldn't change, *I* could. My rude awakening in 1984 provided the missing courage I needed to live the ideas in my head, to be less dependent on the approval of others, to Just Do It. The recidivism to old habits of mind was enormous, of course. Nine days will not undo thirty-seven years of socialization, but it was a valuable start. It took almost a year before I could entirely resume my life again, and no part of it has completely returned to "normal" since then. That close brush with death, the great distiller of what's important in life, provided so many revelations about what I would do differently if I had the chance. And then, at age thirty-seven, I did. A gift.

The coma shook up my routines in every arena—my work, my family, my friendships, especially my motherhood. That June, the kids came to spend the summer with me and Larry in Connecticut as soon as school was out. We had all agreed to postpone their move east for one more year, because my main job was to recover my health, and Howard had promised to take a leave from his studies to support the kids. Aware that the boys would be leaving in September, I gave myself the luxury of a summer without deadlines. We took ferries to Island Beach, had cookouts at Tod's Point, cultivated new friends in their future neighborhood, discovered Arnie's Game Room in Westport, and even got Larry to play hooky from work one gorgeous Wednesday morning to come play with us at Action Park in New Jersey.

I was startled by odd glimpses into the personalities of these two boys I thought I knew so well. After being half there for them all these years, being completely there for those three months was like having a motherhood honeymoon. It could only have been as intense as it was because it was for a limited time—not so long to take anyone for granted, but not so short to miss the point of breaking with routine. We would all emerge from that summer with new insights about who we were and who we weren't anymore.

I know of no shortcuts through the anger and angst of the five-year wasteland, so dense are the lessons of divorce, so slow is human comprehension. The members of my postnuclear family entered the next stage with more spirited cooperation than we had achieved so far. "You seem so *happy*," a friend remarked during a visit that August, pleased to see me in an environment of lush affection again. "I am." I smiled. "All it took was five years and a coma."

WHEN I said goodbye to the kids that September, I tried to think of their departure as no more traumatic than sending them off to boarding school. But "Mom" was so grafted to my identity by then, I had a few disoriented months trying to function without it. After a decade of thinking like a group, an indivisible "we," I discovered the boundaries of my being had melted and merged with the boys'. My feelings were focused on theirs; what I needed to do and be was deeply influenced by what needed to happen for them. Although that liquid merger of selves ten years earlier seemed to happen in seconds, the gradual separation that began that fall would stretch over the next ten years.

This groupness of mind, so expansive and welcome in the early years, had become a burdensome habit, though neither the kids nor I recognized the ways it limited us until we were forced apart. I remembered my displaced homemakers' astounding reports of the rude shocks that await a woman outside her family-defined role, all the work it takes to fill in the parts of herself that were neglected or ignored. Not easy, getting a life.

There were pleasant surprises too, of course. After becoming a long-distance mother, I discovered that a child's love was sturdy and reliable, although often expressed in monosyllables over the phone. We visited often. I either drove the 750 miles to Ann Arbor or flew the kids to New York, and it was fun to be the "goody" parent for a year, the one who supplied the treats instead of the unnoticeable essentials. Even the nonreciprocal love I had grown accustomed to—especially during the chilly winter after the divorce when the kids were most concerned about their dad—underwent some subtle but startling modifications. They saw their dad every day now. Just as Dorothy Dinnerstein had predicted, when men raise children they can be taken for granted as easily as women.

"One imagines what the young male would be like if trained or

initiated by the Wild Man rather than a woman," Robert Bly spec-
ulated in a 1982 interview, although he'd never had time to actually
test his romantic theory in real life himself. Bly's wife raised his kids.
Author Sharon Dubiago, a mother of sons, wishes Bly and other
Wild Men would do more training and less theorizing. When men
tend to the daily needs of children, "the male body becomes the
too-familiar one we grow from, and so reject. Then the universal
turning to the secondary parent would be *to* and *for* the Female, the
only thing that's going to save us. How's that, Robert, for serious
mother severance? The argument for male child care?" Dubiago
asked.

The Father's Day essay I published in the *Times* that so unnerved
the woman's magazine editor described what we learned the year
Howard was a nurturing Wild Man and I was a long-distance
Unnatural Mom. I discovered that much of the contempt for
mothers so evident in the *Psychological Abstracts* was a product of
the institutional structure of the family. Take mothers out of their
exclusive service role, let fathers and sons clean up some of their
own messes, and you eliminate perhaps half of the one hundred-
some problems mothers are alleged to cause their children. In their
all-male home in Ann Arbor in 1984—smack in the middle of my
sons' childhood—men did the cooking, cleaning, laundry, and groceries. More significantly, they had to find ways to articulate their
own deeply complicated feelings since there were no females
around to intuit them. They talked, they argued, they faced each
other's needs without interference.

With their dad in clear view that year, their extracurricular
thoughts about how I was doing prompted some memorable
actions. I was expecting a call from my agent's office one weekday
morning when the phone rang and an operator asked if I would
accept long-distance charges. A distinctly non-9-to-5 voice said, "Hi
Mom, it's me."

"Darren!" I quickly accepted the charges. It was the middle of
his school day. "Are you all right, Honey? What's wrong?"

"Nothing," he said calmly. He offered no more information,

waiting for my next question. At age nine, Darren was a walking demonstration of William Strunk's main advice to writers: "Omit needless words!"

"Well, that's good," I said, relaxing. "So what's up? Why did you call, sweetie?"

"I'm on my lunch hour," he said. "I passed this pay phone in the hall and just thought I'd give you a buzz."

A fourth grader on his lunch hour. These small gestures knocked my socks off. The buzz from Darren kept me high the rest of the day. A mother becomes so accustomed to nonreciprocal love that the little thoughtful things they did during my recovery year felt like enormous bouquets. I *loved* being an unnatural mother—told all my friends they should try it for a year.

ALTHOUGH I remain a strictly nondenominational woman, I acquired a deep, enduring affinity with my sons after that nine-day period when I had been most acutely out of control. That experience in 1984 awakened a spiritual connection to them that feels infinite—longer than the years we will live in the same house together; longer, perhaps, than even the years we will inhabit this planet together. "This great friendship of ours is pretty eternal," Alice Walker once said about her relationship with her daughter Rebecca. "I often tell her that no matter what, I will always be with her. It's my sense that the real incarnation is not necessarily coming back as someone else but, just as you inherit your mother's brown eyes, you inherit part of her soul."

This certain knowledge that we were inseparably connected greatly relieved the urge to "possess" my sons, even after I returned to reality. This bond felt so sturdy, so infinite, it stretched across 750 miles without much strain that year they lived in Ann Arbor. Discovering a new kind of intimacy that could coexist with independence became an exceedingly fortunate prelude to living with adolescents.

FIVE YEARS after my recovery, Ryan and Darren both managed to ignore the fanfare when a memoir about my coma was published.

Ryan didn't pick up the book until a year later, the summer of his sixteenth year, when he attended a hockey camp in Canada and spent a month with my brother Paul. Only later did it occur to me that he'd chosen the safest place in the universe to open his family's most radioactive material. This son, forever crossing interstate boundaries in search of father figures, loved and trusted my brother Paul. Trying to maintain his equilibrium through the sudden mood swings and intense yearnings that regularly ambush a boy of sixteen, he kept himself on ice all day tending goals and wore himself out in his uncle's woodworking studio each evening. During his urgent search for identity that summer, Ryan played hard, worked hard, talked hard. He cried hard, too. His voice was gravelly and thick when he called home late one night, and began a conversation I'll never forget.

"Hey—what's the matter, honey?" I asked, alarmed by his congested condition.

"I'm halfway through your book, Mom . . ." He broke into sobs. He had most of the specifics now. The details were hard on him: He hadn't known the inside facts about Frank's suicide, how devastated I'd been; He was shocked by the mental illness that riddled our family; He was rattled to learn about how poor we had been, how much sacrifice had gone into every pair of tennies he had taken for granted. We talked nonstop for almost two hours.

"I feel so *bad*," he said finally. "I didn't know all that was going on for you. I wish I'd known. I would have done more." He had a terrible case of survivor's guilt, coming on strong five years after the fact.

"Oh Ry, honey . . . You weren't supposed to 'do more' then," I said. "You're reading this history with your sixteen-year-old mind. But you were only half that age when it was all happening. You were a kid. You acted like a kid."

"I wish I hadn't been such a kid," he said, inconsolably older and wiser at sixteen.

"You were being exactly who you were supposed to be. Of *course* you would do things differently if any of this were happening now."

I pictured an unarmored hockey player on the other end of the line, shrunken and vulnerable without his protective padding. I wanted to hug him, wipe his tears, pump him up.

"I know, I know I would," he said, his big heart almost audibly breaking. "Still, I wish I hadn't been such a kid."

"Sweetie . . . don't. Don't take on guilt that isn't yours," I said. "And listen, Bugs. We still have plenty of time. If you really want to 'do more,' I'll save all the dishes and laundry around here until you get home."

He laughed then, letting me kid him out of the blues.

EVERY TIME my young gents and I thought we were finished with the "radicalizing experiences" of 1984, the aftershocks would rumble through our lives in subtle but significant ways. I would be shaken vigorously from a sound sleep on a cozy Saturday morning, whenever Ryan or Darren felt seized by a sudden anxiety: "Oh, sorry, Mom. Just wanted to make sure you were only sleeping." I don't remember feeling guilty that their anxiety level seemed to be rising while mine dropped. The strongest feeling I had in those first months after my breakdown was acute embarrassment. It was a shock to learn I had been asleep for nine days, through lunch meetings and dinner dates, scheduled takeoffs and landings, elementary school plays and college speeches I was to deliver. Finally, however, these large and small humiliations yielded genuine relief. After such a dramatic display of my limitations, nobody, especially me, expected me to leap tall buildings in a single bound. Or even a few bounds.

A near death, unlike the thing itself, leaves all the survivors feeling exceptionally lucky to be alive. For the last ten years, with varying degrees of intensity, the kids and I have shared a mutual attitude of I'm-glad-I-didn't-lose-you. We still had plenty of squabbles about when and how to do chores, but we never had another one about whether they should. It took a cataclysmic event before all the men in my life paid attention to my trivial issues. Moms who

don't break down and go into comas are still expected, alas, to Do
It All. There may have been questions about whether or not I was
an unnatural mom in Manhattan editorial offices, where such
things are decided, but this much was abundantly clear at home:
Mom was no Superwoman.

9

Working Children

"No, really Mom. She wanted to do it. She *asked* me for it," Ry said. I imagined his helpless, I'm-innocent expression on the other end of the line.

"She *asked* for your laundry? She wanted to do your wash?" I asked, swallowing dismay. The fates were tirelessly capricious. In the lottery of human chance, Phyllis Schlafly ends up being the mother of a gay son while my son seemed to be falling in love with the last Totalled Woman in America.

"Yeah. She said she had to do hers anyway; she said it would be no trouble to do mine."

"No trouble? Your laundry?" I pictured the floor of his room the last year he lived at home—a ripe garden of textiles from which he miraculously put himself together every day. "Ry, if this girl thinks your laundry is no trouble, she definitely needs professional help."

He laughed. "Really, Mom, I know you're going to like her. She's an aviation major—she has a license and everything. She's going to be a pilot. And she's got a great sense of humor, too." A young woman who did laundry, flew planes, told jokes, and—though left unsaid, it was obvious from the pictures Ryan sent—had a smile and a body to die for—I heard my son sigh the delirious hum of love-at-last.

"It certainly could be love, Sweetie. But the part about your laundry, that part is probably lust. Lust is a wonderful kind of temporary insanity, but it has a very short life. Eventually, dirty socks go back to being only dirty socks again." The exchange of laundry that's so erotic between college freshmen becomes anticlimactic over time. What used to be "no trouble" can then become big trouble.

"Better not forget how to do your laundry," I suggested. "In fact, you might consider offering to do hers." I reminded him of the startling revelation his brother had made the year before: The way to a woman's heart was to bake a cake and clean up the kitchen, without being asked.

Darren discovered the erotic aura of Guys Who Cook during his junior year of high school, when he enrolled in a Home Economics course for extra credit. The class met right before lunch. He discovered that a jock who brings a tray of truffles into the cafeteria is the most popular guy around. That's when he first got the attention of the beautiful Aly. "You made these *yourself*?" she asked him. The following month, she invited him to the junior prom. The answer to Freud's famous question—What do women want?—probably begins, "A guy who cleans, who cooks, who walks the baby at night . . ."

IT'S SAFE to say that none of us were aware of the potential sex appeal of housework when I first taught my sons to do it. They learned to do domestic chores when they were still young boys because our family, in all its incarnations, never had the essential services of a full-time housewife. By ages six and seven, Ryan and Darren were already solid members of a growing new class of kids: working children, the offspring of working mothers. At night, they looked exactly like countless other generations of children: they slept. By day, however, their lives were entirely different from my traditional childhood in Norwood Park.

At night I looked exactly like other generations of mothers, too. I would tread softly into their darkened room, searching for fuzzy heads to pat and nuzzle. The same ageless questions penetrated the atmosphere: "Well, how are you, Bugs? . . . How was your day?" I would move my hand along their sleeping forms, running a finger across their brows as if it were a Geiger counter detecting anxieties.

Mary Kay Blakely

Keeping watch in their rooms at night, I would contemplate the shifts from my own childhood; how much more independent, responsible, and less innocent theirs had to be. I would try to calculate their happiness quotient, measuring what they needed against what they had. What kind of childhood was this, anyway?

I spent a whole decade weighing that question, ever since it came up during my first compromising moment of working motherhood. Our child-care arrangements, like those of every other working family at the time, were a complicated patchwork of babysitters and car pools and after-school programs. Once, making arrangements to cover business meetings at both ends of my usual working hours, I had to make no less than six phone calls to notify all the members of our extensive support staff. I remember pinning notes to Ryan's jacket, addressed to his bus driver and kindergarten teacher, painstakingly explaining the changes in our routine. I felt like I was sending him out the door that morning routed like an interoffice memo: Please read this child and pass on.

He waved to me from the curb, unconscious of the hot pancakes in the sunny kitchen he was supposed to be having at that hour of the day. I was humbled by his fearless independence. He didn't know how leisurely childhood used to be. Like other working children, he and his brother were encouraged to be self-sufficient as soon as possible. Their home was hardly "childproofed"; in fact, many items were stored closer to the floor than usual so the boys could reach them.

Besides the ABCs and primary colors of childhood, my working sons had to learn how to dial a permanent-press cycle, operate a Touch-Tone phone, use a microwave oven, and load a dishwasher. They communicated in a world of adults, asking for information and leaving messages with answering machines, secretaries, neighbors. Early on, for safety's sake, their innocence had to be sacrificed. My sons needed to know the truth about the dangers of the environment they traveled in. The Grimm fairy tales of their youth were published every day in the newspapers.

What kind of childhood was theirs? It was hard-working, certainly. I remember 3:45 P.M. at the Allen County Auditor's Office, where I worked with Joan and an officeful of working mothers. It was a wonderful place because Joan, with five working children of her own, had a generous attitude toward flex-time and personal calls. Every afternoon, when the kids came home from school to tabletops full of notes, the office phones would start ringing. The taxpayers were put on hold, temporarily: The children were reporting for duty.

We called these conversations "quality time." Any time a child learned another household chore, it improved the quality of our lives. Recipes had to be simple at first, since working children are not, by and large, successful with spices. It takes a few years to make the transition from macaroni and cheese to tortellini and peppers. Walking down the aisle of desks at 3:45 P.M. in the Auditor's Office, you could hear the varied degrees of household organization:

"Take the package labeled 'pot roast' out of the freezer and put it in the microwave to defrost it, Honey. Then—see the pot on the stove?—put in a thin layer of water, and brown it on both sides. Call me back after that, and I'll tell you the rest . . ."

"There's some leftover spaghetti in the refrigerator—let's have that tonight with . . . it's right there on the second shelf, Sweetie, in the Tupperware bowl next to the . . . what? Last night? He ate it last night? The whole *bowl*? . . ."

"Do you see the five dollars on the counter, Sugar? Why don't you and Kimmie meet me at McDonald's, a little after five . . ."

"No, Honey, the water doesn't get brown—you brown the *meat*, you put the *meat* in the water . . ."

They had so much to learn, I used to worry that my sons didn't have enough time for games, time to exercise their fantasies. But playfulness is so inherent to childhood, their imaginations resurfaced again and again. Darren's approach to vacuuming, for example, was highly inventive. One Saturday morning, after a lengthy drone and an alarming number of thumps along the baseboard, I went upstairs to investigate his progress on a hallway rug. I found an irregularly swept pattern, with three large, carefully avoided dust balls in the middle of the floor.

"How could you miss these?" I asked, incredulous.

"I can't suck those up, Mom!" he said with alarm, looking up over the helm of the carpet sweeper. "Those are my energy capsules. If I use them all up, I'll be dead."

Their work was not always a matter of life and death, of course. Working sons don't suffer the same anxiety about housework as their mothers. Ryan and Darren didn't worry much about job security—they knew they would eat . . . eventually. They didn't mind living with dust balls. Unlike me, they seemed to have few regrets about how their childhood was going.

So why, then, did the image of the woman in the apron with the after-school cookies hold such power for me? I indulged that fantasy one winter afternoon, to find out if there was something in that scene essential to a happy childhood. I spent an entire morning rolling out yards of cookie dough, cutting it into little holiday shapes. I finished tinting the frosting just in time, and when the kids came in the back door after school, I was arranging colorful pine trees and elaborate snowflakes on a platter. I was pretty excited, prepared for the dramatic moment.

"Look," I said, pointing to the cookies as if they were a miracle.

"Oh," they said, popping a snowflake into their mouths, "Thanks, Mom."

"You aren't just supposed to *eat* these cookies," I said, crushed. These are *homemade*," I added, as if that explained everything. "God, didn't you even notice the little ornaments on the *trees*, the little silver beads?"

"Oh, yeah," Ryan said, apologetically.

"They're real nice, Mom," Darren added. They were fumbling for their lines—they had no script for this fantasy of mine.

"Maybe next time, though, you could leave the beads off," Ryan said, picking one out of his teeth. "They don't taste very good."

They were right, of course: the cookies were awful. Maybe it was the silver beads; maybe it was the guilt that went into the baking.

Working children have about as much regard for guilt as the children of the '50s had for martyrdom. Those two attitudes ruin almost any party. I discovered it wasn't necessarily the quality of homemade that made the fantasy valuable. I already knew it wasn't the apron—the less laundry working children had to do, the better. It was the affection that made that scene endure from generation to generation, the happy-to-see-you quality that lit up certain loved faces.

These greetings were as frequent as they'd ever been, although they took place at different times and in different ways. Sometimes, they even came long distance. We had a frequent guest those days, a working child of wide experience. Tommy's mother had returned to school full time, commuting 180 miles to Chicago to one of the few seminaries in the country that accepted women. During those three years, Tommy and Margaret became accustomed to delivering much of their news and affection by phone. We all waited for a particularly important call one evening—it was the day of Margaret's first job interview.

"Can I talk to Tommy?" she asked, so excited she forgot to say hello. I passed the receiver to the anxious party.

"You *did*?" Tommy said, breaking into an expansive grin. He cupped his hand over the receiver out of habit, as if shielding her from his bright face. "She got it! She got the job! My mom's going to be the campus minister!"

It was more than a casual excitement. He, too, had an investment in the outcome of the interview. He had hundreds of kid-made lunches in it, many singular walks home from school, lots of long-distance phone calls. Was it worth it? Tommy seemed to think so.

More nights than not I thought so, too, when I stood watch over Ryan and Darren. They never had the innocence and leisure of former generations of children, but I liked their spunk and spirit. They were sassy and worldwise, generous and proud, playful and funny. They didn't seem to mourn the childhood they weren't having; they were too busy living the one they got. I paid my respects during those nighttime visitations. I had to admire the way they earned their sleep.

ALTHOUGH MY sons had mastered most household chores by the time they reached their teens, they began suffering a kind of mental entropy during adolescence. All previous domestic training suddenly evaporated, and they hit a period of household incompetence. They lost wallets and car keys, tracked mud across the living room carpet, forgot that wet towels on a closet floor will smell like dead rats in no time. I understand from friends who are the mothers of girls that "it's just as bad with teenage daughters."

Living with male adolescents was a difficult adjustment at first. Except for periodic lapses with my reading glasses on airplanes, I am borderline obsessive in my own organizing habits. My sock drawer is arranged by color, my spices by alphabet; I used to be comforted by the idea that if I ever went blind I would still be able to get dressed and cook. This carefully ordered home environment disintegrated rapidly once my sons became house-blind. The most trying adolescent behavior for me was not the defiance, not the rebellion, but the profound oblivion. They were simply not there half the time.

"Yo, D.," I called to him once, in a semi-stupor before the TV. "'Come in Rangoon.'" I pointed to the pistachio shells he was dropping on the floor, then to the bowl on the table. "Let's get with the program here, buddy."

"Oh, sorry Mom." He started picking the shells out of the carpet. When I returned later, the shells he'd collected had been placed on the table, next to the bowl. It was a species problem, I decided, rather than a discipline problem. Training a boy of thirteen not to drop things on the floor was like training a St. Bernard not to drool. You could wear yourself out with no appreciable gain. Once puberty took over, my choices were these: I could spend the next three or four years guarding against stains on the antique white chairs, or I could move them out and furnish the living room with indestructible bean bags, built to withstand the indignities of adolescent occupants. That is, I could become a ceaseless nag for the next few years, or I could become utterly tasteless.

Once the boys started traveling in team-sized packs—all of whom were just as oblivious as my sons—the choice was clear. For their peace and my sanity, and because I wanted the jocks to feel at home more than I wanted my home to feel elegant, I postponed all lingering desires to live in House Beautiful. I consciously rearranged the domestic stage so that much of their friend-action could take place under our roof. Larry, for whom cleanliness was not next to godliness but godliness itself, found living with very young teenagers a trial. It probably wasn't a coincidence that he began working long overtime hours at his office after the junior high soccer team adopted our house as their hangout.

Rooms originally designed for the social life of the two-parent family were adapted to our postnuclear needs: the living room became the kids' television room and quasi-gym, furnished with an overstuffed couch and nicked furniture that could accept hard use without complaint; the large "master bedroom" became my home office/library, as well as a kind of nonsecular chapel where various confessions were heard; Larry's bedroom/study was meticulously neat and strictly off-limits; the kids' bedrooms had extra mattresses and sleeping bags for overnight guests; the kitchen became the sole "family room" where we cooked, ate, and exchanged news flashes. The lower kitchen cabinets had long been designated as self-service snack stations, with enough plastic cups and plates to service armies during after-school raids. ("Ration yourselves and your friends—when supplies are gone, you're dry 'til my next trip to Kroger.") The bathroom mirror became the bulletin board for Post-It notes to both sons and guests, since it was the one location I could be sure would have their attention several times a day.

Instead of reshaping the occupants to fit the structure of the house, we changed the building to fit the family. Every room was used, lived in, bent to our purposes. Tacky but user-friendly, our heavily trafficked home took on a kind of hole-in-the-wall quality. Compared to my mother, who had provided an elegant atmosphere for the Ladies' Bridge Club once a month despite five active children growing up under the same roof, I felt like Ma Barker running a hangout for underage rowdies.

Spooky things happen in houses densely occupied by adolescent boys. When I checked out a four-inch dent in the living room ceiling one afternoon, even the kid still holding the baseball bat looked genuinely baffled about how he possibly could have done it. Could the bat be possessed? Had I seen *Poltergeist*? Another time, after the lock on the back door had been splintered from the frame, I asked if Matt, our break-dancing neighbor turned Karate Kid that year, had done it. My sons, hating to be weasels, nodded a probably.

"He'll probably deny it," Ryan said, shrugging his shoulders. "He'll probably say we dared him to do it."

"Did you?" I asked.

"Yeah," he said.

As my once lovely home dissolved into Boys' Town, I dreaded all the additional housework running a hangout implied: more fingerprints on the walls, more litter in the kitchen, more footprints on the rug. Even though the kids were responsible for cleaning up after their friends, pistachio shells could collect dust on a tabletop for a month before they would notice. But instead of more housework, there was actually less. Once I stopped worrying about "ugly black heel marks," the bane of TV housewives, "waxy yellow buildup" and "water spots on the glassware" weren't far behind. Since form followed function, most of the domestic tasks geared toward maintaining House Beautiful became obsolete.

Occasionally, the racket got to me. I tried the ear plugs a friend had recommended, but muffling noises from the living room only made them more rattling. (What was *that*?) There were times I had to clear everyone out for homicide prevention. "Deadline Week," I'd post a warning on the bathroom mirror. This meant, as Darren bluntly translated for a guest, "Be quiet or die."

Most of the time, though, I was genuinely happy their friends made themselves at home in our house. They kicked off their shoes, went directly to the kid-cabinets, knew where to put the recyclable soda cans, and kept chatting, goofing, laughing whenever I drifted through the rooms they occupied. When they were clustered around the big oak table in the kitchen for a game or a snack, I would eavesdrop shamelessly while I brewed a pot of coffee. Sometimes I'd add a comment or two, sometimes risk a joke, then disappear back into my office. Working at home was even more compatible with the kids' adolescence than with their early childhood, when being there and totally not there was just what everyone needed.

Finding myself in the circus atmosphere of a nearly total jock environment, I thought a lot about the freedom Adrienne Rich had described during her outlaw summer in Vermont, when she and her three sons lived outside the regulation of other people's expectations. Would I have given myself permission for our distinctly eccentric home decor if I had not already been relieved of the appellation "good mother?" Certainly, there was an order to our seeming chaos, but it wouldn't have been evident to the Avon Lady, had she ever braved our doorbell.

10

"The Wrong Crowd"

This habit of eavesdropping on my sons and their friends might have been a kind of maternal voyeurism, but I preferred to think of it as part of my job. Observing the boys in the company of their peers was an unfailing source of insights into who they were, what they thought, where the gaps in their socialization were, how the social skills they'd acquired so far were being put to use. Their friends provided a reality check for my own expectations, a reliable measure of what still qualified as age-appropriate behavior and what did not. Worries about crude table manners and clumsiness tended to dissipate in the presence of their burping and stumbling friends. Although these observations would not lessen my desire for a belch-free environment, they would make me understand that other mothers had not achieved it either. Invariably, spending time with my sons' friends made me relax, lighten up, take the longer view.

A familiar background presence, I eventually became largely invisible to the youths who roamed freely through the house—except to the most astute and plotting guests.

"Hello, Mrs. Blakely," Carlos always said politely. Although most of my sons' friends were casual about honorific titles, adopting our Midwestern habit of using first names, Carlos stood resolutely on form. "Mary Kay" made him nervous. "I couldn't call her *that*," he said to Ryan once, "She's your *mother*." To Carlos, a mother had to be some kind of "Missus," married or not. Ever since I first met him, a slender bundle of undisciplined energy at age twelve, the most erratic but talented athlete on Ry's middle school soccer team, I've been "Mrs. Blakely" to Carlos, married to myself.

Back then, Carlos used a nervous, almost guilty mumble, "Hullo-Missus-Blake-lee," as if maybe he shouldn't be in my kitchen at all, let alone helping himself to the cookies. Seven winning soccer seasons later, having doubled in both size and confidence and now the subject of many tantalizing rumors of sexual adventures (started largely by Carlos himself), he has shed all vestiges of shyness. Whenever I walk into the kitchen and find Carlos there today, he flashes his killer grin, opens his arms widely, and tilts his head slightly sideways, the better to charm me with: "Missus Blaaaaaak-ly," he says warmly, deeply, as if I were the exact vision he was hoping to have. "How nice to see you . . ."

It was usually Carlos's braggadocio voice that preceded Ryan's loudest laughs or deepest groans during bull sessions at the kitchen table. It was invariably some remark from Carlos that prompted the most conspiratorial "C'mon's," the most outraged "No way's!" Of all my sons' friends, Carlos took the greatest number of detours from the straight and narrow, and therefore worked hardest to cover his tracks. Carlos was an indefatigable flatterer, our own Latino Eddie Haskell.

"You look very nice today, Mrs. Blakely," he said once when I emerged from my office to refill my coffee cup, wearing a dowdy pair of sweats and a kerchief bandanna around my brow. My sons were both familiar with this fetching ensemble, which usually appeared after I'd been holed up in my office for a day or two, in the final throes of some deadline. They understood this look to mean: She's getting close now, should be taking a shower any day.

"Is that a new hairstyle?" Carlos asked. He wedged his chin firmly into his neck and raised his eyebrows in critical evaluation, either trying to pass for a serious art critic or trying not to blow the joke by laughing out loud. Ryan and I exchanged smiles. I lifted a strand of limp hair.

"It's called 'Fax by five, or Else.' Carlos, do you mistake me for

June Cleaver?" Ryan laughed, delighted to see his friend unmasked. Then Carlos laughed too.

For as long as we've known him, Carlos has fit the definition of a guy from "the Wrong Crowd," as outlined in the parent newsletters—bad grades, connections with the juvenile underworld, early experiments with dope and beer. He was rash and impulsive, questioned and subverted all authority, presented one self to parents and another to peers. What the parent newsletters rarely mentioned, however, is how much fun the Wrong Crowd could be. My sons got a huge charge out of Carlos and, to tell the truth, so did I. For seven years, I've stood on the sidelines while this kid propelled himself down various fields, sometimes recklessly, sometimes brilliantly. I've cheered him on, yelled at him, applauded him, worried about him, helped him with term papers, written him letters of recommendation, filled out his scholarship applications, served him dinners on Fridays, eaten the breakfasts he and Ryan made on Saturdays, and watched him inspire, appall, entertain, and bully my sons. I loved Carlos, Ry's chief bull shitter and confidence man. I also kept my eye on him.

EVEN IF I had tried to filter the companions my sons chose, I doubt I would have succeeded. Ryan and Darren were aggressively friendly. They picked up pals everywhere. From the moment they could walk and talk, they craved the company of other kids as much as they craved food or sleep. As they commuted between Indiana and Michigan, they often belonged to more than one gang at a time. After moving to Connecticut, they formed the East Coast headquarters for "The Rebel Club," their first official gang in Fort Wayne.

Their preadolescent clubhouse, a pair of roomy cubby holes in the attic of our rented house, was outfitted with pillows, sleeping bags, and assorted camping equipment. It became a kind of neighborhood halfway house for other restless middle schoolers in search of a group identity. The daring name was somewhat compromised by a volunteer army of limp, nap-worn teddy bears guarding the entrance. It was never exactly clear what the rebels were rebelling against. Their only raids were limited to attacks on the kid-cabinets in the kitchen, looting their own supplies.

Although I was not eligible for membership, I was invited upstairs after the renovations to tour headquarters and meet the members—largely because I had surrendered huge quantities of paper, cellophane tape, staplers, and notebooks from my office. All the boys were introduced as "general" this or "commandant" that, while all the girls were introduced as "the secretaries."

"You said we were secretaries of *state*," Molly objected, conscious of the sleight. "Besides, I don't know how to type yet," she said.

"That's right, Molly, and don't ever admit you've learned how," I warned her. "Being able to type could lower your salary someday." Just like ten years of raising kids could earn zero credit for teaching experience. Once keyboards were attached to computers, people of the general and commandant persuasion would begin to recognize the value of typing skills, but I cautioned the girl rebels not to perform any task a boy rebel wouldn't do. Ryan and Darren rolled their eyes under the brown brims of their junior Indiana Jones hats. By ages eight and ten, they were beginning to find my lectures on gender politics tedious.

There were heartening signs that the next generation would approach those bristling issues with more generosity and open-mindedness than mine. *My Weekly Reader*, a national magazine for middle schoolers, made news that year with a survey reporting 46 percent of its readership would welcome a female president someday. But the hierarchy of the Rebel Club, which pridefully claimed a policy of admitting girls, suggested that a woman's route to high office was still going to be granted inch by laborious inch.

While I gave myself plenty of legitimate reasons for maintaining close contact with the boys' friends, I had so far enjoyed this part of motherhood immensely. One of my favorite ways to avoid my own keyboard was to take a carload of kids and a camera to the zoo or the beach. With each passing year, however, the fun of these group outings took second place to necessity. As we moved deeper into adolescence, it became more and more critical to know not only the names but also the habits, attitudes, histories, and traditions of their increasingly diverse, increasingly independent friends.

Most literature on the culture of adolescence focuses on peer pressure as a negative force parents should try to defuse. Warnings about "the wrong crowd" read like tornado alerts in parent manuals, advising us to seal children off from potential damage. It is a relative term that means different things in different places. In Fort Wayne, for example, the wrong crowd meant hanging out with liberal democrats. In Connecticut, it meant kids who weren't planning to get a Ph.D. from Yale. Given my own affection for friends of the unorthodox sort, I never felt like I could tell my sons whom to love. But I did try to teach them how to be a friend. To me, friends are essential to sustaining life, a kind of psychological CPR.

The flip side of peer pressure was peer approval, of course, which turned out to be as indispensable to my sons as it was for me. Without the insights I gained from their various gangs—their sociological control groups—it was as easy to underestimate certain spectacular teenage achievements as it was to overestimate their capacity for mature behavior. This was evident one winter when a snowstorm canceled school and gave me an unanticipated day off with Darren and two junior high friends. I fell in with "the wrong crowd" and had to reconcile some former prejudices with a few startling new facts. Until that afternoon, I had been completely unaware that I was living with one of the folk legends of Fairfield County.

Given our outlaw habits, we ignored advisories to stay off the roads after the storm had passed and followed a snow plow down Route 1 to Arnie's Game Room in Westport. I dropped them off, asking them to be in the parking lot in exactly two hours since the trip home would be riskier after dark. I then left to run a few errands. Time flies at Arnie's. The kids weren't outside when I returned. After idling the engine for several minutes to keep the heater on, I finally turned off the car and went inside to see what was holding them up.

Rows and rows of video screens glowed in the cavernous game room, packed with school kids on furlough. The loud electronic beeps and artillery explosions reminded me of why I hadn't come into Arnie's since we'd discovered it two years earlier. Few adults ventured inside. We had errands to run, phone calls to make, commuter trains to meet, maybe newspapers to read over a cup of very quiet custard. Kids lined every aisle like dozens of miniature gamblers, sinking their quarters into slot machines, the younger ones on stools to reach the levers, the older ones hunched over the controls in tense concentration. The better you were at zapping enemies and blowing up buildings, the longer you played. If you racked up enough points before the computer declared "Game Over," you were invited to place three initials in "The Top Ten." This list flashed on the screen at the end of every game, a kind of honor roll for the semi-anonymous heroes of Arnie's.

Adjusting my eyes to the dimmed lights after the blinding snowscape outside, I squinted down one jammed aisle after another without locating my quarry. The last row was empty except for a knot of kids gathered at one end. They were watching over Darren's shoulder as he furiously operated the controls. I recognized the absorbed look on his face, glowing in the blue illumination of the screen. I'd seen that look in game rooms at every service plaza on Interstate 80 between New York and Ann Arbor.

Every time we pulled off during our many twelve-hour drives between their dad's home and mine, I gave the kids a few quarters for video games while I took a newspaper into the coffee shop. Half an hour later, Darren would still be on his first coin. That was the same period when questions about whether Nintendo nerds would grow up brain damaged first surfaced in the press. Indeed, I disliked the themes of most of the games my younger son enjoyed. Like most cartoon shows for children, the entertainment depended on shooting or chasing or destroying somebody or something— all in friendly animation. There had to be adults involved in the design and manufacture of these aggressive games and bullying cartoons, since an enormous amount of capital was involved. Were they all cases of arrested development? A few games like Tetris offered challenges with geometric shapes, but the majority employed the player's logic and skill in some violent objective.

Darren excelled at all of these games, but, aware of my dim regard for their aggressive goals, he didn't share his enthusiasm with me. He didn't expect me to be among his fans. Neither did I, until I stood behind his young audience that afternoon at Arnie's and watched him work the levers from another perspective.

"You know who this is?" the boy in front of me whispered to his companion, in the hushed voice of a sports announcer trying not to break the concentration of a golfer desperate for a birdie.

"Who?" his friend whispered back.

"It's Doc," the boy said reverently. I recognized the phonetic pronunciation of Darren's initials.

"No way!" his friend said. He looked skeptically at my son, the back of his faded denim jacket hanging loosely from his slim, angular shoulders, a shock of unruly hair springing up around his cowlick. It was hard to imagine this slight competitor with the delicate features as a serious threat to the heavyweights banging away in other aisles.

"I'm positive. It's Doc alright. Just saw him put his initials on the Pac-Man down the aisle. If he breaks this record, he's got every screen in this row." He waved his arm down the empty aisle, where some thirty computer screens flashed invitations to compete.

"No way!" his friend repeated. "Straight flush?

The announcer nodded solemnly, pursing his lips as he returned his attention to the screen. Murmurs, hushes, aha's!, more murmurs. The Arnie's audience sounded like indoor Wimbledon spectators as Darren moved both hands across the levers and buttons with astonishing speed, his eyes never blinking from the screen, dipping a shoulder in one direction to bank a series of slap shots, straightening, then swiftly dropping the other. When "Game Over" finally flashed on the screen after a last tense round of bonus time, the crowd broke into loud applause. Darren entered his initials, D.O.K., in the number one slot.

"The whole damn *row*," the announcer said as the audience dispersed. He looked at my son with awe.

Before that afternoon, I knew this son mainly as the kid who couldn't make it across a room without knocking over everything in his path. Perhaps because his remarkable dexterity had not yet extended to his feet, I hadn't noticed the lightning quick communication between his head and his hands, the intense concentration he could hold through forty-two unbreakable minutes. For years I had watched him leaving his mark on computer games along Interstate 80 like Zorro. But it was only in the dim interior of Arnie's, watching the faces of admiring young strangers, that I finally understood the source of this quiet son's confidence. Here, there could be no doubt he was good at something; maybe terrifically good at something, at just the age when he needed it most.

It was dark on the way home, and I had to keep my eyes on the road. But I stole looks in the rear-view mirror whenever I could, studying Darren in the back seat between his two friends. Being cool required young teenagers to assume a posture of "no big deal" at all times; the bigger the deal the flatter the response. The car chatter assumed its normal petulant tones as I aimed the car south along Route 1, covering the usual trials of boyhood: oppressive teachers, dorky coaches, scary girls, hopelessly out-of-it parents. His friends said goodbye that evening with the requisite jabs to the shoulder, the ubiquitous "Later, dweeb." Then came the awed look I'd seen before among D.'s hacker friends, the nickname I'd heard him called that year but hadn't really understood: "Way to go, Doc."

I REMEMBER reading Christmas letters from Fort Wayne friends a few weeks later, bringing me up to date on children who had taken a semester off from college to build homes in Nicaragua, or just returned from a Fulbright fellowship in the Middle East, or completed a dissertation on child welfare in undeveloped countries. I did not know exactly how to share my joy in a son who had become a video Zorro. My own peers would hardly recognize the odd thrills known only to the patrons of Arnie's and truckers at Ohio service plazas. It was a thrill I might have missed entirely myself, but for a snow day when I holed up with the wrong crowd.

Whenever the racket from the backyard or the kitchen penetrated my home office and made me wish for older, more modulated daily companions, I had to remind myself that I needed these neighborhood gangs almost as much as the kids. I needed them to provide entertainment while I worked; I also needed their eyes, their murmurs, their cool appraisals because my own judgment of my sons was becoming entirely too unreliable. Especially as they experimented with new identities, their peers supplied both pressure and validation. It seemed that Bubber and Pork Chop had barely left center stage when the Ry-man and Doc came on. These new incarnations were born without my participation, without even my perception of them. These were the selves that bloomed only in the presence of friends.

Since Ryan and Darren now traveled frequently between two states and had close friendships in two cities, and since our steadily downward mobility drew us ever nearer to the urban centers of young male rage, I felt an enormous need to stay tuned in to their inside chatter. Just when it became more important than ever to hang out with their friends, it became increasingly difficult to maintain this longtime habit.

It was easy and cheap enough to keep our dinner table and guest rooms populated with neighborhood friends; everybody liked macaroni and cheese, and nobody minded sleeping in bags. Maintaining vital contact with out-of-town friends was harder and more expensive. Sometimes, to keep my sons in close touch with positive influences from a distance of 750 miles, I had to violate some cherished rules of high school attendance clerks. When vacation breaks in the Midwest did not neatly coincide with those on the East Coast, it became necessary to wire around the system a bit. Periodically, I called the school secretary to exempt them for "a family emergency."

We referred to these self-declared holidays as "personal days," borrowing one of the more humane concepts of corporate personnel policies. To remain eligible for the privilege of truancy, the boys had to maintain a certain grade-point average—although even that rule was broken once, when it became clear that nothing would relieve a dark depression more than a long camping weekend with a best friend.

The rules and boundaries became ever more liquid in the last trimester of motherhood, when the jocks entered their teens. "Be consistent," the parent manuals advised over and over. "Trust your instincts," I remembered again and again, the vow from Kay's trial at ISPI twenty years earlier that was permanently imprinted on my brain. It took me the first fifteen years of motherhood to merge the wisdom of these competing principles, fifteen whole years before I could be consistent about trusting my instincts. By then we were routinely breaking the rules. Just after Ryan's fifteenth birthday, we took an illegal spring break to host a week-long "family emergency" with four Michigan pals. Although I did feel some sense of emergency about keeping the boys connected to their Midwestern roots, I couldn't lie to Mary, the high school secretary who had become my friend.

"The truth is," I confessed, "we have some out-of-town guests and I'm taking the whole gang to New York. We're going to the movies."

"If I write that on the attendance report, the kids will both have to serve a detention," Mary said. "It's better for them if you give me a legal excuse. Let's see, the movies . . . I think that would be 'sick with the flu.'"

The flu season that April caused some of the most infectious laughs we ever had. I played hooky from work myself that week, since it was the last year I would be serving as their chauffeur. One more birthday, and Ryan would have his own license. My eavesdropping days were numbered.

Larry and I drove two cars to the airport to collect our four guests and their luggage, since I'd been strongly cautioned against renting something so pedestrian as a station wagon for the week.

"A *station wagon*?" the jocks groaned in unison, "Oh *Mom* . . ." A look was exchanged between them that said, "The guys will be here in a matter of days; how are we going to shape her up to pass for cool by then?" It was an instant reminder of the enormous power of "mom." By the time Ryan and Darren reached adolescence, I acquired a random, almost unconscious ability to kill them of embarrassment. I've tried to use this power sparingly, but it has come in handy.

Most of our trips that week, sans luggage, were made in my small but sufficiently "cool" black Impulse. Somebody's elbow or knee was generally interfering with the circulation in somebody else's arm or leg, but I quickly learned that comfort was not nearly as essential as form during the embarrassment-prone years. Traveling in a close pack with the six boys—aka "The Posse"—reminded me of the preschool car pool I drove some ten years before. The pitch and depth of the voices, as well as the topics of discussion, had changed radically, however.

In the first conversation from LaGuardia to home, members of the Posse reviewed plans for the week. Between highway signs requiring my complete attention, I caught snatches of plots to stay up all night, raid the refrigerator, host a wild party. The word "girls" descended and commenced a round of intense queries about whether they were "dogs." Or perhaps the dogs were in the car. In any event, the prospect of being seen with a dog was an even greater compromise than being seen in a station wagon. Threats to young machismo cropped up just about everywhere.

What I'd estimated to be a week's supply of soda and Oreos was exhausted after twenty-four hours. A brief fact-finding mission revealed that nobody remembered consuming them. It was suggested that the drain on supplies was probably caused by the enormous traffic that had begun coursing through the house once word got out in the neighborhood that we were hosting a week-long party.

There was, in fact, a party atmosphere about the house all week. Ryan and Darren enjoyed having their two worlds merge, friends meeting friends. When we took a trip to Westport to blow some dough at Arnie's game room, two Greenwich friends were invited along. Squeezing eight almost-teenagers into the Impulse made intimacy between strangers automatic.

The gang accumulated members through the week. One afternoon I counted nine bodies sprawled on the couches and floor in front of the TV—an entire baseball team. What do you see when you look into a room populated by nine young, forming males? Limbs. Limbs and feet, astonishingly long and large, draped over chair arms and pillows. The human body undergoes a peculiar shift in adolescence, entering a dimension of time and space physics has yet to identify. The pull of gravity becomes so powerful, it causes them to lumber, trip, stumble down the street. I felt a raw admiration for their sheer will to keep moving against all odds.

We went to Chinatown in Manhattan one evening, shopping and eating our way down the crowded streets. It was tough, six guys out on the town trying to be cool with a mom in tow, especially a mom with a camera. We swung a few good deals on watches and a cool pair of shades, and one of our party actually bought a souvenir for his mother. We reviewed menu selections in Chinatown and neighboring Little Italy, and I encouraged them to choose a restaurant for dinner where they could sample something new. Their final consensus was McDonald's.

We visited the World Trade Center later that night for a look at Manhattan with its lights on. I pointed out the Statue of Liberty and the historic Wall Street cathedral, showed them Ellis Island, and told them what it once meant for our distant relatives. The main attraction, however, proved to be the gift shop. As we crowded into the elevator, other passengers curious about our group had a bold clue in the six-inch red button attached to the lapel of one of our denim jackets, which had caused great guffaws in the gift shop:

Roses are red
Violets are blue
I'm schizophrenic
And so am I

That was the Posse's slogan as they exited through the revolving
doors at ground level, jamming all six bodies into one compartment. This seemed to be the compulsory method for exiting any
building, and escalators had to be approached backward and from
the opposite direction they wished to go. The troops were weary
on the way home; clowning around was exhausting. But the theme
of the week was "never say die," let alone sleep. The front-seat passengers had control of the tape deck on the way home and led the
back seat in a rousing chorus of "The Limbo Rock." They achieved
a rare harmony with David Lee Roth's rendition of "California
Girls." Although we were driving along the wrong coast for such
fantasies, it gave me goose bumps to realize we were only a few
slim years and one driver away from those dreams. How did they
get those deep voices in those young bodies so fast?

My reveries about their coming maturity were interrupted when
a loud shriek suddenly burst from the back seat—one of many during the week. Inevitably, it meant somebody farted. The effect of
this commonplace biological event on a carful of adolescent boys
demands immediate action. It calls for opening all windows,
including the sunroof, followed by a vigorous search for the
offender. Nobody ever did it.

We rented many videotapes, for that seemed to be the only
means to rest. Sleep for the Posse meant turning on the TV. The
tasteful movie selections included *Spaceballs* and *The Lost Boys*. We
almost appeared in a movie ourselves. In Central Park one afternoon, a crew was filming scenes at the band shell and needed an
audience. A producer invited the boys to be "extras." There was
great enthusiasm at first, until it was revealed they would not be
paid $100 per hour, as they expected. When the producer said
they'd have to stick around and remain motionless for three hours,

the thrill wore off. It was a gorgeous afternoon in the park, with jugglers and entertainers warming up for the crowds, and the boys preferred to roam.

It wasn't always easy to travel as a tight pack and make everyone happy. During our visit to Manhattan, in the middle of our debate about whether to use our last hours in the city to visit the World Trade Center or check out the night action in Washington Square Park, Ryan and his sophomore friends tried to pull rank on Darren's freshman trio. "The older boys don't get a charge out of big buildings anymore," a senior member of the pack drily stated. One year of life experience, in teen time, is the equivalent of a whole generation. But the "big boys" eventually gave in, discovering some amusement in becoming kids again themselves. The journey back didn't prove too difficult.

The civility of their conduct would have surprised their parents. Living with adolescents often brings a sense of humiliation or defeat over the slowness of human development. The initial "anything we can get away with" attitude was revised almost immediately, and the boys largely policed their own behavior. A midweek shopping spree brought an arsenal of squirt guns into the house—the perennial springtime weapon—and gun control laws were quickly established: "Not in the house, you dope." It wasn't exactly how I would have put it, but it did the job. Some remarkable things happened without any direction from me: The boys cleaned up after themselves in the bathroom and kitchen; and they offered to help with the cooking and serving. It shouldn't be amazing when six boys go on vacation and reveal that major parts of their socialization have actually taken hold. But to me, perhaps because I spent so many hours in the dean's office trying to right the course of backsliders and deviants, those glimmers of actual maturity seemed genuinely miraculous.

Although I had once been a specialist in teenage delinquency, the forms of rebellion an adolescent had to choose from by 1988 were mind-boggling. I envied the parents of the '50s and their worries about their children "talking out of turn, chewing gum in class, not doing homework, stepping out of line, not cleaning their rooms." By the time Ryan and Darren entered high school, most of the top five problems listed in *USA Today* were evident among their classmates: Drug addiction, teenage pregnancy, suicide and homicide, gang violence, anorexia and bulimia. They had friends who had to be hospitalized, who disappeared into recovery programs, who had brothers in jail, who had pregnant sisters. We'd traveled a long way from their early, charming inquiries ("Mom, how many chews are there in a stick of gum?") to their frightening questions now: "Mom, can you really get addicted to crack after only one try?"

I longed for disciplinary infractions the size of chewing gum: "I just don't know what to do about this kid." I imagined consulting my friends, fonts of wisdom on managing gum crimes. "I've tried reasoning with him, grounding him, banning MTV for two weeks . . . nothing works. Doing the laundry yesterday—what do I find in his jeans? Two packs of Wrigley's. What's a mother to do?" But those were not the questions that kept my long-distance conversations going with friends, sometimes for hours.

"I found a gun in his room," a longtime friend croaked into the receiver late one night, barely audible. It was just a few months after her only son had celebrated his fifteenth birthday. She sounded like she was calling from under her bed, her mouth full of dustballs. "Do you think this is something to worry about?"

"A *gun?*" I asked. "Do I think this is something to worry about?" I repeated, astonished. "A *real* gun?" Was she out of her mind? Yes. Yes, she was out of her mind and had been heading in that direction for some time. She was one of the most intelligent, competent, compassionate women I knew, facts that served her successfully in every arena of her life except motherhood that year. Two years ago this son who had always been difficult—restless, hot-tempered, brilliant, needy in the extreme—became completely out of control when his parents' divorce collided with his own rocky adolescence.

By the time she found the gun, so many other impossible words and phrases had attached themselves to his brief history that she lost her bearings entirely. In her private conversations, she now employed a vocabulary she'd never imagined: "uppers, downers, speed, shoplifting, coke, suspended sentence, burglary, therapy, drug rehabilitation, high school dropout, attempted suicide." She was as unprepared for the delinquent world from which these surreal terms came as Kay was for the unreality of Ward B thirty years ago. After spending vast worry on uppers and burglary and attempted suicide, where did a gun fit into the anxiety scale? Was the gun a big worry or a middling one? Wasn't it true according to Channel One, the commercial cable network pumped into schools across the country, that more than 50 percent of American homes now had one or more guns? Didn't the National Rifle Association send membership applications to male high school graduates in Fairfield County, inviting them to exercise their inalienable right to bear arms? Couldn't a gun in your son's bedroom, in 1990, be considered "normal?"

When a high school teacher twenty-five years ago said, "Hand over that piece, please," it used to mean "Give me your gum." Now "that piece" means "the gun, please." Is this something to worry about? Is my friend having migraines because of a typo? For the sake of her younger daughter, a frequent target of her son's bullying but so far only verbal threats, should she force him to leave home, send him to the equivalent of the Culver Military Academy, the place worried mothers used to send boys who didn't do their homework? And how could it even be true that such crushing questions had become so personally relevant to her, a "good mother" for fifteen years, a completely "normal" person?

It happened so fast, the two-year trip from drugs to the gun. She was utterly baffled about who and what to blame. She knew he hadn't fallen in with the wrong crowd. There was no crowd at all. "He's such a loner," she wept one night. "Other mothers won't let their kids spend any time with him anymore." Just when this brilliant but troubled boy was most desperate for friends, just when my friend most needed other adults to reinforce her, they were both ostracized by parents trying to protect their kids from "the wrong crowd." Whenever I came across those warnings in PTA newsletters and magazine advice columns, I would think, "And what if the wrong crowd is us?"

A POPULAR poster in the early '70s pictured Whistler's mother in her rocker, holding a machine gun across her lap under the caption, "The Women's Movement is gonna get your mama and your sister and your *girlfriend*." Before I hung it next to my desk in the auditor's office, I painted over the machine gun and drew in a picket sign instead. (As strident and hysterical as feminists were reputed to be, we've never opened fire with anything more lethal than words.) Women who read the poster generally laughed, but men almost never did. They would hike up their pants and cross their arms over their chests, as if thinking, "Not *my* mama or girlfriend." If the poster were still on my wall today, I suspect the reaction of my sons and their friends might be: "Yeah, well, I guess I expected that."

Although my sons found their place in the subcultures of sports and computers through gangs of guys, their involvement with social issues has been mainly through female friends. Ryan's hunch that I would like his laundry-washing aviator girlfriend turned out to be right. I love what I see so far in this next female generation, which seems to be entering womanhood with a healthy sense of entitlement: "Sure, I'll do your wash . . . and you'll make my dinner, right?" Maybe that's what the anthropologists actually had in mind when they gave women the task of taming and civilizing men. Instead of opposing sides, however—you try to change me, I try to resist you—there's heartening evidence that the partner model is finally catching on. Darren attended the local March for Choice last spring with Aly, who didn't regard abortion as a "women's issue." If you cared about women, it was your issue too—you surrendered your Sunday, you held up your sign.

Although I never thought I'd be the kind of mother who would count on future wives to teach my sons what I could not, I now understand how young men can learn twice as much in half the time when love is involved. Girlfriends have inspired some of my sons' most transcendent moments. Although Darren had plenty of courage on the rugby field, charging fearlessly into lines of beefy thugs intent on breaking both his knees, he depended on Aly to get him through his Thursday evening jitters last spring, when he came face to face with the skinny, disorganized, often loony population lined up at St. Luke's soup kitchen. Initially, he'd gotten onto Aly's volunteer team as a Guy Who Cooks, helping her prepare dinner for 125 people and dropping it off at the shelter. He didn't like to go in because, as he once said, "I'm not good with crazy people." They scared him to death.

When an autistic friend came for a visit the year before, I tried to prepare him by explaining her symptoms and reviewing the behaviors that could trigger them: any kind of physical touch, sudden movements, raised voices, profuse gestures, direct eye contact. He became so alarmed that he might forget and accidentally initiate a "shutdown," he excused himself that weekend and stayed with a friend.

"I'm sorry, Mom" he said, feeling gutless for wanting out. "I'm just so uncomfortable around mentally ill people. I'm not like you."

"It's okay, D.," I said, "but everyone's uncomfortable at first—I certainly was. I don't know anybody who isn't—except maybe Betty."

At Betty's Consignment Shop, a glorious junk store around the corner from our rented house, the proprietor was an unflappable dispenser of cheap goods and incomparable kindness. Betty's was a regular stop for Crazy Eddie, a large, unkempt figure who stood in front of her store every day directing the overhead traffic, waving his arms, sometimes yelling loudly to the spaceships and aliens who visited him there. Unable to persuade Eddie to find another landing strip, Betty eventually put him and his invisible aliens to work. Every morning he set up a display on the sidewalk—the same broken chairs on either side of the same St. Francis bird bath—and every afternoon he carried it all back inside. He couldn't really hurt the merchandise since it was already junk, Betty said, and having a routine seemed to comfort him. It was true that on his most agitated days he sometimes frightened customers away. But whatever fate had paired Betty with the madman, it had been kind enough to provide her with a sensible detachment from faint-hearted customers and neighbors. Betty had a genius for charity.

Whenever I drove past Eddie, I would call his name and wave, exactly the same way every time. He would wave back, sometimes shouting an incomprehensible warning. My sons would usually look the other way during these manic greetings, embarrassed for both of us—for Eddie, because he was clearly and loudly crazy and for me, because it looked like I could be too. I didn't expect them to participate in these foreign exchanges, but it seemed essential to expose them, to pass along the lessons I'd learned from the matrons at Dunning: Look, listen, learn the routines. Pay attention and "sustain the gaze" as Joanna Macy described it, and you can eventually diffuse the pain of human suffering. Direct involvement was more effective than trying to avoid or deny human tragedy. Like a flu shot, direct contact with the virus itself provided a kind of inoculation against vague fears and depression.

My sons had so far preferred avoidance when it came to mental illness, perhaps because it was so close to home. So I was surprised when Darren started volunteering at St. Luke's with Aly that year, deliberately putting himself in close proximity to the mentally ill. They served dinner every Thursday, and once a month, they cooked it as well. They would haul a trunkload of groceries into the kitchen after school, chop and stir and talk for two ceaseless hours, and then haul three barrels of spaghetti and large ice chests of salad back out. It was clear from his chatter that Darren had gotten to know his clients quite well.

"You know the guy I mean," Darren said to Aly, looking up from the loaf of Italian bread he was slathering with garlic butter. "You know—the guy who always puts his earflaps down when he comes *inside* the building?" He stopped his knife-work briefly to snap an imaginary strap under his chin. Aly smiled and nodded for him to go on. "Well, he goes right up to her, puts his face about two inches from hers, and yells, 'Shocka-shula, you been singin' that same damn song all night—you drivin' me nuts!'" He laughed. "No kidding! Shocka-shula—that killed me. God, she *does* drive you nuts. I'm telling you, these crazy people . . . " He stopped then, apparently deciding not to tell.

These crazy people, I thought, could be your own relatives.

CARLOS WON a soccer scholarship and enjoyed his first semester of college immensely—so much so that the president sent him a letter over Christmas break informing him there was no point in his returning unless he had some explanation for his nearly nonexistent grade-point average. We spent a long evening at my computer, working on his reply. First, it was his coach's fault, who scheduled practices in the only hours he had to do his English papers; then it was his English professor's fault, who docked him a grade for being late with assignments. Then there was his roommate . . .

"Carlos?"

"Yes, Mrs. Blakely?"

"What about you? Can you think of any way you might have fucked up here?"

"Beg pardon?" In Carlos's strict code of parental behavior, the June Cleavers do not swear.

"Carlos, this guy is not a dummy. He's going to recognize this bullshit a mile away. If you want him to take you seriously, you've got to be honest. Did *you* do anything wrong?"

Well. Maybe. A few too many beers. Maybe too many parties, he said. Too few classes. Did he really want to go back? What for? After several hours of interrogation and cross examination, we had a two-page letter to fax to the president. I named the document and saved the file before printing. The computer hummed as the screen flashed me the message, "Saving Carlos." And so it goes.

We have lived in good neighborhoods and bad as our class status changed, and most of the stereotypes I once entertained proved to be wrong. In the best neighborhood we inhabited, Vernon Jordan was shot; in the worst, we made some of our lifetime friends. It seems to me that anywhere I went in the Kinder, Gentler Nation in those days, whether I allied myself with the girl Rebels or escaped to Arnie's or rode with the Posse, whether I dropped in at Betty's or heard Shocka-shula's monotonous song, or even answered my own telephone late at night, I found myself in thick with the wrong crowd in no time at all. Oddly enough, the wrong crowds have been as valuable and instructive and necessary as all the right crowds we have become engaged with again and again. We all want exactly the same things: To love, to be loved. And maybe, if you are a young male, to own your own car. It seems so incredibly simple, but of course it's not. Even if we manage to avoid the Big Five catastrophes that could cancel happiness, there are a hundred lesser ways a human being can lose sight of the horizon.

IT WAS snowing hard when Carlos left our house late that night. Ry and I turned off the lights and locked the door behind him. Before closing the drapes we stood at the picture window for a few minutes, watching his friend trudge through the thick powder toward his car, buried like a raisin in a loaf of rising dough. I felt a peculiar yearning as I followed Carlos's solo figure, tough and vulnerable at once, advancing through the beautiful, treacherous snowstorm. The flakes fell soundlessly under the pink lights flooding the park at the end of our street. He got into his car and turned on the engine, then immediately got out again. He walked around the front and stood at the curb under a stand of oak trees.

Over the roof of the car, we saw him hunch his shoulders, then tilt his head back and sigh with obvious relief. Ry and I both started laughing.

"Too bad Robert Frost never knew Carlos," I said. "He would have inspired a poem, 'Pissing in the Woods on a Snowy Evening.'"

11

The Importance
of Being Imperfect

One of the more interesting facts I uncovered in my research about brain damage in coma patients is that after awakening, we often exhibit an inability to feel depression. It is as if our sadness circuits have burned out. In my case, I think several anxiety fuses might have blown as well. After I recovered from my near-death experience, I had trouble working up my usual angst about deadlines, and even all the champion worrying I'd done about the kids during the years of divorce had dropped down to minor league status. I was mainly grateful: We were all still alive. I continued to feel immensely connected to my kids and my work, but the lines of attachment were no longer around my neck, as it were. The pressure of time had melted.

A magazine editor called one afternoon from the manic interior of Manhattan to declare an emergency in the art department—she needed a rewrite, and fast, because Prettyface or Slimdown or somebody had just pulled a major ad. Half a dozen people were putting in serious overtime to rework the whole "back of the book," as they say in the magazine biz. It meant dropping everything, including my dinner with a close friend whose son was on the verge of flunking out of high school. (His executive dad, not coincidentally, had left home that winter to live on a houseboat in the Florida Keys.) I couldn't see canceling our critical dinner talk and shifting into overdrive to avert the dreadful consequences of going without mascara advice for a month.

"If nobody dies, it's not an emergency," I said to my editor. I promised to supply the rewrite copy the next day. I would tell my friend almost the same thing at dinner that evening, suggesting that if her son did flunk out, she might consider sending him to live on the houseboat with his father for a semester. Since they were both in dropout mode, driving her crazy from different directions, why not put them together and let them be responsible for each other? I would eventually tell whole audiences of working mothers the same thing during subsequent lecture tours. I became a kind of talk show missionary for a while, warning women still laboring under the impossible expectations of three-point moms that they could be rapidly approaching ground zero. Half of the emergencies constricting our hearts and raising our blood pressure were fakes. In the final exam awaiting all of us in the end, who's going to look back on their life and think, "The world would have been a much better place if I'd only gotten that Prettyface ad and persuaded more women to color their cheeks."

After my own anxiety fuses had blown, I could no longer think of myself as indispensable to any civilization, either the small one at home or the big one out there. During those immobile months I spent in the hospital while life in the greater world proceeded without me, I acquired a more accurate perception of my significance on this planet. After my medical emergency forced me to give up the business of being everything to everyone, I eventually abandoned the guilt and need for approval that kept working moms like Alice and me running in place. My new role model during this transition phase was an unlikely one, no doubt influenced by the young male company I was keeping.

Being recovering Hoosiers, Ryan and Darren were big fans of Indiana Jones. Outfitted in khakis and his signature brown felt hat, a Christmas gift from their aunt Regina, they looked like two undersized claim jumpers in a frontier gold rush. Because they were too young to be admitted to the movies starring their hero without an accompanying adult, I saw more of Indy's rakish adventures than was probably healthy for a woman already inclined toward outlawdom. For years afterward, one particular scene kept replaying in my head. Like Darren's fortune cookie prayer, it popped into mind whenever I needed it.

Indiana's already had a busy day rescuing women, escaping assassins, climbing out of snake pits when Harrison Ford, looking attractively worse for the wear, is suddenly jumped by yet another menacing enemy in a public market. White robes furling and eyes flashing, the evil sheik draws a huge, gleaming saber as the crowd shrinks back in terror. Our hero looks around and sees no way around the duel. Someone tosses him a saber, the regional weapon of choice, which he receives in unaccomplished hands. The bystanders gasp as the sheik shows off his sword-twirling talents. Slicing the air like a high-speed propeller, the blade whistles with the sound of imminent death. The crowd hushes and looks to Indy, clearly waiting for him to match the sheik's incredible performance.

Indiana looks at his puny, borrowed saber, tries a bumbling half-loop with the unfamiliar weapon, considers the odds of coming out alive. Not good. For a brief moment he tenses his jaw, bracing for a confrontation with the whirling, swinging, slicing blade. Then abruptly, he has another idea. He draws a revolver from his belt and pulls the trigger. In classic minimalist Ford, he shrugs his eyebrows to the crowd: "No show today, folks."

That, I think, is what my calling cards might have said if I'd had any printed in those first years after my coma. When I was invited back into the snake pits of guilt—at work, at home, at PTA meetings—I couldn't think of any compelling reasons to go. Who would die if my rewrite copy arrived on a Wednesday instead of a Tuesday? Sure, there would be some chagrin if I didn't get the kids to the barber before their school pictures. But how guilty would I really feel, ten years from now, when we came upon them again in a yearbook? If they looked like two escapees from a hippie commune, maybe with parents named Moonbeam and Pluto, wouldn't we probably laugh? Couldn't we afford a little laugh now? These were the kind of thoughts that made depression more difficult after my coma; so many things that once made me worry now made me laugh. I could see why the neurologists called it "brain damage." What else could explain a middle-aged, semi-married woman with two children and a job who felt neither guilty nor depressed? Unfortunately, it wasn't permanent. After the first easy year of being happy-to-be-back-among-the-likes-of-you, I had to concentrate on maintaining this delightful brain damage.

The Indy scene reminded me to keep assessing the given terms, to see if there wasn't another way to meet my various obligations without walking directly into the propeller. As my own recent breakdown indicated, if I didn't change the expectations of my family and my colleagues, and didn't redirect the ensuing guilt, I faced more than a metaphorical possibility of death or dismemberment.

By the late '80s, media commentators interpreted the fall of Superwoman as the end of feminism; women's magazines declared that "having it all" was out. Headlines were now reporting that professional women were leaving their jobs in droves because a mother "can't do both." A cover story in the *New York Times Magazine* featuring a photojournalist identified as "one of the top three or four in the world" explained why she decided against motherhood: "I don't see how a woman in documentary photography could have children," she told her interviewer. "I think it's a very difficult thing to raise a family, and I have enormous respect for people who do it. I'd hate to do something like that and not be good at it. It's for a long time." The famous photojournalist had chosen, with some regret, to remain childless.

Headlines declaring that mothers "can't do both" were happily received by folks who hoped women had finally come to their senses and would be soon resuming their rightful place at the ironing board. They were not so happily received by those who had no choice about doing both—that is, all the mothers in the middle and lower classes of our Kinder, Gentler Nation. If the most well-positioned and influential women were either going home or remaining childless, there would be less pressure for the institutional changes the rest of us needed in the echelons below. Even for those lucky few who did have the luxury of choice—you needed money or a well-paid mate to do without a job—being asked to decide between your passion for work and your passion for children was like being asked by your doctor whether you preferred him to remove your brain or your heart.

A PREGNANT Jane Pauley once asked me on the air, apparently oblivious to her own impending reality, if women shouldn't limit themselves to either work or family. Weren't women inviting stress by "trying to do too much"?

"Women aren't trying to do too much," I said. "Women *have* too much to do." Jane, whose intelligence must have been under the ecstatic spell of heightened estrogen that morning, imagined such fulfillment in motherhood she said that she might not return to the "Today Show" until her children started school. Jane had twins and was back at work in less than a year. Celebrity mothers who provided advice and role models for my generation were about as impossible to emulate as the Virgin Mary and Mother Cabrini were for my mother and Brownie leader. Those celebrities who did brave "doing both," as Jane did, usually had the income and staff to do so without making any serious amendments to the status quo. Most of the rest of us were still laboring under the cliché: "A woman has to work twice as hard as any man to be considered half as good." That equation kept us so frazzled that hundreds of women from coast to coast thought my coma sounded like something they might want to try.

"You slept for *nine days*?" a woman in Portland asked, with obvious envy. "How *was* that?"

There had to be healthier ways of relieving our national stress. I was struck by the realization that a man in documentary photography faced no such dilemma about having children. To put it in modern cliché, a father had to work only half as hard as any mother to be considered twice as good. "Though it's very important for men to marry and have a family," Dr. Daniel J. Levinson of Yale University said, "the big difference is that a man feels he is taking care of his family by working." A woman, on the other hand, feels she is depriving her family by working. Most women think that motherhood or any other significant love relationship involves some element of being there.

I see no way around the "twice as hard" part of the given formula, at least in my lifetime. In terms of economic clout, men's salaries are the sheik's gleaming saber and women's are Indy's puny sword. For all the stridency and hysteria about unequal pay in the last two decades, women have narrowed the 35 cent wage gap—and therefore our working hours—by only a dime. We've won a coffee break, as it were. Although we have limited power to change the economic part of the equation, we have some control over the self-esteem part—the "half as good" judgment that keeps us going at a burn. Maybe half-approval was too much to wish for in these trying times.

Maybe I could live with only a quarter's worth of approval, since it was so hard for working mothers to come by. And what would my life look like if I needed no approval? My joint passions for motherhood and writing had already compromised any claim to be a "good mother" of the three-point quality. From the beginning, I belonged to the category psychologist Bruno Bettelheim labeled "Good Enough Mothers," a kind of subspecies of imperfectionists. For women who were accustomed to achievement and success, becoming imperfect required enormous concentration. Striving to be a Good Enough Mother sounds slightly shameful when compared to being "one of the top three or four in the world," but imperfection has not turned out to be as hateful as the photojournalist imagined.

The anticipation of getting a "C" on one's life transcript was worse than the actual fact. My first one arrived the September we finished Phase III of our custody plan, the year after my recovery, when the kids finally moved east to live with Larry and me in Connecticut. There was a lot of adjusting, accommodating, listening, and talking to do that fall, which coincided with my return to full-time work. When the kids weren't having a sleepless night in those first three months, I was having one. Since then, as now, there was no such thing as nightmare leave, I reported for work each day with what working mothers I know call "soft brain."

Being slow of mind during those months, I proofread all my assignments twice before handing them in. Nevertheless, I armed one copy editor—an arrogant young man who relished my errors with unsettling glee—with this ammunition against my brilliance: In a single essay, I described "a white house with green shudders" inhabited by a person who was "fearful down to the souls of her feet." For the next six months, the copy editor performed a little green shudder and laughed every time I handed in an assignment, as I felt my soul relocating in my feet.

As compromising as it was to be an imperfect writer, the humility of being an imperfect mother was even greater. The year I began moonlighting to write a book in addition to my regular magazine assignments, I returned home from the library one evening two hours later than promised. I found four messages on the answering machine from Darren, then eleven, reporting that he was in the emergency room of the local hospital with his older brother. He left no information about Ryan's injury—each time he obediently gave his name, the time, and the same "brief message." The moment every working mother fears had finally arrived: I was "not there" for an emergency.

After more than a decade of practice, I easily imagined the worst. Heart pounding, I barreled into the emergency room, anticipating the horror of finding my older son on a stretcher. Instead, I found him sitting calmly in the waiting area, holding an ice pack around a swollen hand. Since the minor fracture wasn't life-threatening, the hospital staff couldn't X ray or set the small bone without parental permission, and the boys had to wait in the lounge until I arrived. The major discomfort Ryan felt during the extended wait came from his long distance from the refrigerator. The hospital cafeteria was closed so he called Matt and Eric, two friends in the neighborhood, who brought supplies from a nearby McDonald's. When

I arrived, the four boys were camped out in couches eating hamburgers and french fries, as if a hospital emergency room were as genial a place as any for an impromptu picnic.

Is it heretical for me to admit that, once my heartbeat returned to normal, I was actually *pleased* that I had not "been there" for my sons? The photojournalist is absolutely right that motherhood "takes a long time." Or, to put it another, blunter way, it can take thirteen years to see what kind of picture you've got. In the hospital that night I saw two boys, long accustomed to answering machines and pay phones, confidently and ingeniously filling in for me. Although they had managed the crisis ably, I did not escape contempt for being a Good Enough Mother.

"So you finally got here," the resident remarked disdainfully, "we've been trying to reach you for more than two hours." He looked at the boys with pity, two nearly motherless children. I saw two hatless hero-types, braving an adventure in the snake pit as if it were all in a day's work. When the young doctor returned his gaze to me, I felt the rising tremor of a green shudder. But I didn't apologize. My perpetual urge to apologize was like the "existential hum" Kurt Vonnegut once described, "the uneasiness which keeps us moving," the feeling that "I have somehow disgraced myself." To live with the hum of imperfection, I had to stop regarding my many professional and familial absences as cause for apology. I began to see them as opportunities for my family and colleagues to exercise compassion. Unfortunately, the resident in the emergency room missed his opportunity.

As compromising as it seemed, it was nevertheless essential to keep offering these opportunities for compassion. Nightmares, after all, were not solely the province of frightened children; adults coping with divorce, or keeping vigil for a dying parent, or watching a teenage son flunk out of school have them too. In my dream for the revolution of the work place, men as well as women would have the courage to become provocatively imperfect because they, too, would develop the desire to "be there" for someone they loved.

It happened dramatically at the magazine I was working for that year, when one man's personal tremor moved an entire institution.

He was a senior editor at a national news weekly—a pressure-cooker position in an institution famous for its tradition of once-a-week all-nighters. Anyone who expected a long tenure in the organization was expected to be there. After almost ten years of nearly perfect attendance, he began taking exceptionally long lunch hours and leaving promptly at five every night, deadlines pending or not. He said nothing for three months, until he returned from lunch one day and walked numbly out of the elevator. Eyes vacant and face blanched, he walked past his office and down the carpeted corridor, stopping finally in his boss's doorway.

"Listen, I have something to tell you," he said abruptly. "My best friend just died of AIDS." He paused a moment, letting the weight of this admission sink in, disclosing the most important secret of his personal life. "He died this noon," he said, then added ironically: "He conveniently waited for my lunch hour." He shook his head in disbelief. "I just want you to know . . . I'll be a little off-center for a while." His boss, unlike the resident in the emergency room, did not miss the opportunity for compassion.

She was a woman who'd been off-center herself, and she understood the exact location of his soul as he leaned against her doorway. In the face of actual death, all the fake emergencies paled.

"I'm sorry," she said. "Take good care of yourself. We'll take care of your desk." For the next few months, the senior editor was astounded by his colleagues' generosity as they covered him through weeks of all-nighters. There were others who didn't join the effort, of course, operating from the attitude of "We all have our crises—why should you be any different?" But mostly, the staff recognized that we all needed to be different at one time or another—that is, if we cared about the people in our personal lives. A peculiar thing happens when people who work together risk becoming imperfect and share an opportunity for compassion. They begin to feel a mutual investment in the outcome.

The willingness to risk imperfection, in fact, might ultimately be the most valuable contribution my generation of women can make to the work place. After all the congressional studies on the glass ceiling depressing women's wages, all the media reports about the paternity leaves men are not taking, all the sad stories about day-care shortages in a country that still wants to think jobs, and therefore day care, are a "choice" for most parents, we know now what people need. But from my observations, our work habits have become even more stressful than they were in the unenlightened days of my own young motherhood. The separation of spheres is as oppressive as ever, since the economy is still largely unrecognized as a *family* issue. The massive layoffs that depressed my Midwestern community have now blighted families from coast to coast. Those friends who are still employed after the hostile takeovers and stockholder greed of the '80s are in worse straits than many of our unemployed peers.

"Nine P.M. and I'm still at the office," a friend called to say recently, dead-tired after her fourth double-shift in a row. She still had Easter baskets and a family reunion to prepare when she got home later that night. For most of my friends today, a forty-hour work week would look like a part-time job.

"Go home," I advised her. "If you get fired, at least you can put 'Easter Bunny' on your next resume."

If all 48 million working women took the risk and stepped even slightly off the center of prevailing attitudes—revising the professional and personal expectations of both men and women—the center would move. That enormous tremor might not happen in my lifetime, but I can feel it coming each time I contribute a solitary green shudder. I imagine myself as part of a vast mediocre majority, and it elevates my soul right up to my knees.

12

The Brownie Revolt

Larry seemed not to have noticed by 1987 that Ryan and Darren had moved in permanently. Our blended family had the persistent separation qualities of oil and vinegar: unless I kept shaking everyone up, each sought his own level. Larry continued to operate as though we were primarily a couple, except one of us had two sons; the boys regarded me as their single parent, although there was another adult in the house. Larry was polite with the guys, much as a concierge might be to guests camped out in his hotel lobby, whenever he asked them not to let friends with sticky fingers handle the remote controls for the TV. But his regular habit of pouring a glass of wine when he came home from work, talking to me about his day at the office before dinner, continued as if we were still just a twosome. Everything about his demeanor that year seemed to carry a warning: If you want to raise my consciousness about familial tasks and nurturing responsibilities, a forklift might be necessary.

Ryan and Darren became scrupulous observers of Larry's routine habits—the least powerful members of any small civilization understand how the hierarchy works better than the hierarchy understands its subjects. They stopped coming into the kitchen to help me make dinner, which used to be our "quality time," since the conversation there now rarely included them. Their relationship with Larry seemed to be taking on the uneasy accord of an exceptionally neat and fastidious New York executive caught in the same elevator with two sweaty midtown messengers.

Howard, meanwhile, was having trouble structuring time in his suddenly unhinged days. Two years after the boys moved east, his dissertation was dead in the water. His own move, as well as the job that would provide child support, appeared to be indefinitely postponed. During visits to Ann Arbor, the kids naturally noticed his depression. I had to keep reciting Dr. Whiteside's advice like a mantra to myself, "You have no business planning Howard's life— you can only change your own." It was hard to stay on track with that bit of difficult wisdom, especially under the mounting pressure of the kids' bills.

Larry and I had established a pattern of splitting our joint expenses the first year we lived together, with each of us covering our own personal expenses. I was not aware for several years that I'd achieved another hybrid of "concept equality." No adjustments to our financial arrangement were made when the kids joined us; they simply became two more of my personal expenses, as it were. Larry noticed the financial strain I was under, but blamed Howard for not contributing any child support. He reminded me, in case it might have slipped my mind, that Howard had been in graduate school for six years now. Larry was super-responsible about his own obligations—his life insurance, his dental care, his annual cholesterol tests—but he felt that paying any portion of the kids' costs would be the equivalent of paying Howard's bills, which violated his principle of self-sufficiency. Larry was a lead alto in the chorus of friends who thought I should take Howard to court and cease my useless belief in holistic divorce. I didn't, mostly because I doubted that the courts would achieve what anthropologists had been urging women to do for centuries: harness men into the role of husband and father.

Howard was completely irresponsible about money that year, and Larry was super-conscientious about his obligations, but both came to the same conclusion about paying the kids' expenses. For wildly different reasons, their separate decisions had exactly the same impact on me: I had to cover everything. It took me several years to recognize the double default because, to be fair, I first had to answer these questions: Why should Larry support my sons, since he was neither their father nor my husband? Why should Howard support his sons when he "didn't get to live with them," as he had proposed? Why shouldn't I, who freely chose both to have children and to divorce, not be solely responsible for the results? Depending on which point of view I accepted, the answers shifted.

My problem didn't merely involve untangling questions of responsibility, however. It led me to consider the question of kindness. How could men who genuinely loved women watch us labor "twice as hard" year after year, and not volunteer to ease our load, *whatever* the circumstances that got us here? What is love, if not "common decency"?

Since Larry's salary was nearly double mine, our joint household soon resembled a microcosm of the class divisions that formed after the first six years of Reaganomics. In our two-story, two-class household, the kids and I lived in the lower class while Larry lived above us. Despite the long discussions we had about family before we moved in together, Larry and I had not escaped the "her kids, his money" of marriage. Nor did we appear to be living the terms of a good divorce.

ALL OVER the United States in 1987 there were images of the New Domesticated Men: Parks on weekends were full of fathers pushing strollers, TV sitcoms starred single fathers who could give toddlers a bath and teenagers good advice, life insurance commercials featured daddies saying how important it was to support their offspring even beyond death. But these public scenes represented a private reality that was still in the I-wish stage. Even today, it still isn't unusual for men to excuse themselves from familial responsibilities because they think women can do them more easily. A recent article in the life-style section of the *Boston Globe* reported that, although many men have learned to perform domestic tasks their fathers never dreamed of doing, calling a baby-sitter is still an unsettled frontier. The fathers interviewed—some of whom ran national businesses, big-city hospitals, and major universities—all said, without evident embarrassment, they just can't call a baby-sitter as well as a mother could.

"If my husband started hiring the baby-sitters, I'd have to stay involved anyway," Jane Adams, a mother of two, was quoted. "It's in my nature." Careful, Jane, I thought. This nature business will backfire on you.

The persistent "instinct" theory is partly to blame for the continued difficulty my generation of men is having catching on to the rudiments of being a husband and father. If women's natural instincts drive them to feed, clothe, nurture, launder, and spot-remove twenty-four hours a day, why would a man whose natural instinct propels him into an easy chair with the newspaper want to upset this delicate balance by voluntarily taking up half her load? Nor does it take an anthropologist to know why men might be reluctant to change this arrangement, why they might not be self-starters in this particular area of evolution.

If acquiring the baby-sitter is a biologically determined talent, it's logical to assume that driving the junior high car pool before work and picking up supplies for the Halloween party after work should also come naturally to women. The *Globe* noted that Jane, who is presently working at home, planned to resume her professional career sometime in the future. Since more than three-fourths of her peers will be taking on paid employment before their children reach sitter-free years, Jane might soon be wishing her husband would find it in his nature to call a baby-sitter once in a while.

I LONGED for a dual-career father as a role model for my sons, a man who could earn a living and plan a birthday party at the same time. This wish dominated my thoughts the year I became the room mother of Mr. Baldino's sixth grade class. It had been Ryan's idea in the first place—"Mom, please? We're the only class that doesn't have a room mother! Nobody volunteered!" But at the end of my tenure, he asked me not to reenlist. I remember the turning-point day.

"Hello, Tony? This is Ryan's mom. Is your father there?" It was 7:30 P.M. on a Wednesday evening, and I was sitting at my desk with a list of twenty-four names and numbers in front of me. Larry was still at his office, working overtime on a project that had consumed him for six weeks. The kids and I microwaved something with noodles and gravy for dinner, because I had a critical deadline of my own that night. Working alphabetically down my list, I was only on the Ds. "Nobody keeps answering," as Holden Caulfield once said.

"He's watching TV," Tony replied.

"Great," I said, making a check mark next to his name. "Tell him I want to talk to him."

While Tony notified his dad, I scanned the list and looked up at the clock. I still had a lot of work to do that evening—my assignment should have been express-mailed two hours earlier. Late that afternoon, I had called Ellen, the editor at *Ms.* waiting on the other end, who wasn't at all surprised to receive the message: "I'm running late."

Ellen is a mother too, so she had herself experienced the chagrin of uttering that phrase to colleagues. She was kind and gave me another day. But by doing so, she made her own job harder—at 5:00, she had to step into her boss's office and report, "We're running late." My motherhood changed from "I" to "we," becoming plural again, thanks to another woman.

Tony's Dad was taking his time. I tried to remember what programs were on the air at 7:30 P.M., but the last one I remembered watching was "Marcus Welby, M.D." Leisure time had disappeared from my life, which was how I got drafted into being a room mother in the first place. I couldn't volunteer to be a field trip mother or a cafeteria mother because those tasks required daytime hours, but room mothers could make their phone calls at night.

I had honored Ryan's request because I still tried to do my share of PTA-type assignments. I didn't want to fuel the flames between mothers who work at home and mothers who work outside. Mrs. Laura L. Luteri, of Mount Prospect, Illinois, had just fired a tiny grenade into my camp, in a letter to the editor of *Better Homes and Gardens*. She wrote that she was sick and tired of hearing the excuse "I can't, I work" from working mothers. Mrs. Luteri resented women like me for depending on women like her to fill in. In fact, I was depending on school administrations to recognize that room mother and cafeteria mother and field trip mother should all become paid positions.

"Hello?" a male voice interrupted my thoughts, with a touch of boredom. The voice didn't sound as if it were dressed in a suit and tie; it had a sweatshirt and jeans on, but managed to talk down to me nevertheless. Perhaps I had been referred to as "Ryan's mom," so I sat up a little straighter and introduced myself.

"Mr. D., this is Mary Kay Blakely. I'm the room mother for Mr. Baldino's sixth-grade class," I began in my most professional voice.

"Hold on," he interrupted, "I'll get my wife." The professional disguise failed. "Room mother" gave me away—he recognized this as a woman's call.

"No, wait," I replied instantly, keeping him attached to the receiver. "I've already spoken to your wife several times this year . . ."

A mental image of Mrs. D. flashed into my mind. Like all the mothers of the children in Mr. Baldino's class, she was making dinner. I called during dinner to save myself time dialing repeat calls; working mothers were usually home at dinner time.

"Oh, God," they sighed whenever I mentioned my name, "let me get a pencil." Four times this year, I had made requests of their time and heard their fatigue. The cumulative guilt of twenty-two sighs repeated four times led me to revise the message I was asked to send out that night. I only changed one word, inspired by the argument I had that morning with Larry.

"We're asking the sixth-grade fathers . . ." I began, and faltered slightly. It was an editorial we, but in fact I had no authority behind me. The other room mothers were not asking for fathers tonight. It was a "we" to make me bigger than "I," a "we" representing the plurality of motherhood, a "we" to give some power to the request I was about to make.

"We're asking the fathers to make brownies for the class party next Wednesday. Will you send a dozen to school with Tony?" I stopped, letting the request sink in.

"Me?" he asked incredulously. I imagined Mr. D.'s eyebrows rising up on his forehead. After twelve years of fatherhood, he had apparently never been asked to make brownies, never been a room father. Perhaps he was a father who spent "quality time" with his children on weekends and evenings, but he didn't sound like a man who knew his way around the kitchen. In 1986 the kitchen was where mothers generally spent their quality time, helping children with homework while making dinner and taking phone calls. Running small civilizations.

"Oh, I don't know, I've never made brownies," Mr. D. chuckled, as if I were teasing him. But I was not.

"It's easy. All you have to do is read the box." I was prepared to give him detailed instructions, over the phone, on how to make brownies. Fudge brownies, brownies with nuts, blondie brownies . . . suddenly, Mr. D. had twelve years of knowing nothing about brownies to make up for with me. I realized I was getting worked up. I imagined I was late on my deadline because I'd been making brownies all day.

Be patient, I cautioned myself. If Mr. D had never been asked to do his share, how could I expect him to know? He could know, of course, if he observed Mrs. D.'s fatigue, if he noticed the diminishing quality of her time in the kitchen. Perhaps he didn't see her exhaustion because women in kitchens have always looked exhausted to him. Maybe he thought exhausted was a normal state for us. The mothers in Mr. Baldino's class had been forgiving fathers on the grounds of "how could he know?" for twelve years. Mr. D's learning time had just expired.

"I'll see what I can do," he said, taking me for a fool. "I'll see" was not the same as "I will." Those two words and their lack of commitment were why the phrase "working father" was still unfamiliar to the culture, ten years after the women's movement began; why men and their newspapers filled up the early morning commuter trains, in time for power breakfasts, while women caught the later ones, after driving car pools; why executive women were telling the press they were leaving their jobs because they "couldn't do both," while their executive husbands were never even interviewed. "I'll see" was just inches above "I won't"—the phrase given up with reluctance by fathers in the '70s.

"We need a commitment tonight," I insisted, keeping him on the phone. I was speaking to Mr. D., but I was thinking about the anthropologists who would like me to do a better job of socializing men. They cannot possibly know the size of this request.

When Howard and I reversed roles during his years of unemployment, he was shocked by the cumulative fatigue of running a microscopic society. He felt he had obtained valuable insights into the infrastructure of domestic life; he said he even knew what it felt like to be thought of as "just a housewife." But he never had to do the most draining part of that job. He would look at me with gratitude when I came home from work—an expression I recognized as "Thank god! Relief is here!"

If we had truly reversed roles, I would have kissed him on the cheek, taken my newspaper to the living room, and waited for dinner. But instead, without his having to remind me, I would start making it myself, involving the kids in small tasks for some quality time. He never had to ask, remind, plead with me to notice when the bathroom needed cleaning, the kids needed laundry, the dishes needed doing. Maybe he knew something about the invisible status of "just a housewife," but it wasn't coupled with the contemptuous feeling of being thought a nag. Men rarely have to nag their domestic partners. Women come prepared to help.

My argument that morning with Larry, who was also working under a crushing deadline, had been another rousing chorus of this familiar song. He hated these arguments, as did I, because he had already recognized the dual pressures of work and family I kept bringing to his attention. We both recognized them, but I was the one who met them. His deadline had meant a month of sixty-hour weeks at the office, a month of brief appearances at home. "I have no *choice*," he had said apologetically, listing the emergencies. "I have to work."

"Tell that to Laura Luteri," I replied, although he knew nothing of the debate in the letters-to-the-editor column in *Better Homes and Gardens*. "You *see* no choice," I corrected him, naming the other available alternatives. He could quit his job, I suggested, but I didn't mean it. I couldn't argue persuasively for that choice, since my salary could never cover our joint expenses. He made more money, and making more bread was partly why men were exempted from making the brownies.

Or he could quit the family, I offered, as a second alternative, although I didn't mean that either. They were the kinds of statements that get blown out heatedly during arguments, born of injury or jealousy. But he *had* temporarily quit the family, and by empathizing with his deadlines I lost ground on my own. What good did it do us to think equality if we didn't get to live it?

Or, finally, he could introduce his boss to the term "working father" and the phrase "I'm running late." It would diminish his considerable esteem at work, and it wouldn't be easily accepted. There was no plurality of working fathers in the business world yet, and he would undoubtedly have to run late alone. But in a month of sixty-hour work weeks, the subject of home responsibilities had never come up at his office. How could his boss know he needed time for our family if he never asked? His boss could know, of course, if he chose to see the family portrait on Larry's desk and consider for a moment how such pictures are developed. They take enormous time and care.

"Mr. D., we need to know tonight," I repeated, asking for brownies but wishing for a revolution in the priorities of men. "If you can't bake them yourself, Sara Lee offers a good alternative." While I waited for his answer, I thought about opening a new business, a consulting firm to help fathers see the many options to "I can't, I work."

"Okay," he said, recognizing the only answer that would let him return to his TV program. "A dozen brownies, next Wednesday."

I then dialed the number for Mr. F., repeating my message, then Mr. L. and Mr. M. I was thrilled to raise the eyebrows of the fathers of Mr. Baldino's class. I imagined I was healing some tensions among women, between mothers working at home and outside it. I began to think of my room mother job as a public service to mothers, helping them socialize fathers.

I started with brownies, but I intended to ask men to volunteer to chaperon field trips next. I wanted fathers to know everything about the family pressures they leave to mothers. When working fathers finally have the same needs as working mothers, corporations will begin to see the need for day care, flex-time, sick days for family. The truth: When working fathers need the same benefits and institutional policies as working mothers, we will have them.

My deadline was still ahead of me when I finished the last call. But I felt successful, having secured pledges for 144 brownies, all from fathers. I couldn't be certain Mr. D. or Mr F. did not immediately delegate the responsibility to their wives: "Tony needs a dozen brownies." Or that their wives did not reply: "I don't do brownies." But that evening, I realized that I was through excusing fathers who "understood" but "had no choice." Understanding was fine, but it was time now for fathers to put their brownies where their mouths were.

13
The Brothers K

It's hard to get a clear picture of the chaos that exists in every family, since we rarely let our chaos be caught by the camera. When I hauled out all the cardboard boxes of photographs I'd been collecting for the last two decades, during my serious bout of what Dr. Oliver Sacks described as "incontinent nostalgia," I reviewed hundreds of images of the boys posed together as babes, then as the boys, the guys, the jocks, the gents, and now, the coming men. I decided to make a collage of "The Brothers" for the family photo wall. In roughly chronological order from top to bottom, I filled a poster-sized frame with shots of them horsing around, draping arms over each other's shoulders, mugging for the camera in twosomes as tight as Bert and Ernie, Beetle and Sarge, Seymour and Buddy. Although I had countless photos where they appeared to be the best friends I always hoped they would be, there were almost none showing the parallel reality of them aggravating each other nearly to death. Maybe pictures never lie, but neither do they tell the whole truth.

After I had finished The Brothers collage, slightly chagrined by its Rockwellian half-truths, Darren's lovely girlfriend dropped by and reviewed her loved one's history. She smiled at the charming pair of young yodelers in the yard, the only two kids in Indiana wearing liederhosen; laughed at the Two Stooges where Darren, his baseball beak turned to the back of his head, is jamming his face and hands against Ryan's chest to prop him up on the back of the couch, as Ry aims a power drill into the ceiling during my last home improvement project. She grinned at one of Ryan working his way into a tuxedo on prom night as Darren, in a flannel shirt and cut-offs, secures the clasp of his older brother's bow tie, concentrating on his task instead of his envy. Then Aly pointed to my favorite picture, a long-distance view in the center of the collage, and hummed softly.

Two middle-aged boys of eleven and twelve are sitting on a huge granite rock overlooking the Central Park lagoon, trees leafing high above them, their reflections rippling in the water below. In their grass-stained jeans and brightly colored jerseys they look like they might have come fresh from a ball field somewhere, but their bowed heads and hunched shoulders do not suggest a fun-and-games conversation. Their distance prohibits close scrutiny of their faces, but a pair of poignantly raised hands invites speculation that—youth and innocence aside—they are edging up to the kind of soul searching, intimate talk only siblings can have.

"So *sweet*," Aly said quietly, almost reverently. Darren smiled. It was a drag when his mom thought he was sweet, but it was okay if his girlfriend did.

Once the rivalries of early childhood subside, siblings have a greater chance of establishing lifetime intimacy than is possible in almost any other human relationship, since they have known each other as peers from birth. Ryan, an irrepressible extrovert even at eighteen months, was thrilled when we brought Darren home from the hospital. He thought this funny, entertaining, yielding brother was the best gift we had given him so far. Postponing the rivalry stage, they became inseparable buddies as soon as Darren could walk and talk. Even with a year and a half between them and dominant physical characteristics from opposite parents, they've been mistaken for fraternal twins most of their lives.

"CATHERINE WAS surprised to find out there were two of them," my friend Carrie said after the guys baby-sat one evening for her two year old. "The way we always talked about them, she thought

Ryan-and-Darren was one person." Whenever they were together, they projected an electric, almost neon aura that notified pedestrians, teammates, rivals, girl friends, and neighborhood bullies: "We are Brothers. First there is my brother, then there is you."

The Central Park photograph Aly found so sweet had bittersweet memories for me, for I knew what happened just before and several years after the shutter clicked. At a distance, Aly couldn't see that Darren's body was aflame with a raging, oozing, bleeding rash that covered his face, neck, his entire chest, and all four limbs; she didn't know he had been in the emergency room four days earlier, writhing in agony. Nor could she feel the shadowy presence of the man standing beside the camera as I focused the shot. That was the summer after the kids and I had moved in with Larry. When I look at this picture now, I wonder why it hadn't been obvious to me from the start that he and the boys would have a serious allergic reaction to each other.

I missed a lot of signals from the kids those first years we lived in Connecticut, when Larry dominated my attention. Two years after I had settled in for many long years of happily-ever-after with Larry, I convinced myself the kids were settling in too. I interpreted it as a healthy sign when their first serious sibling rivalries erupted with the crocuses in the spring of '87. It rattled them completely, since they had such limited experience with fraternal conflict. For their first twelve years, they practiced everything on each other first—new personalities, bravado, smarts, jokes. When divorce split the family, they became so close I worried about whether their intense bond was entirely healthy. Darren depended on his brother's social skills through the most harrowing transition stages, and Ryan relied on his brother's easy acquiescence. I worried that these tendencies were the early warning signs of a master/slave relationship. I interpreted the sudden fights that began cropping up that year as a sign of their maturation into separate identities. I even told myself this: They feel safe again for the first time in years—they can finally risk a fight with each other.

IT WAS Ryan, finally, who split the atom again and started the next chain reaction in our postnuclear family. As he approached the end of seventh grade, he waited for exactly the right moment to drop the bomb. One evening that spring, I sat down on the edge of his bed to say good night and he rolled over on his stomach, a signal that he wanted me to do the ritual we'd been performing since he was two years old. As a baby, whenever he was too wound up and over-stimulated at bedtime he used to put himself to sleep by rocking back and forth on hands and knees in his crib, banging forcefully against the bumper pads until he dropped from exhaustion. He mowed the sheets with the top of his head, pressing down so hard he'd worn a bald spot on his crown. After trying everything else to calm him down—a low-sugar diet, warm milk at bedtime, musical teddy bears, nighttime stories—I finally stumbled onto something that worked: I gave him a massage while I talked in a quiet mono-logue, trying to put the tensions of the day into some kind of per-spective for him.

He'd lie perfectly still as I kneaded his tight little muscles, lis-tening hard as I tried to unknot any lingering anxieties: the fight at the playground, the terrible accident he'd seen on Lafayette Street, even his own "vicious mom," who wouldn't buy the plastic tommy gun he craved at K-Mart. He would become especially still at the end, when I brushed my fingers in featherlike strokes from his soles to his scalp, over and over, telling him to imagine my hands "taking out all the bad feelings," as though I were vacuum-ing tension from his psyche. Since the boys shared a room as tod-dlers, when I gave Ryan a massage it meant giving Darren one, too. Throw in a bath and bedtime story, and putting them to bed could easily take more than an hour. One night, too tired for full-service relaxation rituals, I gave them each a massage but skipped the med-itation. "Do the *words*, Mom," Ryan said. "It doesn't work without the words." I remember being surprised that he was actually pay-ing attention to them. By the time the boys reached their double-digit years, I performed much abbreviated versions of this old-time ritual. Whenever one of them asked for it, he always used its childhood name: "Mom, would you do 'Take Out All the Bad Feelings' tonight?"

After giving Ryan a brief massage that night, I stood up and stretched, my back aching after leaning over his now sizable twelve-year-old body. He rolled over and studied me hard, his face so full of anxiety he looked like someone who'd just gotten out of a dentist's chair. Some massage, I thought.

"Mom, I have something to ask you, and I don't want you to take it the wrong way," he said. This usually meant, "I want to try out for football and you're going to do the mother-thing about broken necks and brain damage." I sat back down on the edge of his bed, noticing how roomy it was now that his stuffed animals had been retired to the attic along with other relics of childhood. Something was clearly Up, and it was unusual for Ryan to have much difficulty saying what was on his mind. Unlike Darren, my quiet and sometimes spookily mysterious son, this son was the "blurter." I rarely had to guess what he was thinking. He volunteered most of what I needed to know, as well as quite a few things I didn't want to hear.

"I won't take it wrong," I promised. "Shoot."

"I don't want you to think I don't love you."

"I won't, buddy. Shoot."

"It isn't that I'm not happy with you, Mom." He sat up and adjusted a pillow behind him, making this the longest goddam execution of my life. "Okay, honey. Shoot."

"I'd like to go live with Dad in Ann Arbor next year."

Bull's eye: straight through my heart. Suddenly, I saw myself behind the wheel of the Dodge heading north on Route 23 as the kids disappeared from the rear view-mirror, flung forcefully into the back seat by the bullet of divorce.

"Wait, Mom!" Ryan said, as if he feared I might pass out. "Only for a year! Only for eighth grade—then I'll come back, and Darren will go," he explained. "We've talked it all out."

"You and *Darren* worked this all out?" I asked dumbly, wondering where I'd been during the coup. I'd noticed an ominous shift from the fights back to their hushed and conspiratorial discussions that month, but I had thought they were plotting another Nintendo campaign since I was still convinced we could survive without one.

Ryan said they'd been talking ever since Christmas about how lonely Howard seemed, how much their dad would probably enjoy their company. They also thought it would be nice to be an "only child" for a while—a concept we'd discussed at length that year as I tried to explain why Larry was sometimes slow on the uptake of family rhythms.

"Don't decide tonight," Ryan said, asking me to "please sleep on it." He knew from experience that when I slept hard on things, they invariably looked different in the morning. Sleeping on this one, I thought, could threaten my previous nine-day record.

"You have Larry," Ryan had said, "but Dad has no one." By splitting themselves between us, he thought family affections would be more balanced all the way around. An unspoken, maybe even unconscious part of his plan was undoubtedly a prepubescent version of Robert Bly's wish to live with the Wild Man. He pictured a singular version of "My Three Sons," imagining a freewheeling bachelor life with his dad. Although he didn't say so, I thought his nonrelationship with Larry could have made his strong yearning for his funny, affectionate Dad even more intense.

NEITHER OF the boys felt the anger toward their father that still infected my thinking, as the dissertation remained unfinished and hopes of fulfilling our child support and domicile agreement looked ever more remote. I went to bed hating Howard that night. It wasn't conscious yet, but I knew I was going to have to honor Ryan's request. I must have known for some time that it would be coming, just as the kids knew divorce was inevitable long before it was announced. The boys loved Howard as much as they loved me— maybe more, since I was back in their direct line of vision again, the too-familiar parent who could be taken for granted.

Two out of the three conditions for mortal sin I'd memorized in the Baltimore Catechism now seemed to apply: It was a grievous matter to separate growing sons from their father; I had a strong temptation to do so, knowing I could win a custody battle against Howard. Though I was deeply opposed to the "her kids, his money" bias of marriage, that's what governed divorce judgments and could be used to my advantage. I knew I could manipulate the system: A bankrupt breadwinner stood no chance of winning custody, even against an Unnatural Mom.

Fatally, I recognized a moral obligation to honor my sons' paternal love. Because I loved them and they loved their dad, I had to bite my tongue when their loyalties to Howard prompted treasonous thoughts from me that spring. But before I could consent to Ryan's plan I had to believe everything he said, including, "I don't want you to think I don't love you."

MY EARLIER hunch that Howard and I might be divorcing each other for the rest of our lives seemed more true now than ever. I was continually ambushed by sudden recognitions of his personality and influence on our sons, especially Ryan. As my older son grew out of his boyhood body, he looked more and more like a prepubescent image of his dad. You can hardly get away from a man once his genes are planted in your children. Being reminded of someone I thought I hated by someone I knew I loved threw me into a state of psychological chaos. Against the immense pull of my own wishes and dreams, I struggled to get "right think" on this request. Could I now "give up custody" of my firstborn son? Could I love the boys in the next kind of family they wanted to try? How did they need to be loved by me now?

The editor-in-chief who found me wanting for giving up custody that year didn't know that, after thirteen years, I didn't have it to give up. By then, no mother does. Beginning at birth, we have a little less "custody" every year. By age thirteen, it is absurd not to include children in decisions about domicile. When the biological parents of Kimberly Mays, switched at birth in the hospital, discovered the error fourteen years later, they filed a custody suit against the father who had raised her. The first innocent tragedy in the hospital was compounded by a second deliberate tragedy in the courts. A media obsessed with "sides" reported ugly hostilities from both families and cast Kimberly in the role of the sainted, cherished child. (Who's winning? Who's losing? Who's missing the point completely?)

Before her adoptive father was granted custody, fourteen-year-old Kimberly had to swear before a judge that she wanted nothing to do with her biological family or step-siblings, and would never change her mind. As the celebrated case played out, both her biological and adoptive parent claimed, "I'm best for her, I want her." Only in a society where children are property could such a custody suit be filed to decide who had "rights" to Kimberly, who owned this young person. Century by painful century, the concept of slavery has been outlawed. The laws and scripture once supporting human ownership by reason of race or gender have been repealed and reinterpreted; so too, eventually, will the entitlements of age.

Meanwhile, it was hard to imagine grown-ups more naive about the immediate future. Give Saint Kimberly a few more years, I thought. One lively adolescent could wear out half a dozen parents, and here were three trying to cancel out the others. If she followed the usual hierarchy of human development and reached the she-wolf stage of female adolescence, both her adoptive and biological parents could be saying, "I'm exhausted . . . could you take her this year?"

BY THE time Ryan left for his year as an only child in Ann Arbor, Howard and I had discussed the plan at length with the boys, agreed on timetables and finances, and resolved knotty problems with school transfers. Despite all our careful planning and negotiating, I had an uneasy feeling from the start that real life would not go according to plan. For one thing, writing down promises offered no guarantee that we'd actually keep them—so far, all our written agreements had only guaranteed that we had a record of what we meant to do. For another, teenagers grow so rapidly after they enter the double digits that any judge who asks a fourteen year old what she will be feeling in a year might as well put the question to a Ouija board. Who knows, at fourteen or forty-five, what she will be feeling next year? Wouldn't it depend on how everybody behaves? Although Ryan and Darren could both be breathtakingly mature in their discussions that summer, they also both asked me to "Take Out All the Bad Feelings" with greater frequency that August than during the whole previous year.

BY HONORING Ryan's wish, we once again had to maintain a close relationship across a 750-mile distance. Although I doubt I would ever have suggested this prematurely empty nest myself, the longer view we gained of each other that year—not to mention the startling revelations we had about ourselves—supplied essential information about how to navigate the turbulent rapids of adolescence coming up just around the bend.

Any mother who searches the culture for inspiring examples of adult mother/son relationships will be depressed by the paucity of happy survivors. Everything in the culture conspires against the longevity of mother/son love. "Freud, Jung, Jones, all the boys, tell the dangers of insanity for the son if he gets too close to his mother," Sharon Dubiago writes. "Our dominant psychological notion, that the male must cut himself off from his mother—we never quite get that this means *all* women—is so embedded in our culture that it feels dangerous to question it. But the Truth, as with all patriarchal reversals, is the other way around: The male is *not* supposed to break from his mother. *This* is the wound that paralyzes his soul, all our souls, the 'male wound' we all suffer from that lies at the heart of our sadomasochistic human dysfunction." The delicate surgery of my separation from Ryan during his thirteenth year required maximum concentration, yielding to his need to live with his dad without permanently severing his emotional attachments to me.

As Ryan-and-Darren began dividing into two distinct personalities that autumn, they noticed distinct differences in their parents as well. When Howard and I lived as a couple, Mom-and-Dad existed as one in their minds. After ten years of marriage, even we had trouble distinguishing ourselves as two separate people. Our instructions to the kids usually began, "we think" or "we don't want" or "we believe." I noticed that, even when speaking to each other, the editorial we replaced you and I: "We'll be out of money by the end of the month—we have to do something, and fast." Under the cover of the anonymous we, it was never precisely clear who was responsible for what, or when.

So fused are the identities of parents that neither divorce nor, apparently, death always makes us distinguishable to our children. The personalities of Larry's mother and father were so merged in his mind that his parents were forever coupled in his stories of a deeply unhappy childhood: "They" were depressed, hypercritical, morose, defeated. When I finally met his mother, I was astonished to discover an eighty-three-year-old woman with a great sense of humor and zest for life. She remembered Larry's childhood almost exactly as he did, except in her stories, the gloomy adjectives were attached to the deceased "him." Larry's father seemed to have the same effect on his wife that he had on his son.

"I should have left him," she said. "I thought about it every day when Larry was little. But where would I go?" For a while, she fantasized living on a ranch in Wyoming with Art Linkletter—probably after hearing a sales pitch for a '50s development tract on the radio. Art Linkletter and talk radio were her main companions during those silent years of marriage. This dream of a better life in Wyoming got her out of bed every morning. She would have been an outlaw, I'm fairly sure, if her motherhood had coincided with less punitive times. The easy giggle I heard again and again during our visits couldn't have been wholly absent for her only child—"my only joy," she called Larry. But her laughter and affection were entirely suppressed by his father's overwhelming unhappiness. Larry couldn't wait to leave home, and he never wanted to go back. Although his father had been dead nearly thirty years, his aging mother still labored under the judgments made of "them."

AFTER BECOMING a postnuclear family, our continuous separations and regroupings made it easier to notice individual differences and keep up with changes. Like Howard's radicalizing experience the year I attended the Ohio conference, when he learned more about his two young sons in one weekend of solo fatherhood than in the previous two years, Ryan returned after being his father's only son with a new name and a greatly altered sense of self. Finances had been so tight in Ann Arbor, Ry had gotten a job as soon as he turned fourteen, scooping ice cream at a family-owned dairy to help with expenses. His fantasy year with his dad satisfied his hunger for one-on-one attention and rescued their relationship from becoming myth. His father was a real guy, as it turned out, an earthbound hero with talents and problems a lot like his own. It gave them both a rich trove of stories and a language they would draw on for years. And Ryan came back having experienced the happiness of being useful to someone he loved.

Ryan entered his freshman year at Greenwich High School that September, sure he knew nearly everything he needed to know about life. He had become Darren's much older brother again; the significance of that eighteen months between them could shrink and expand from issue to issue, almost hour to hour. If D. found his brother's benignly paternal attitude annoying at times, he also admired it. Generosity looks terrific on a fourteen-year-old kid. Like the pure, goofy pleasure on a toddler's face when he discovers that legs are for walking, it makes you smile, almost burst into tears.

I remember noting this more expansive self at a soccer game that autumn during Ryan's first season with the junior varsity. Most of his sports events were scheduled during working hours, making regular attendance difficult. After a year of missing him, I redoubled my efforts, acutely aware of the finite time we could count on living together. It was probably for this reason that mothers were the main occupants in the bleachers for the freshman games.

Since I had only limited knowledge of the game, I relied on cues from other mothers, the way I once watched people in the front pews at church to know when to kneel or stand. Wherever the ball was, I was usually watching the goalie—a clear leader on the team, loud and passionate, hollering orders and shouting cheers. Ry trotted off the field at half time, slapping congratulations onto the backs of his teammates and receiving many blows of praise in return. Seeing that he was busy, I waved a wordless greeting. Startled to see me, he broke into a delighted grin.

"Hey, Mom!" he yelled. "You *made* it!" He separated from the pack and trotted over to the bleachers.

He asked when I'd arrived—had I seen his spectacular first-period save, Humza's fabulous break, Carlos's amazing run? I nodded and smiled. I *thought* I had seen these things.

"Okay, well. That's great. I gotta get back," he said, breathless and excited. "Thanks for coming." Then he kissed me on the cheek and returned to the huddle.

The other freshman mothers were stunned.

"He *kissed* you," the woman next to me said. "He kissed you in front of the whole team." A plump woman on the bench below us turned around. "I don't think my son has noticed me for three years," she said. The bleacher crowd chuckled. We all knew what being invisible felt like. "So c'mon, what's your secret?" she asked.

"Neglect," I said. How to explain the unexpected rewards of an unnatural mom to these mothers who had been there for their sons, day after day since birth? Clearly, I'd gotten a reprieve from some of the mother-loathing that so afflicts teenagers making their first mad break from home. With the new sense of independence and self-assurance he earned that year with his father, Ryan could afford sideline kisses to me. It would be temporary, of course—everything with children is temporary. But it was a scene I would be pleased to remember again and again.

WHEN DARREN left for Ann Arbor the following September to do his solo year with Howard, I expected this wrenching departure would also yield some valuable growth. My younger son had a much harder time leaving his familiar life in Connecticut. Although Darren had also made some dramatic changes the year he was my "only child," acquiring more nerve and daring than he had in the company of his aggressively protective brother, he approached his move back to the Midwest more out of duty than desire. He loved Howard but had some questions about how lovable his dad would find him. I remember a conversation on the way to Baskin and Robbins one summer evening, the week before he left.

"What's there about me for Dad to like?" he asked. "I'm not as good as Ryan at sports," he said, aware of the close bond between Ryan and Howard. "What have I got? Good grades," he said, and shrugged. He thought of himself mainly as the family nerd that year. Although everything would change with the flash flood of hormones in the next two years, his body filling out to go with those enormous feet of his, he still had the clumsy proportions of a puppy with big paws that summer.

Howard was nervous himself. Unquestionably, he loved this sweet, thoughtful second son, but Darren was much harder to know than "the blurter." I knew they would rediscover their affinities. What I never, never imagined was that this agreeable younger son would initiate the bloodiest chapter of family history. At the end of his year in Ann Arbor, he announced he wasn't coming back.

He'd reunited with his two closest buddies in Ann Arbor, Pete and Tynan, his best friends since second grade. Ty was a computer genius and had a technological wonderland in his basement, where this tight trio spent uncountable hours being Masters of the Universe. As I'd anticipated, Darren and his father found their bonds. They shared the same whimsical sense of humor, and the sweaty challenge of computer games provided more than enough competition. They had discussed the possibility of his attending high school there, and by the time I was informed of "Darren's Plan," it was presented as a done deal.

I felt betrayed. How could Howard encourage a plan that meant the kids would probably never live together again? In his thirteen-year-old mind, Darren was thinking of Howard's loneliness, my comparative happiness, his two close buddies; he felt useful to his dad and saw no injury to his brother or me. I was convinced Howard had manipulated this move, however unconsciously, by his need for "another year with the kids." I was furious that he never acknowledged all the accommodating we had done for this need so far: I had moved to Ann Arbor, Ryan had moved to Ann Arbor, Darren had moved to Ann Arbor—all to accommodate Howard, who hadn't moved an inch. The heated thought pulsing through me in that summer of '89 was this: *it was his goddam turn*.

That was the open mind with which I brought my sons into therapy during Darren's vacation in Connecticut that summer. He would be fourteen that August, and any intelligent judge settling a "custody battle" for a child that age would have to ask what he wanted to do. Up until now, all domicile decisions had been made for him. Darren was smart and honest and fair, and certainly was qualified and entitled to make his own decision. I told Darren I would accept whatever decision he made, as long as it was an informed decision.

The kids *hated* these sessions with a passion. They didn't want to talk about their mother and father, their unacknowledged conflicts, the history they didn't know—the who and how and why of their family that kids don't question until a crisis splits everything open. I knew certain kinds of knowledge never arrive without crushing blows to innocence. I also knew that this son, like his mother, had an enormous quantity of innocence to lose.

My most painful memories of motherhood occurred in that white-walled office on Summer Street, watching my kind, yielding, most innocent son turned inside out with despair. It was the first time he had strongly asserted his will in the family, and he was met with the most ferocious and passionate resistance. Ryan and Darren and I met with the therapist singly, in pairs, and also as a threesome, uncovering ugly facts and feelings that were impossible to disguise in the subsequent weeks. Having shielded the boys from the gruesome details behind the divorce, Howard and I had given them the most unanswerable question of their lives: Why?

"What really kills me is that when they're together, they get along so well," Darren once said to his brother. "So what did we have to go through all this pain for?" It had been a rhetorical question then; he didn't really want the answer. That summer, we became The Family Who Knew Too Much.

Whatever Darren decided, it became clear to him that someone was going to be hurt. I asked Howard to join us for some of the sessions. When he couldn't come, the boys and I traveled to Ann Arbor to have a few sessions with Howard there. Darren's pain and sorrow were palpable on Interstate 80 that July as he wrestled with his decision. He sat glumly in front of the TV all month, unseeing, unhearing, his natural wit and smarts buried in a rubble of doubt. I grieved with him. Welcome to real life, I thought, where suffering is part of the human experience.

Teaching children how to handle pain is one of the hardest tasks of motherhood. It is harder still to be the source of the pain itself. How can you take in their suffering without guilt? Guilt, too, is a teacher, and mine told me that my own anger, my years of impotent rage, were improperly spent in this battle. Darren was too inexperienced for the maelstrom of passion he released during our family's civil war. Maybe there was no way to usher him through that awful summer without damage; maybe the pathology in our family could never be healed without pain. Whoever said "The truth will make you free, but first it will make you miserable," didn't tell us "How free? How miserable?"

At the end of the summer, Darren proposed a compromise: He'd go back to Ann Arbor and Howard for one more year, graduate from junior high with his classmates, then return to me and his brother in Connecticut to finish his last three years of high school. This was a thoughtful plan, and everyone surrendered unconditionally to his peace treaty. I know he used the information he obtained that summer to make his choice, and eventually he felt confident he'd made the right decision. But from then on he and I both felt the seismic shift in affections, whether we were living together or not. We'd had a seamless and easy affection between us until he met my buried rage that summer. I can't say whether it frightened or repulsed him, or both. He still can't talk about that awful summer, keeping a veteran's silence about his war memories.

IN THE nuclear winter following the brothers' separation, deep fissures riddled the whole family structure. Ry, now familiar with the further amenities of human relationships after his summer of therapy, started complaining openly about his frustrations with Larry. In one form or another, they had lived together for almost five years. The odds of turning Larry into a family man now seemed risky. Whenever I thought about spending the next three years—the last I had with the kids—negotiating, arguing, pleading, and encouraging him to become someone he obviously didn't want to be, I closed my eyes and saw Indiana Jones, facing the twirling, slicing, threatening saber of the sheik. My choice, as I saw it, was to accept a challenge I couldn't possible win; or to forfeit the duel, shrugging my eyebrows to say, "No show today, folks."

Although we had never married, Larry and I began couples' counseling during the winter of '89 to help us shape a "good divorce." There have been periods in my life, and this was certainly one of them, when my family could have kept a live-in therapist busy all day. Intellectually, we had both acknowledged the end of our intimate relationship, but emotionally, we each had to resolve separate questions about "what went wrong?" Since this was not the first time that a love commitment died before I did, I had to address a pervasive sense of failure. My therapist, a kind woman who allowed her personal life to inform her work, suggested I reframe my assumptions: "When you began this relationship five years ago, you were in shaky emotional and financial shape. Now, you're both so much better than you were." Be sad, she said softly, mourn the losses that come with growth, "but don't call that a failure." With those words guiding broken hearts, Larry and I agreed to part the following spring.

ALTHOUGH I can't be certain what Ryan and Darren's private discussion was about that afternoon in Central Park, whenever I look at the evocative image of their talk on the rock I imagine they are negotiating the Children's Divorce. While they were eager to have the experience of being an "only child" for a year, they also had to be aware—given the copious evidence of fraternal bonding surrounding the picture—what a high price they would pay for that experience. Of all the separations from parents and friends and relatives, splitting The Brothers was the most delicate surgery. "The membranes between us are so thin," Seymour once wrote his brother Buddy. For Ryan-and-Darren, independence from each other was the most painful passage of adolescence. Was Darren's unforgettable outbreak that summer a violent reaction to poison ivy, an allergic reaction to Larry, or an explosion of grief when his brother and best friend announced he was moving 750 miles away?

Listening to their chatter the winter we sifted through family pictures at the kitchen table, and especially to the silences that gripped them periodically, I am now certain they have plenty of material for their unhappy childhood stories if a therapist should ever ask some day. In photo after photo I could see how wrong I had been, and how often: Here I am smiling into the eyes of a man I loved, thinking we would live happily ever after; there I am standing alone having survived another "learning experience." One year I bear the confident look of a woman who knows exactly what her young sons need and has no questions about her competence; another year I wear the almost startled humility of a woman confronted by her ignorance, wondering what else I might not know.

Every professional has to make some regrettable errors, especially over a twenty-year career. But I felt my mother-mistakes so much more keenly than my professional lapses. Those unyielding, maternal regrets were my most insistent teachers, the most demanding prods to keep thinking and striving. As I arranged the finished collages of family history above the fireplace, exposing our half-truths and heaving passions and deep regrets, I thought if I'd given the photo wall a title it would probably be, "We Are Still Alive."

PART THREE

THE COMING MEN

*We have to face the fact that either all of us
are going to die together or we are going to learn to live together
and if we are to live together, we have to talk.*

—Eleanor Roosevelt

14

Here They Come, Hormones Raging

The altitude of Ryan's voice had been dropping, an octave at a time it seemed, for six months. By his fourteenth year, a rapid burst of growth had zapped the remainder of his boyish energy. He extracted himself wearily from the couch each evening and shuffled to dinner like a man wearing a backpack of bowling balls. The sudden elevations and drops in mood had him rising and falling willy-nilly, leaving him in a state of emotional vertigo. So there were plenty of signs. It isn't that I hadn't seen the coming man approaching.

For months in my mind I'd been sitting in a Tilt-A-Whirl car, the crash bar drawn up safely, waiting for the time to throw the switch and reel us off into the spins and loops and whiplash jerks of adolescence. "Adolescence," author Kurt Vonnegut once suggested, "is children's menopause." I thought I was prepared for the thrills and jolts, the lost equilibrium and breathtaking speed. Nevertheless, when the switch was finally thrown at the Junior Varsity Football Banquet that November, it took me by surprise. It's one thing to imagine the coming man; it's another thing entirely to meet him.

I had my seat belt on, so to speak, because I knew these football things were rough on my psyche. Standing on the sidelines those Saturday mornings that fall, I watched my son delight in ramming the life out of the other players. I knew I was supposed to cheer whenever this happened, but my shouts invariably got caught in my throat, as if the wind had been knocked out of me.

Sometimes, it was the Cardinal red jersey I was rooting for that

crashed to the ground in a lifeless heap, and I knew I wasn't supposed to be alarmed then either. I wasn't, by all means, supposed to
rush out onto the field to check his pulse. My usual anxiety about
their mortality was compounded by an assignment for *Life*, about
comas caused by head injuries. I listened to heartbroken mothers
whose lives changed completely in a split second, when a car or
motorcycle accident left a daughter or son with permanent brain
damage. Male adolescents were the most vulnerable population—
the most reckless, the most impudent, the most oblivious to the
fragility of life.

After finishing my research, I was obsessed with head injuries.
Every time Ryan or Darren headed out the door for such dangerous destinations as the mall or the movies, I would say: "Be care-
ful/Wear your seat belt/Use your helmet."

"Bye Mom, . . . Going to work," Darren said last year, then held
up his stop-the-speech hand. "And yes, I know, 'Wear your helmet.'" He worked as a clerk at an office supply store, not a high-
risk job unless you count paper cuts. My fear of head injuries was
strictly a Coma Mom worry. Neither my sons nor any of their
coaches could share this preoccupation with mortal injury.

All of their coaches in soccer and wrestling and baseball taught
them to accept pain unflinchingly. But for football and rugby players, the marines and green berets of male sport, pain seemed to be
the very objective. For a young football player, the sight of a mother
rushing across the field in alarm was worse than death itself. The
main thing I had to remember, as I stood on the sidelines that fall,
was to repress all my usual instincts.

At the banquet that November, after helping serve enormous
quantities of chili-dogs and soda, I took a seat at a back table as the
coach cleared his throat and the twenty-some players lined up to
receive their awards. I donned the all-purpose, general-interest
smile parents frequently wear when their children are on stage, but
I let my mind drift out the back door.

It was only fourteen years, I thought nostalgically, since I held
the infant this now solid boy used to be. Wholly absorbed in the

miracle of "having a baby," I was only dimly aware then of just how much life I'd given birth to. Very quickly, the baby disappeared into a toddler, a child, a teenager, a jock . . . possibly one day a Hari Krishna, maybe even a Republican. Once you've launched your genes into orbit there are no guarantees about where they'll show up. I certainly never imagined my child on a football field. No woman is ever totally prepared for all the births that begin with "having a baby."

Joan had five babies by the mid-'60s and woke up the mother of five teenagers in the late '70s. She blames Gerber. "Instead of those adorable babies on cereal boxes and jars, they should picture what children will look like after you feed them." She thought pictures of tall, gangly youths with guitars hanging from their shoulders, woozy with weltschmerz, would reflect more truth in advertising.

If you feed them, they grow, and Ryan—the apple-cheeked baby, the freckled child, the witty boy—grew an explosive three inches that year, developed biceps and pectorals, and outfitted himself with shoulder pads and a helmet for his new life as a tackle. He experimented with various personalities to go with this tough new image. Turning up the collars of his jackets Marlon-Brando style, he practiced facial expressions in the hallway mirror. In his school pictures that year, his lips are curled in a lopsided grimace and his eyes narrowed in an apparent effort to look like Clint Eastwood. But among the frankly cheerful smiles in the freshman year book, he looked more like a stroke patient suffering temporary paralysis. Masculinity comes hard to the baby-faced.

"God, Ry, you look gargantuan," a dinner guest remarked when he lumbered in the back door in full battle gear one evening. He beamed. "Thank you," he replied instantly.

I sensed his growing detachment from me that year, catching his absorbed profile as I drove him and Darren to school each morning. He would stare distractedly out the windshield, listening to the radio, absorbed in thoughts about the day ahead. There were friends to amuse, enemies to outwit, an English teacher to placate, a coach to impress. His world was populated with names I didn't recognize, events I didn't know about. Trees could be falling in his forest, and I would never hear them.

There was a time when I was privy to every word he spoke in a day. Fourteen years ago, I could count them all on one hand. Conversations bloomed between us over the next decade, amazing me with each new development in vocabulary and intelligence and sensibility. By last November, we had circled back to our roots, speaking in monosyllables again: "Hi, hon, how was school?" I would ask.

"Fine," he'd reply. End of conversation. The "blurter" now had other, more relevant audiences for his stories.

Clearly, he was more anxious for the switch to be thrown than I was. In anticipation of the coming changes, I had given both boys a copy of *The What's Happening to My Body? Book for Boys* by Lynda Madaras (1984). Usually, any book about bodies or sex was immediately devoured, spine creased, pages turned down for ready reference. But *What's Happening to My Body?* sat unopened on Ry's nightstand for months.

"Do you want to talk about it—maybe read it together?" I asked one evening as we said goodnight.

"What for?" he sighed, sinking into his pillows, "Nothing's happening."

He looked at me with pure gloom. Things were happening to bodies all around him, and he was anxious for some changes in his own. His best friend Carlos, a walking encyclopedia of sexual misinformation, described nocturnal emissions of the most sublime sort. Even "dumb old Matt"—another close pal who had been valiantly resisting the nerd reputation attached to musicians in the school band until he achieved local fame as a break dancer—had betrayed Ryan, gone ahead without him and sprouted chin hairs as well as a visible, fuzzy shadow on his upper lip. Full of impatience and despair, Ry longed to wake up in damp sheets, to need the electric razor he'd bought with his allowance, to have an actual reason for the antiperspirant he had started applying every day.

His mind was a few seasons ahead of his body; throughout childhood, mental and physical development rarely ran on conveniently parallel tracks. Darren was still a little guy of three or four when he came apart in a shoe department one afternoon, after the sales clerk brought the tennis shoes he had picked out and tried to put them on his feet. Darren's protest was instant and loud. "No, no, no!" he yelled. He wanted the exact shoes he'd picked out on the shelf. I tried to explain in clear toddlerese that this pair was exactly the same style, but in his much smaller size.

"I don't care about style," he wailed, "I want big shoes!" His misery was so complete, I was almost persuaded to buy the gunboats that would have immobilized him. I think he imagined that was how you got to be Walt Frazier—you got yourself some big shoes and grew into them. In Darren's imagination, "big shoes" fit who he wanted to be.

MERE MONTHS after Ry's late-night lament, the tables turned again and his physical development leapt ahead of his head. The fourteen-year-old mind suddenly found itself in the unfamiliar body of an adult. Like a new driver behind the wheel of a rental car, he lurched and stalled through his days, unaccustomed to the controls. This time lag between physical and mental development naturally caused some incongruous scenes. I remember his deep, low laugh erupting from the living room one afternoon—the still-startling baritone of the coming man.

"What are you watching?" I asked, as he grinned into the TV.

"Porky Pig," he said, then smiled sheepishly and laughed at himself. At fourteen, in a body growing to Rambo proportions, he was still amused by Porky Pig.

The effects of this time lag are not always so harmless and amusing, as he discovered in a wrenching experience with Darren one afternoon. With the ever expandable and contractible eighteen months between them, one year they would be almost exactly the same height, two fuzzy heads at the same level in my rear-view mirror, sharing the same interests in soccer or Cub Scouts; the next year, one of them would have grown two inches, lost all interest in

Big Bird, and gotten "bossy and crabby" all of a sudden. Then the year after that, they would change places again. "Okay, you're the tallest but I'm still the oldest," Ry said that year, when Darren's loose-jointed, beanstalk frame gained an eighth of an inch over Ry's senior bulk on the growth chart inside the broom closet door.

For the first decade of their lives, the differences in size were only minimally significant. From the time they were toddlers, they indulged in vigorous physical play. The two boys would roll across the living room floor, wrestling and laughing, like two bear cubs releasing excess energy. When they were watching television I could always tell, from another room, when a commercial came on. They loved to "lose it" in these manic outbursts. But in a memorable episode that year, a playful shove from Ryan carried much more thrust than he'd intended. It sent Darren reeling across the floor, crashing into the living room wall with a forceful thud. He sank in a heap as blood poured from his nose.

"Are you al *right*?" I heard Ry's shaky new baritone ask, genuine panic threading his voice. Darren's nose wasn't broken, but the bloody accident frightened them both.

"I'm sorry, God, I'm *so sorry*," Ryan repeated over and over. He put a comforting arm around his brother and then, suddenly distrusting this familiar gesture, dropped it limply to his side. He wore the look of a boy having a bad brother day, staring numbly at his hands as if they had betrayed him. "Gargantuan," he learned that afternoon, had its dark side.

Now that he was no longer a bear cub, his increasing strength meant certain boyhood habits and attitudes had to change. This particular reality—the unseen power behind his punches—was not a fact he had all the time in the world to absorb. He was still largely unconscious of the ways men have abused their physical strength, still mainly oblivious to the threat his muscle implied. After witnessing the blood and recognizing its source, however, another "accident" wouldn't be so innocent.

If this new physical power was frightening, it was also exhilarating. For a young teenage boy who's struggling for a place in the world, it changes everything. The bully behavior that young males are so famous for takes root, I suspect, in these adolescent canyons between psychological and physical growth, when an immature boy who still gets a kick out of Porky Pig wakes up one morning with the power to impose his will on anyone who gets in his way. The most trying part of human development is that power often comes before wisdom.

Ryan had to experiment with this sudden surge of power in a safe arena, and for him, that arena was the football field. I watched the experiments that fall with mixed emotions. During the first games of the season, the inexperienced junior varsity chased the ball down the field, running in random confusion like a dozen excited, oversized gerbils. By the end of the season, they moved together like pieces of smooth machinery, mowing down their opposition to reach their goals. For me it was far easier to cheer for the gerbils than the relentless machine.

Although my son unflinchingly accepted the punishment of the field, I wrestled with strange sensations on the sidelines. I observed the camaraderie he shared with his team, the affectionate grins and pats they exchanged throughout the games. In a peculiar way, I understood this willingness to undergo physical pain to achieve group affinity. I guessed it was a male version of the female urge to have babies. The pain itself was rarely a deterrent in the pursuit of human intimacy. I witnessed this male bonding the way an empathetic father might see an infant at a mother's breast, trying to fathom the chemistry of the scene, knowing it would never be exactly my experience.

Most of his words and affections were directed to his own world now—so obvious, that November, at the football banquet. He was proud to be in the lineup at the front of the hall, joking with friends, aiming to please. When the coach was down to the last six presentations, he noticed only four trophies were left on the table and announced that two of the players would have to receive theirs later. "Later," for a fourteen year old, translates to "never," and the boys at the end responded immediately by pushing up to the front.

Under pressure from the rear Ry took two small backward shuffles, letting his teammates move ahead. Quite voluntarily, he ended up last in line. This, from the boy who helped himself to the biggest slice of cake, took the window seat in cars, got the first serving at dinner.

When the coach introduced him in the last speech of the night, they exchanged their respects without props. It was a brief glimpse into how life was playing out in his world, and it gave me goose bumps. A mother yearns for such proof that her child has the social skills to navigate the larger world out there, but there is that disorienting, peculiar grief when it comes, when the switch gets thrown and we all lose our place for a while. *He doesn't need me anymore*, I thought. It was my first encounter with the feeling Joan wished for on that frantic afternoon in the Auditor's Office, "to be unnecessary." It was nice; it was also weird. In the ongoing dialectic of motherhood, where opposite realities could be simultaneously true, I welcomed it and dreaded it.

When Ryan left the stage that night, it felt like a large ocean liner had just cut berth from my small harbor, churning the water and pushing out mightily for open seas. Listing precariously in his wake, I rocked unsteadily between awe and regret, the love and detachment such launches require.

15
Hey, Stupid

"Where did we go wrong?" Joan asked after reporting the stunning news about Carolen. "Wasn't she listening all those years in CR? She's smart, she's happy, she's got a great life—what can she be thinking? She's forty-two years old and sounded as addle-brained about having a baby as any twenty year old. She's ecstatic about this pregnancy. Thinks motherhood will be wonderful. I feel responsible."

I laughed. "C'mon, Joan. You were almost forty-two when you had Patty."

"I was a practicing Catholic then," she said. "I wasn't myself."

Although our Fort Wayne consciousness raising group now stretched from Colorado to New Hampshire, from Chile to Connecticut, we planned "war buddy" reunions whenever we could and stayed in touch by phone in between. So when Carolen got the surprise of her life and discovered she was not infertile after all, despite nine years without birth control, we closely monitored her pregnancy from month to month. It was my job to start the telephone tree the minute I had a report from the hospital.

Her voice reverberated with wild joy the morning she finally called, and I burst into tears of relief. Normally calm and dependably mature, Carolen released a bouquet of exclamations as she described the flawless beauty of Alice Louise, one day old, asleep in her arms. Oblivious of long-range consequences, she was under the spell of the most extraordinary creature she had ever seen. Since I'd had two similar sightings in maternity wings myself—in what now seemed another lifetime—I knew her state. A woman never forgets the burst of passion that floods her being in the wake of those first, untameable contractions.

I felt a twinge of envy. The happiness Carolen was experiencing in these euphoric beginnings of bonding reached me as I stood on the brink of emancipation. Capsulized in that phone call between Missouri and Connecticut was the great irony of motherhood: A mother starts out as the most important person in her child's life and, if she's successful in her work, a mere fifteen years later she will become the most embarrassing.

It is not a journey for the weak. Of course, I didn't remind Carolen just then that the thrills attending infancy are exceedingly transient. I didn't mention Joan's latest report from the front lines, where her five kids were now bouncing through adolescence en masse. Joan finally understood why women her age often became fond of saying the rosary, she said. "It's just like playing solitaire. Gives you something comforting to do while you wait for the sound of tires in the driveway."

In her delirious state in the maternity wing, it was impossible for Carolen to imagine that the baby planted in the receiving blanket would grow with breathtaking speed into toddler, child, teenager, adult. A mother spends more years navigating her relationship through the last category than all of the others combined—at least three or four decades, if statistics apply. Keeping the joy alive for the duration is the supreme challenge of motherhood.

There is a wealth of information guiding mothers through the work of infancy and early childhood, but the experts offer little advice about how to ensure a successful adult relationship. As if our interest in children dies after adolescence, mothers are "disappeared" from the literature. But if the early bonding has taken and if the groupness of mind and body has become habit, the separation during adolescence is as wrenching for mothers as it is for children.

"Have you become stupid yet?" my friend Jeanette asked as we watched her daughter Erin, a fourteen-year-old girl with the body of a woman bursting through, depart from our table in a restaurant and head for the ladies room. "Sometime last summer, I became stupid," she confessed, adding that there was little she could do to deflect the force of Erin's contempt. When she was invited to deliver a prestigious lecture at an international conference, Erin sat in the front row, her arms crossed defensively over her chest. The lecture went well, followed by a lively question-and-answer period. Jeanette thought she had scored some points with her daughter, but Erin's evaluation was this: "If you had explained yourself better, there wouldn't have been so many questions afterward."

I nodded, acknowledging that stupidity had become epidemic at my house, too. I'd begun, for example, to fail at public appearances. That same week Ryan, who'd been so extravagant with his sideline kiss just one year earlier, found it necessary to put the length of an entire cafeteria between us at a high school orientation program because I'd neglected to cuff my jeans according to current sophomore standards.

I was regularly coached on my vocabulary, encouraged to incorporate terms like "chill out," and cautioned against posing embarrassing questions in front of friends, such as the noxious "What time will you be home?" If I had been impressed with the vulnerability of an infant in Parkview Hospital fifteen years before, I was dazzled by the fragility of a teenager. I'd nearly killed Darren of embarrassment that week by asking a stranger for directions.

These near-fatal humiliations are part of the strike for independence, of course, all part of the clumsy but earnest search for an answer to the omnipresent adolescent question, Who am I? Unfortunately, my sons' identity crises occurred when I was asking the same question: Who are *you*? Who am *I*? Just as their bodies were surging with the wild disturbances and excitement of new hormones, I was undergoing a similarly passionate transition at my end of the reproductive cycle. This construction of human biology clearly shows that God is not a woman; otherwise, adolescence and menopause would not occur so frequently in the same family at the same time. Two simultaneous identity crises while our bodies move irrevocably in polar directions? No, this could not be the work of a woman.

Fortunately, mother love is strong stuff and allowed me to be amused, sometimes even delighted by the first awkward assaults on my intelligence. Luckily, too, women of my generation had the means to nourish their own self-esteem in ways the housewives of my mother's generation could only dream about. After twenty years of talking, breaking silence, being strident and hysterical, all the friends in my CR group had sturdy support networks, creative work that mattered, a genuine possibility for life after motherhood, and, God knows, the support walls of our sanity—our women friends.

What worried me was that so many mothers never regain any intimacy with their grown sons after the disdain of adolescence has set in. As a woman standing on the brink of stupidity myself, I was shaken by the odds of escape. The break for independence that my own peers had conducted in their youth had been so inept, most of them had sorry relationships with their mothers. One friend didn't feel she could risk revealing her lesbianism; another couldn't share her feelings about an abortion; another couldn't get through a Mother's Day dinner without biting his tongue. Would my sons consider me hopelessly ineducable twenty years from now?

The danger of being thought stupid, of course, is that you begin to act that way. During a trip to the mall with the kids once, I tried to divert their attention from my driving in "the retarded lane" on the expressway by asking Ryan how things were going with his beauteous girlfriend Gretchen: "So, Ry, how's Gertrude?"

The wrong name. It was the most embarrassing error a dumb mom can make. I did not have to look into the rear-view mirror to know the effect "Gertrude" had on my son.

It would be an early version of the disbelieving look Larry shot across the table during the last dinner we had with his mother, the woman I thought witty, bright, and wholly admirable. With her son, however, whose judgment had been formed some thirty years ago and remained unaltered, she was nervous and cautious, unsure of what to say to him. Relying on old, dusty conversation, she asked—in a petulant tone she'd never used with me—"Aren't you going to finish your vegetables?" He delivered a look that could have melted lead. I saw her shrivel and felt her instant regret.

BECOMING UNSTUPID means relinquishing some of the power that arrives with the receiving blanket—the power of role, the power that passes for love. "Because I'm the mommy, that's why" is a swift and handy conclusion to difficult discussions but ultimately meaningless. Although it remained appropriate for me to assert rules with Ryan and Darren at ages fourteen and fifteen, we all recognized by now that they had the right—I would even say the obligation—to question those rules.

Still, relinquishing the power of her role doesn't mean a mother becomes powerless, especially if she emerges from the dual identity crisis with her self-esteem intact. My sons would never be my peers—there would always be that quarter century wedged between us—but equality wasn't the prize at stake. After my fifteen-year investment, my goal was three or four more decades of deep shudders.

During a candid discussion with Kay about the ongoing conflicts of love and independence, she asked how I would handle the crisis if either of my sons rejected a belief I cherished: feminism, say, or civil rights, which figured as prominently in my life as the Catholicism I had rejected did in hers. I admitted I'd have a hard time enjoying myself at a Mother's Day dinner with the next Larry Flynt or David Duke. But the grievances I observed among my peers didn't stem from a wholesale rejection of maternal values. Rather, the differences came from the changes one generation made to fit those values into the new information of another age. Independence required grown children to reject part of who we are, but just as inevitably, my sons would take part of who I am with them.

I told Kay that I thought the most enduring gift of motherhood was the opportunity to see what your soul might look like in the next generation, to see how it performed under the mores, customs, and beliefs of another age. Maybe part of her soul would commit a holistic divorce, or try to live honorably in sin, or introduce the notion of women priests. Maybe someday part of my soul would fall in love with someone of the same sex, or try to eradicate homophobia in the marines, or introduce the culture to the concept of working fathers. Imagine: This is how your soul might look if you had come of age in different times. At least, I told my mother, that's how I like to think I'll react if Ryan's and Darren's future choices appear mysterious or strange to me.

In the meantime, certain phrases—"Finish your broccoli" or "I'm the mommy, that's why"—had to be deleted from my vocabulary after the boys became "gargantuan." Not only because they'd both reached a size that made such commands a useless form of persuasion, but also because those phrases were unlikely to usher in a future of friendship. It wasn't too early at age fifteen to practice speaking to my sons as adults.

After all the names I'd been called since the beginning, from Zero Mom to Unnatural Mo   I didn't think Stupid Mom was a healthy place to linger indefinitely. How does one change a given identity? In *Recreating Motherhood* (1989), author Barbara Katz Rothman suggests that it might be helpful to drop role titles altogether for a while. Especially while new identities are being forged, "Mother" can be oppressively anonymous. As Rothman points out, a child screams "mommy" on a playground, and a dozen women turn around; an agitated teenager moans "*Muh*-ther" at a high school orientation, and six of us immediately hear the existential hum, the uneasy feeling that we have somehow disgraced ourselves.

"Every time you use the word, you are reinforcing the cultural expectations of what mommies do and what daddies do," Rothman wrote. "As those notions change, it might be better to drop the archaic language." Certainly, she notes, we rarely address our offspring by role: "How was school today, Child?" My own siblings' habit of calling my parents Kay and Jerry began in adolescence, initiated mostly by my older brother Paul and me. When Frank's cat-astrophic illness threw the familiar routines of our family into chaos, everyone had to assume new identities. My parents' pain was so visible during those years, despite their determined efforts to pretend otherwise, Paul and I became as vigilant about squelching conflicts as Ryan and Darren had become during the post–divorce years.

We policed the squabbles of our younger siblings with the same zero tolerance. Even in the basement—the only place in our tradi-tional household where the kid–society could play itself out—sib-ling outbursts were no longer allowed. In all the we/they conspir-acies between kids and parents to date, Paul had always been a reliable ally to the "we's." That year, he defected and became a loy-alist to the "they's." If he caught Kevin teasing Gina at the Ping-Pong table, he would look up from his book with irritation and say, "Shut up, you guys." He would point through the raftered ceiling and then lower his voice as if the place might be bugged. "They can *hear* you down here. Can't you see they have *enough* on their minds?"

My own retreat from "mommy and daddy" was more ambigu-ous. The eleven-year age difference between me and my youngest sibling put me somewhere between "sister" and "mom," just as my intimate talks with my mother at the kitchen table during all those years put me somewhere between "daughter" and "friend." I solved my role confusion by specifying Paul's "they" as "Kay and Jerry." I identified my parents by name rather than role to establish a mid-dling authority of my own: "Kevin, put Jerry's hammer back where you found it. It drives him berserk when he can't find his tools—and this is not a good time to drive him berserk." Or, "Gina, remember to leave Kay a note when you stay at Julie's for dinner—she had to call about forty of your friends to find out where you were last night."

To my parents themselves, however, I used their names uncon-sciously and unevenly. As my mother once pointed out, I called her "Kay" except when I wanted something from her, and then she was

"Mom" again. She was "Mom" quite often as I moved closer to menopause and my sons plowed through adolescence. I discovered a growing number of things I needed to know from her. My mother, like Mark Twain's father, was becoming wiser every year—or I was becoming stupider.

Whenever I felt my maternal self-esteem slipping or suffered a cognitive hangover after a high school orientation meeting, I would call on friends for a reality check. A few days after a long chat with my friend Marti, I received a postcard with the message I tacked on my office wall that year: "In a woman-hating culture, self-love is an act of rebellion." I would eventually pass the message on to Carolen, since I knew Baby Alice, angel that she was, would give her mother's self-esteem a vigorous workout someday.

TALKING TO my friend on the phone, aware of her delirious state in the maternity wing, I understood why Kay chose not to mention on the first morning of my motherhood all the trials and frustrations that lay ahead of me. A kind of amnesia about the pain of motherhood is essential to the propagation of the species. Unlike pandas, we have to forget we're living in captivity. Even in a woman-hating culture, we have to keep risking belief in our own endurance. "You'll be surprised," my mother had said that morning fifteen years ago, "how much that baby boy will make you forgive and forget." I would never have believed there was that much mercy or stupidity in me.

Soon enough, Carolen would be surprised too. If she wanted to pick my brain about how to prepare for her future dumbing down, she had my number. I was surprised again myself, the very next day, when I stopped in the baby shop to find a gift for the smallest libber in our CR family. I instantly became infected with Carolen's giddy exclamation points. The tiny pink tennies—I remembered Ryan's red ones—size *zero!* The little French sun suits—I remembered Darren at the shore, his first encounter with ocean-sized waves: "They keep coming—and Mom! They're *free!*" He thought having that much fun required a pocketful of quarters. Oohing and aahing through the store aisles, remembering all the little hands and feet I had put in so many mittens and boots, mourning all the "gone children" I have loved, recalling the memories they had imprinted on me, I realized how much they had shaped the answer to "Who am I?"

I left the baby shop loaded with memorabilia, grinning like a fool. A woman in this addled state was vulnerable to reenlistment, so when Carolen invited me to become Alice's godmother, I didn't hesitate. I might have been stupid that year, but I was in for the whole fifteen years. Or the whole fifty yards. That is, I was in for the whole chilling out.

16

A Wrestling Mom

A writer I much admire said in an essay about the trials of being the feminist mother of sons that it *pained* her to see her adolescent son suffer abuse from thuggish friends for sticking up for the rights of gay sailors and American Indians. Good God, I thought, those are the joyful moments for a feminist mother. The painful moments come when she hears her son issue a wolf whistle or talk about joining the army.

My sons have wanted to join the army, to be like Tom Cruise in *Top Gun*. They have wanted to swagger. Like Clint Eastwood, they've hankered after the respect and awe a man gets when he leaves a wake of death behind him. I have seen these macho personas come and go with my sons. So I didn't take all these theatrical characters too seriously—Indiana Jones, Luke Skywalker, Rocky Balboa. They usually didn't survive beyond the year. One did, however, and I realized after the third year that it was probably a keeper. It was not a part of my son I had grown, and it did not cheer me. Of all the role models I imagined for my sons, Hulk Hogan was not one of them.

"It's not the same as TV, Mom," Ryan said. Wrestle-Mania was just theatre, he said. "It's a joke. That isn't real wrestling." His passion for this sport would eventually engage me in a male culture for which I would never have imagined developing an affinity.

EVERY FRIDAY morning during his senior year of high school, Ryan stood before the bathroom mirror carefully knotting his tie. A strictly jeans and T-shirt guy at age eighteen, he followed the high school athlete's tradition of wearing ties to notify classmates: I have a game today. Friends would wish him luck in the halls, but few would attend the afternoon meet. Unlike the football and basketball teams, wrestlers attract about the same size audience as, say, the chess club. It did not matter. His teammates and coaches—the close fraternity he aimed to please most—would observe every move. A sparse population of parents would make up in volume what we lacked in numbers.

The button at his neck fell a half-inch short of its mark, although his eyes withheld any pleasure at the measurable results of all the iron he'd pumped. Nor did his eyes concede any regret when he combed his hair around the swollen, tender tip of his "cauliflower" ear, in full bloom again this season. Admitting neither vanity nor chagrin to the mirror, a young wrestler strives to become utterly unconscious of his body—its muscle, its pain, its hunger, its sweat. It was the wrestler's mom, approaching the end of an eighteen-year intimacy with this body and this boy, who openly admired and winced through mornings such as these.

"How do I look?" he asked, more out of habit than any need for my approval. He patted his black tie familiarly.

"Like a pallbearer with a tic," I replied. He laughed.

In fact, I thought he looked splendid, but saying so would have been meaningless that day. We had come to the outer edge of unconditional love, and wrestling taught both of us what some of the future conditions might be. For a boy who'd always known how to charm parents and teachers out of final ultimata, for whom friendship and fun came easily but deadlines and due dates were hard, I suspected he loved this sport precisely because it was so merciless. Give in to temptation, skip a practice, allow a distraction, underestimate an opponent—you lose. In a six-minute match, there is no room for excuses. Preparing for a test that would take him to the limits of his strength and his will, he had no use for easy praise that day.

Before he left the bathroom, he weighed himself one last time, apparently to see if combing his hair had worked off another ounce.

Wrestlers are relentless dieters—if you're good at 152 pounds, they maintain, you should be dynamite at 145. Despite the saunas and workouts in layers of polyurethene, there would be high anxiety when, stripped down to mere ounces of clothing, he stepped on the scale to qualify for the meet. "Enjoy your Thanksgiving dinner," his head coach advised in November. "It will be your last full meal for three months." Not making weight was the worst kind of defeat, providing opponents the free points of a forfeit and disappointing teammates with a failure of will.

All family dinners became testy events during wrestling season. His scorn for calories interrupted my long habits of the heart, equating food with love. Rejection was inevitable. "What's *in* this?" he asked suspiciously before applying his fork to his plate. "How many grams of fat?" For someone who once thought there was no greater heaven than helping himself to a full bag of Chips Ahoy, a stick of celery held little bliss. That morning, he had a glass of water for breakfast. He would probably skip lunch.

"Are you coming today?" he asked before heading out the door, aware of my conflicts with work. Four years ago, I hadn't comprehended the urgency of his repeated invitations to the meets. As a single mom, I preferred other ways of spending our limited "quality time" together than by losing circulation in the bleachers twice a week. Initially, duty rather than enthusiasm brought me to the gym. It's hard for my family and friends to believe I became a sweaty-palmed fan of high school wrestling.

The team had already begun their stretching exercises when I took my seat in the bleachers that afternoon. Ryan sat in the center of the circle with the two other captains, Enrique and Will, surrounded by their black, white, Asian, and Hispanic teammates— all dressed in red. Like a military drill team, they moved in unison to the captains' calls: "Down . . . up . . . again . . . up . . . left . . . up . . . down . . ." The goofball antics that regularly erupted during practices were not indulged here. Under the scrutiny of opponents with names like the Rams, Bears, Wreckers, Vikings, or Warriors, the Greenwich Cardinals gave nothing away.

Although their movements were graceful and disciplined, adolescence lent a distinctly amateur quality to their performance: there was always a limb flailing here or there with a too-large foot. Already my throat swelled with involuntary emotion, like the buried patriotism that reveals itself when a parade marches by. An almost primal longing for a united humanity surfaced as I watched this colorfully diverse team moving in a single, unified direction.

The youngest wrestlers, smaller by half than most of the fans in the bleachers, approached the mat first. The lightweights, usually in their first varsity season, were all limbs. In any position, their eight entangled appendages resembled a dense thicket of pickup sticks. During Ryan's first season four years ago, I could never tell exactly what he was supposed to be doing down there. My cheers were feeble, limited to "Go, Ry!" But where? To what end? The rapid development in a boy between fourteen and eighteen can give a mother the bends, however prepared she may think she is for the coming man.

I had, of course, observed the results of his body-building, but until I attended a wrestling match I'd never watched him use this power on another person. At eighteen, he had the capacity to level most of the people in the gymnasium. There was a part of him that loved this power; there was a part of me that regretted it. I couldn't witness this obvious strength in my son, his joy in using it, without thinking about the ways it would change his social relationships with women. His habitual friendliness with strangers on the sidewalk, with clerks in stores and cafés, was not as readily returned anymore. Some women—not because of anything he had done but what had been done to them—automatically feared him. The "collateral" damage of violence against women: It costs all men smiles on the street.

When the weight class below him was called to the mat, Ryan shed his warmup sweats and secured the straps of his singlet. One of the reasons he kept inviting me to his meets, I finally understood, was that he wanted to announce: "This is who I am now. See me." And see I did. Confronted by all that lycra and muscle, the various states of dress and undress, the mothers in the bleachers hardly knew where to rest their eyes. When I looked away from my own son, I soon realized that I was admiring the son of another mother, perhaps the one sitting next to me. I looked down at my feet and thought about human sexuality. I wondered if it was the same for fathers who observed their daughters in bikinis for the first time. It was hard to know the appropriate way to acknowledge the stunning physical changes in a child of the other sex, and yet not to acknowledge those changes was to ignore the most important developmental issues of the moment.

He put on his headgear and then began the sideline dance that wrestlers do, the loose-limbed hop from foot to foot that simultaneously pumps them up and calms them down. His eyes were focused utterly inward, concentrating on some private vision inside his head. If he knew I was watching, if he knew how much I studied and enjoyed this unselfconscious, rhythmic, juice-up dance, he would stop instantly, as if he had been caught exploring his face for morning stubble in the bathroom mirror. I thought if he kept up this freedom of expression, there was a good chance he'd be spared the urge to beat drums as a Wild Man twenty-some years from now.

For all the mockery Robert Bly's tribal rituals in suburban America have inspired, he has hit a cultural nerve in his argument for exclusively male companionship and ritual. In a lecture four years ago, Bly implied that a single mother's close relationships with sons—especially firstborns—often made it difficult for them to come to terms with the aggressive and competitive parts of themselves. He suggested there were some truths men must learn that mothers cannot teach them. Ryan learned things in the company of his coaches and teammates that I could never have taught him. This recognition brought an element of pain, as separation invariably does.

The week before, still pumped up after an invigorating victory, a phrase commonly used in the locker room slipped out in the car: It was too bad his best friend had to lose to that "fuckin' fairy" from

Darien. He was sorry the minute he'd said the F-word—not the first one, which has thoroughly saturated the culture. ("The word 'fuck' is uttered 102 times during the film *The Last Boy Scouts*," according to the *Harper's* Index.) No, it was the second F-word that prompted the apology. Only in the environment of the car did he remember that our extended family of friends included several fairies. The word meant nothing, he assured me. It was army.

"It's only language," I reminded him, " . . . only the stuff we think with." I knew crudeness was a prerequisite in the world of the locker room; he knew sexism and homophobia were enemies in mine. His defection didn't seem so innocent, so temporary, to me because this phrase was acquired during his first real experience with power. How that power was defined, for and against whom, had everything to do with how it would eventually be used. Still largely unconscious of the bigotry that began with a word, he didn't want it to matter. "Trust me," I said. "Words matter."

If my son had some discomforting moments with the language requirements of a feminist mom, I had a few unsettling months with the service obligations of a wrestling son. According to tradition, the captains' moms were responsible for raising funds for the team. Consequently, I spent most of my Saturdays that winter in the corridor outside the gymnasium serving chili-dogs with the other mothers. We were real estate managers, bank cashiers, journalists . . . women who had not served coffee to the men in our offices for the last ten years. Yet there we were, catering to sons who stood on the brink of "emancipated minor," fully aware that serving men leads not to gratitude but to oblivion.

I had some difficulties with the unfair assumption that a captain's dad belongs in the bleachers while a captain's mom is happiest behind the refreshment stand. Nevertheless, I felt a peculiar satisfaction fulfilling my chili-dog duties. Maybe it was a fit of nostalgia, savoring every ritual of our last season together. Or maybe it was the greater generosity one generation affords to the next. Fifteen years ago, I was a consultant for the Amax Coal Company when the first women employees entered the mines, amid great hostility and resistance. "I can get behind this liberation stuff for my daughters," one of the miners confessed privately, "but not for my wife."

My thoughts were suddenly interrupted by loud hollering below. The two coaches leaped up from their seats and were leaning over the edge of the mat as the referee crouched low, eyeball-to-eyeball with the wrestlers on the floor. Before I could join the rallying shouts, a hand slapped the mat, a whistle blew. The wrestler in blue jumped up ecstatically. A defeated Cardinal sat on the mat in limp disbelief. He threw off his headgear angrily, then quickly picked it up and left the mat before tripping into the penalty points of unsportsmanlike conduct. The head coach shrugged and raised a pair of helpless hands—sign language for "shit happens." Slipping out of his wet singlet, he put on the T-shirt bearing this month's slogan: "PAIN—It is better to give than to receive." A junior varsity player was bounced from the bench to make room for the higher ranked, defeated teammate. Membership had its privileges.

Whenever a Cardinal left the mat in despair, a grim and wordless exchange rippled through the eyes in the bleachers. It was a humbling moment to witness a son in defeat, to contemplate how much more loomed ahead, how powerless we were to prevent it. Every mother I know has battled the irrational craving to spare her children disappointment and heartache. When Ryan exploded in enraged frustration on the golf course last summer, one of my relatives advised me to teach him our family philosophy that it's just as honorable to be a good loser as it is to be a gracious winner. "I can't teach him that," I said, empathizing with his suffering. "It isn't true."

The two wrestling team alumni who came to every meet were whispering some private, last-minute advice to Ryan before he stepped onto the mat. Pete and Pat—whom the Cardinals referred to as "Pete and Repeat" and who might be eligible to found the first chapter of Adult Children of Wrestling Moms—still arranged their business and social lives around the high school team, not yet having found a fraternity as satisfying as this in the outside world. I was grateful for the straightforward affection they gave my son.

Whatever the content of their private conversations, it introduced me to what complete comprehension looked like on his face. It was not an expression I'd ever seen at home.

The coaches met him at the edge of the mat. They had the credibility and authority—all but expired for most of the parents in the bleachers—to demand discipline and give orders. It was a challenge to feel entirely happy about this natural turn of events. I couldn't help wishing this authority were directing him, "Do your homework! Think about your future!" But instead I heard, "I know you can *kill* this guy! I want to see it in the first period!"

As Ryan crouched into his stance, my heartbeat accelerated, my skin dampened, my own muscles became taut. Sitting in the bleachers was an aerobic experience for me. As usual, I sat myself next to the Puebla women, Enrique's mother and two sisters, who taught the tweedier New England residents how to behave at a wrestling meet. The team loved them: "You can really *hear* them," the coach said.

I liked to sit next to the Pueblas because I never had to feel like an emotionally embarrassing relative in their company. Enrique's mother Marcia, one of my fund-raising teammates at the refreshment stand this year, spoke only Spanish while I spoke only English. We understood each other's sign language and facial expressions adequately enough to conduct our chili-dog business, but our communication in the bleachers was seamless. She screamed, I screamed, we all screamed.

An aggressive takedown in the first period resulted in a reversal. Alarm flashed into Ryan's face and stayed there. As he fought with everything he had—every muscle straining against the hold, every fiber of his being resisting defeat—the Cardinal fans tried to outshout the deafening cheers from our opponents. The buzzer sounded, ending the period in the nick of time.

Unless someone got a bloody nose—a painless and welcome time-out—it was usually necessary for one of the wrestlers to tie his shoe between periods. It was a lengthy process, tightening laces and wrapping the ankles, then taking a drink for revival. It was usually the losing wrestler who discovered he needed to relace a shoe, who needed to break the momentum of his opponent and rally his own. Perilously close to defeat, Ryan painstakingly attended his shoe. My thoughts drifted back to the first time he dressed himself, the gorgeous look of satisfaction on his three-year-old face . . . until he got to those damn shoes. Defeated by a shoelace, he cried in frustration. Vulnerable again, the lone figure bent in concentration on the mat raised an identical lump in my throat. If he lost his match that day, I knew he would not let himself cry.

After a second punishing round, his total exhaustion was evident: spent muscles, sweaty limbs, airless lungs, a worried face. With time running out, the third period was always the most reckless. Already, mat burns colored his cheeks, blood trickled from his mouth; his ear, I thought, must have been swelling under his headgear. He said he never felt these injuries when they were happening. I did. For the last four years, emergency rooms had been a regular feature of my existence. In these stark, tiled rooms of reverberating tensions, there were no crowds, no cheers, no coaches. Emergency rooms were where mothers wrestled alone against monstrous fears.

I thought back to the prior December when Ry's teammate, Will, grabbed my elbow before I paid my admission at the Staples High School tournament and reported that Ryan had just been taken out on a stretcher. My heart squeezed fiercely as images of broken necks, brain damage, and comas flooded my brain. "It's only his arm," Will assured me. Only an arm, only an ear . . . only the young can be so cavalier about their bodies. Armies are made up of youth for a reason. Ryan was a casualty of friendly fire that day: The injury happened during warmups with a teammate. When he lost consciousness after severely dislocating his right elbow, the trainer called an ambulance.

Fifteen minutes later, after a record number of moving violations on I-95, I reached Norwalk Hospital. Despite my wish to remain calm, I had trouble with simple interrogatory sentences at the information desk: "My son, Staples High School, about fifteen minutes ago—his arm (a spastic gesture to my right elbow) . . . is he here?" The nurse looked quizzically, then brightened.

"Oh, you mean *Ryan*." She smiled and pointed down a long corridor. A burly paramedic pushing an ambulance gurney noted my hesitation in the hallway. I repeated my garbled question. "Oh," he said, grinning, "you want *Ryan*." He accompanied me to his room.

Obviously no longer unconscious, my son was propped up in his bed, a very pale Cardinal in a nest of white sheets. The doctor, still smiling from some joke that preceded my arrival, picked up a pair of scissors to free the wounded arm from his pullover jacket. Their amiable chatter concluded abruptly.

"No way!" Ryan said, the color returning to his face. He sat bolt upright and insisted on pulling it over his head. When the doctor rejected that suggestion as too painful and risky, the paramedic, a former high school wrestler, came to the defense of his fellow jock.

"Doc, you can't cut his jacket—read this," he said, pointing to the word embroidered on the right shoulder: "Captain." The doctor looked at me, the only nonmember of this religion.

"Knock him out," I said. "Cut the jacket."

The patient prevailed. It took three of us to slip the jacket, undamaged, over his head and arm. It seemed a foolish kind of bravery, risking enormous pain to salvage a symbol. But in the whiplash emotions of his final wrestling season, nothing stayed the same. As the fear of permanent physical injury receded into the background, I recognized the enduring psychological benefits he'd earned from this sport. If wrestling gave him one oddball ear and six weeks in a sling, it also produced a confident, witty, capable young man, the *Ryan* instantly recognized by the hospital staff. He was willing to put his body between the scissors and the "Captain" because, he reminded me, "words matter."

Going into that third reckless period, he knew he needed a pin. Handicapped by the limited flexibility of this now-bandaged arm and a longer limbed opponent, he had trouble securing the leg he needed for a take-down. With thirty seconds to go, he lunged for a knee in a sudden rush of adrenalin. Now he was in a cradle, now he was out, now he had freed his arm, now he was on top pressing down . . . three inches to go, two inches, oh-my-God-*one*-inch! My laryngitis would inform me later that much of the thunderous noise in the bleachers came from me. He got his pin, seven seconds to spare.

Tradition required each wrestler, after the referee raised the winner's arm, to shake the hand of the opponent's coach. Although Ryan might not yet have mastered the good loser part of our family's honorable equation, his relatives would have been pleased to have seen him in the role of gracious winner. On the way back across the mat to his own bench he always stopped, win or lose, to hug his opponent. This hug was no formality but full of emotion. After four years of rising up in the same weight classes together and witnessing each other's most glorious and humiliating moments, his mortal enemies from other schools had become his friends. During long breaks at all-day tournaments, they empathized with injuries and bad seasons, traded tips about summer camps and clinics, talked scholarships and women. The hug said "congratulations" or "sorry I had to pin you." In his last year, it had the bittersweet tinge of "so long."

Like the handshake of peace at the end of a church service, each team lined up after the final match and walked in a single file across the gym, shaking or slapping each hand from the opposite direction. Only once, when a racial slur tipped the defeated Cardinals beyond a strained control, did the handshake erupt in a brawl. Wrestling on a multi-racial team required coming to terms with every myth about racial superiority or inferiority. On the mat, you could hardly know a man better, be closer, understand more thoroughly that his immediate goals are exactly the same as your own.

Maybe it was this quality that wrestling had given my son—the camaraderie and experience of navigating the high tensions of an interracial world—that caused my palms to sweat so. The civil wars among our children, race against race, are so heartbreaking. Watching this handshake of peace, it became excruciatingly clear that if all of us would only do the same—if we would only mobilize our wills not to give in to temptation, skip a practice, allow a distraction, underestimate an opponent, or be careless with language— we would not have to keep losing the next generation to wars.

As the team rolled up the mats, the moms in the bleachers conferred on final plans for the annual awards banquet. Moving as far away from chili-dogs as possible we agreed on a Chinese menu, then decided to hire a caterer to serve it. We packed our gear—the video cameras, the coolers of Gatorade, the ace bandages and aspirin and ice packs we were never without. If we were entirely sane, we would not need these semibarbaric rituals to break our hearts and thrill our souls. But we were not entirely sane. We would be back next week.

17
Sex, Lies, and Parental Consent

All human beings are doomed to live and learn, suffer and regress, recover and try again. The blissful innocence we are born with is probably essential to human survival. If we knew in advance how much pain and grief we'd have to endure before acquiring any genuinely useful knowledge about love and independence and sexuality, the toddler's persistent "But *why?*" would become, "Never mind." By adolescence, it's usually the puzzled parents who are asking why. The answer, depending on what response that question elicited before the tables turned, is often a surly rendition of "Because I'm the teenager, that's why."

The hardest part of being human is that our most critical self-knowledge comes from experience—some of it truly painful—and parents want more than anything to spare their offspring painful experiences. Hence, long after our legitimate authority has expired, we are still tempted to make rules, levy sanctions, even pass legislation requiring "parental consent" before allowing young people access to certain information and experiences—particularly sexual information and experiences. Like trying to preserve an artistic sensibility by keeping a painter blindfolded, this controlling impulse thwarts the very development it means to encourage.

Almost every adolescent will break almost every rule, at least once, before understanding why the rule is there. This reality became obvious fifteen years ago in the Dean's Office at Bishop Luers High School, when it was my job to police adolescent behavior. Had the kids' parents heard the private confessions that I heard, they would have had—as one junior who swore me to secrecy said—"about forty hernias apiece." When my own sons reached this perilous stretch of life, it was hernia time for me.

Having once been a specialist in adolescent crimes and misdemeanors didn't fill me with confidence that I could usher my own sons through this thicket of passions without encountering any trouble. My experience, in fact, had exactly the opposite effect. I knew the chances that Ryan and Darren would break home rules were 100 percent. The only thing I didn't know was how many, how long, and how damaging those breaks would be.

My estimates were based on my former work with that fraction of the adolescent population at Bishop Luers who stepped outside the boundaries of civilization outlined in the Student Handbook— a volume that carried about as much weight with my juvenile offenders as, say, *Miss Manners' Guide to Excruciatingly Correct Behavior* might hold for the truckers at the service plazas along Interstate 80. Their offenses were largely the result of hormonal energy exceeding the speed limit—certainly, propelling them beyond their capacity to consider probable consequences. It was impossible to contain this energy, although the faculty certainly tried.

Trying to anticipate all the bizarre ideas that would crop up in an adolescent mind, a team of teachers and administrators met each summer to revise and expand the guidelines. None of us had the foresight to include such sanctions as: "Any freshman who drops lighted firecrackers out the window of the school bus will be suspended for three days" or "Any senior who celebrates the last week of school by drinking Boone's Farm apple wine before lunch will serve a final detention for bad taste." As adults far removed from the excessive energy and stupidity that routinely afflicts teenagers, we couldn't imagine all the rash acts a youth might conceive, and we tended toward amnesia when remembering our own.

The underlying assumption behind most of the rules was that adolescents were "out of control" and it was our job to save them from themselves. This should have been an alarming idea for the faculty, who shared responsibility with parents for teaching self-control. In truth, the students were rarely out of control but were frequently immature and ignorant. More than knowledge and experience, we gave them rules to keep them under our control, confusing obedience with "mature behavior."

The Handbook required parent conferences for serious offenses, and these were the most wrenching moments of truth for everyone involved. I met with wounded, guilty, worried mothers years before I became one myself, and I learned that parents had as much trouble establishing separate identities as their children—maybe even more. Universally, parents felt embarrassed or remorseful over crimes they didn't commit, regarding their children's behavior as direct reflections of themselves. Recommending detachment (as only a nonmother could), I reminded one apologetic mother who frequented my office during those years not to blame herself: "Please don't . . . It was your son who anonymously contributed the tray of marijuana brownies to the Junior Class Bake Sale, not you. When kids do these things, I don't assume they learned it at home," I assured her. "Personally, I blame it on high-humidity days."

When grave problems with drugs or alcohol or truancy erupted, I sat with mothers outside emergency rooms and courtrooms, feeling their sorrow, mourning our mutual helplessness. I thought of myself as an ally to these vulnerable women, caught in an emotional warp of love and anger. Since I believed wholeheartedly in the Handbook's philosophy of working together with parents when trouble came, I was deeply conflicted whenever I had to abandon this principle. Yet I did so, deliberately, at least once a week.

I dealt regularly with a special category of young errants who bound me to confidentiality, asking for help not only without their parents' knowledge but probably in violation of parental values. From the moment these tense and distraught students appeared in the doorway of my office, I could distinguish them from the class cutters or graffiti vandals. They always arrived solo, without notes from their teachers, their guilt and anxiety so great they turned themselves in. I knew the problem was sex before they said a word.

Technically, the students' sexual behavior was outside my venue. In a Catholic high school, premarital sex was classified as sin and assigned to the Religion Department. Beyond the mandated etiquette at high school dances, there were few guidelines about sex in the Student Handbook. It was understood—or rather, misunderstood—that no students were to have sex with anyone, ever. This was the operative assumption in the Religion Department, which is why the "sex criminals" brought their confessions to me.

Humble, never defiant, stumbling for explanations, they had trouble naming the problem: "I'm not sure, but I think I'm . . . six weeks ago, after the homecoming dance, Tommy and I . . . it happened so *fast* . . . if it just went in an inch—we didn't go 'all the way'—can you still get . . . ?" I would put the Do Not Disturb sign on the knob and close the door, then sit down on the threadbare sofa across from the shelf where I kept a sizable collection of confiscated pea-shooters and whoopie cushions, and help them out with the impossible word: "Pregnant?"

The sex criminals were perhaps the most troublesome students for me because, still a young woman myself, I had not fully recovered from my own Catholic girlhood. I felt shakiest in my ability to be helpful on sexual matters. What did I really know? Since my own repressed youth, I'd gained a whole new intellectual understanding of human sexuality. But emotionally, my sensibility was framed by a parochial education. This religious education collided with the sexually repressed '50s, when information was scarce and girls were taught to loathe their bodies as "vessels of sin." The overwhelming guilt I grew up with was not useful either in teaching morality or in managing human desire. Although boys acted on the normal, oaty urges of adolescence without losing their self-esteem, sexually active girls fell straight from virgin to whore. The notion that young men "scored" in the back seats of Chevys while young women "sinned" was ruinous to both sexes: If a girl spends twenty years believing her body is a vessel of sin, that she is responsible for any sexual crimes committed against her, that her own desires are harmful and wrong, when she finally puts on a white dress and walks down a church aisle, the subsequent one-hour ceremony will not alter a lifetime of wrong-think. If a boy spends twenty years believing that girls who enjoy sex as much as men are sluts, that he is owed relief once he becomes aroused, that only bad girls "do it," when he finally puts on a tuxedo and marries a "good" girl, the holy vows he recites cannot erase the contempt of his formative years. How, in this mine field of self-disgust and alienation, could either sex achieve genuine affection for the other? Still removing shrapnel from my own adolescent wounds, I listened to the confessions of the sex criminals with a mixture of rage and pain over my own youthful ignorance.

Instead of straightforward information, the high school's sex education program offered more myths and confusion. The celibate friar who taught the senior course on human sexuality demonstrated the difference between male and female sexual responses by placing two glasses of water on the podium, then dropping an Alka Seltzer into one and a Bufferin into the other. "This is the male sexual response," he explained, holding up the frothing, effervescent Alka Seltzer. Then he pointed to the sodden Bufferin disintegrating quietly in the other glass and said, "This is the female response."

"I must be a freak," a perfectly healthy young woman confessed after witnessing the friar's scientific demonstration. "I'm an Alka Seltzer trapped in a Bufferin body."

I would have been amused at the absurdity if I didn't see, week after week, the harmful results. The misinformation about human biology may have caused headaches, but the absence of information about birth control caused more than that. I will never forget the tearful months a bright and thoughtful eighteen year old spent in my office, weeping in despair over the disgrace she imagined bringing to the parents she loved. Feeling deeply deviant for acting on normal sexual feelings, she punished herself with unceasing guilt. Too ashamed to schedule the pregnancy test that would have brought relief and knowledge, she was suicidal and depressed for three long months. She finally got her period—but not before most of her hair had fallen out. Covering her head with a red bandanna, she underwent extensive diagnostic tests without ever telling her worried parents the cause of her distress. Bound by my promise of confidentiality, neither could I.

The private traumas of the sex criminals were so heart wrenching, I was moved to break the Handbook principles myself. When students asked me to help them obtain birth control pills and diaphragms, I made appointments at the women's clinic downtown, issued passes from study halls, and lent them my car keys to get there. I would then spend the next hour in immense anxiety, thinking about their parents, my betrayal, possible accidents, losing my job, vowing not to place myself at risk again. But the very next week I would make more phone calls and turn over my car keys again.

One senior girl who came for help was the daughter of a close friend. I urged her to confide in her mother, assuring her of my continued support. When she refused, I couldn't talk to my friend without her agreement. I knew her mother to be understanding—but then so was mine, and I could never have discussed the particulars of my early sexual encounters with her. Kids can rarely imagine their own parents riding the wild, hormonal roller coaster of adolescence, and amazingly, parents barely remember it themselves when their kids are going through it.

Children terrify us when they become sexually active because it presents so many opportunities for hurt. Parents who count solely on a policy of abstinence, especially given today's statistics on teenage pregnancy, are a study in wishful thinking. Reverend Pat Robertson, the leader of the Christian Coalition who opposes sex education and promotes parental consent laws, seems to have forgotten about his own shotgun marriage. St. Augustine, Mary Magdalene, the heroes and heroines in *The Lives of the Saints* offer plenty of proof that good men and women can emerge from a wild youth. But today, you can die of a wild youth before you have time to grow up. Sexual ignorance has never been so lethal.

Recognizing that a parent cannot play the leading role as confidant is even more difficult for parents who consider themselves "modern." I was stunned by the arrogance of an acquaintance who, proud of her close relationship with her daughters and her enlightened attitudes about sex/birth control/abortion, said, "There isn't anything my girls can't discuss with me." Her liberal sense of entitlement to "know" was indistinguishable from the conservative position on parental rights—even if it came from the desire for intimacy rather than control. To her, it was a sign of bad parenting and poor communication when adolescents sought outside help or advice. To me, such thinking seems dangerous.

Although most of the Luers parents were good people who cared about their kids, my students swore they would "rather die" than reveal their private sexual experiences to their parents. Tragically, this was not an adolescent exaggeration. Where accurate information about a child's sexual activity is concerned, liberal and conservative parents are in essentially the same position. Laws requiring parental consent for birth control and abortion put all children's lives at risk. In Indiana, such a law became fatal for seventeen-year-old Rebecca Bell. Pregnant and afraid to confide in the parents she loved, she had an illegal abortion instead. When her mother, Karen, became alarmed by her daughter's subsequent flu symptoms and persistent fever, she took her to a doctor and finally learned what happened—too late to save Rebecca's life. A young woman died of an untreated infection because of a talk that didn't happen, a talk that should never have been required by law. Karen Bell has since become an ardent opponent of legislation that would drive young women to backstairs abortionists.

Parental consent laws, based on the presumption that a parent's right to know supersedes an adolescent's right to privacy, are not only dangerous but futile. It would be as impossible to write legislation that anticipated all the necessary exceptions we'd be obliged to make as it would be to draft comprehensive rules for the Student Handbook. We'd have to be wise—and honest—enough to include exceptions for incest and rape, for immaturity and inexperience, for honors students who would rather risk baldness or death than disappoint beloved parents. Even parents who have reached the highest level of consciousness on Abraham Maslow's famous hierarchy of human development can't claim a wisdom that comprehensive. Nor, from the evidence so far, can my generation of parents claim to be that honest.

An article in the *New York Times* described how my contemporaries—many of whom were active participants in the sexual revolution—felt either regressive or hypocritical for imposing rules of conduct we oncerejected. The distance between what we did then and what we say now is evident everywhere: We smoked dope in liberal quantities then but now insist we "didn't inhale"; we resisted the draft and protested war then but now reject political candidates who can't prove themselves "patriots"; we exercised sexual liberty then but now pass laws prohibiting the same freedom for our children; we have yet to tell the truth about our own youth but tell our kids to confide in us.

AS A young mother and wife during the height of the sexual revolution, I was not an active player in that social rebellion. As a former SDS model, my youthful experiments were mainly a daring exposure of cleavage and knees. I remember the disbelief one evening when a group of middle-aged friends, reminiscing about the bad "good old days" of their wild youth, asked me how many sexual partners there were in my past. I confessed that I was still in the low one-digits.

"Really?" the group said in unison, totally incredulous.

"Really," I admitted. On the subject of sex, I regarded myself as Remedial Mom.

Since Howard was not much more experienced than I, our sons, entering the dramatically altered sexual culture of the '90s, had the collective knowledge of a nun and a monk for personal guidance.

I was grateful for the comprehensive sex education programs at the public schools Ryan and Darren attended, and I had supplemented this information with illustrated books since early childhood. Sex was easy to talk about when they were little, before terminal embarrassment set in. By the time they entered middle school, Larry suggested using visual aids. The first packages of condoms he gave my sons were received enthusiastically—for all the wrong reasons. The boys and their friends filled them with water and dropped them from the second story window. Too soon, we supposed.

Nevertheless, I made several subsequent trips to a local drug store to buy safe sex paraphernalia. I wanted them to become familiar with these items long before it might be time to use them. A clerk once eyed me curiously when I put my copious supplies on the counter—Today sponges, spermicidal jellies, applicators, and dozens of condoms—lubricated and not, ribbed and smooth, thin and super strength, in every conceivable size. (As author Barbara Seaman observed, "Condoms are sized like olives—'Jumbo, Colossal, and Super Colossal'—so nobody has to go in and ask for the small.")

"You must be going on a long vacation," the clerk said as she rang up the sale.

"No," I said, offering no further comment. I didn't encourage conversation during these transactions. I let her think I was a silver-haired Greenwich matron who was into group sex.

After my sons' interest in water balloons had given way to a greater interest in girls, they were mortified when I emptied another bag of supplies and initiated a discussion at the kitchen table.

"Mom, just because we have girlfriends doesn't mean we're having sex," one of them said. They looked at each other and shook their heads, which I understood to mean, "Here she goes again." Not yet, they wanted me to know.

I was making no assumptions about their private sex lives, I assured them, and they had no obligation to tell me any details. But, just like driving lessons, it takes more time than you imagine to master the necessary maneuvers. I'd begun putting the boys behind the wheel before the legal age because I was acutely aware that they would be navigating some of the busiest highways in the world, among some of the craziest drivers, at the most impulsive and least coordinated age. I wanted to give myself extra time in the co-pilot's seat to fill their heads with rules, advice, warnings, and confidence. They are both terrific drivers today. Practicing safe sex in these perilous times, I felt, couldn't begin too early or too often.

Whether or not they were sexually active, I told them, it made sense to become familiar with how to use a condom. It wasn't something they wanted to encounter for the first time in the heat of passion. The packages had useful diagrams of the male and female body—deliberately unsexy line drawings of angles and openings and organs so they might one day "know thy partner" in a more biblical sense. I advised them to practice and become experts with prophylactics not only because they needed to protect themselves from sexually transmitted diseases, but also because men as well as women have a moral obligation to prevent unwanted pregnancies. Centuries before AIDS compelled us all to worry about the consequences of sex, half of us worried and suffered alone. It was impossible to calculate how many women lost their lives, literally and figuratively, before unprotected sex was recognized as unsafe.

Ryan and Darren maintained eye contact with the ceiling whenever I delivered my sermons on sex. My moral advice was necessarily brief: No means no. Using a condom is a sign of respect, and you should never have sex with anyone you can't respect. Responsible sex, ironically, met the exact same qualifications as mortal sin—one had to recognize strong temptations, grievous matters, and full consent of all wills.

GIVING KIDS information and access to birth control, as the current debates over sex education across the country make painfully clear, is frequently confused with giving them "permission." Permission isn't the issue. I could neither give nor withhold permission; it wasn't mine to give. I could give advice, warnings, knowledge, and information, but the actual decision to have sex belongs exclusively to the owners of the bodies involved.

As a dean, it was never easy to trust the decision-making capacity of adolescents, but it was even harder as a mother. Can young people who still have an active interest in whoopie cushions and Boone's Farm apple wine be considered mature enough to make intelligent decisions about sex? Of course not. We would all prefer to wait until they were further along Maslow's scale of human development, to delay sexual activity until they had mastered the most critical lessons about love and empathy and wisdom. But intelligent or not, with or without our knowledge, decisions will be made and sex will happen.

Frankly, I am baffled by parents who argue against sex education in schools and require consent before allowing a teenager access to condoms. Are there really people who want to know every detail of adolescent sex? I found it trying enough to endure the minor flirtations of the young and the lustful. Teenagers are mindless of discretion. In love with their own bodies, they are oblivious to how all their giggling, bumping, poking, patting, tickling, and smooching might not be as much fun for the nonparticipating witnesses.

The nineteen-year-old son of a friend exposed an entire dinner party to the intimate sounds of his sex life when, home from college for the holidays, he thumped away with his very verbal girlfriend in his bedroom while his mother served guests in the adjoining dining room. There was acute embarrassment all around as each of us wondered whether to acknowledge the squeaking bedsprings or pretend we were deaf. The lovers finally emerged, sweaty and tucking in shirttails, as we quietly applied our forks to dessert. They headed into the kitchen, ravenous and giggling, no doubt amused by his mother's uptight and scandalized guests. It became clear to all the grey-haired sexual revolutionaries at the table that liberty without discretion was not what we meant. So what did we mean?

"It's his home, too—what can I do?" my friend asked, shrugging her shoulders helplessly. "Ask him to park in the driveway and use the back seat of the car?"

Under the circumstances, yes. During his mother's dinner party, the back seat of his car would have been a more appropriate location.

I remember describing this scene to Ryan and Darren, hoping to impress them with the need for dignity and discretion. The message I apparently relayed instead, as an incident in my own home made evident a few years later, encouraged secrecy and covert activities. Late one night, I heard several voices erupting and shushing each other as the garage door opened and footsteps hurried into the boys' den downstairs. Nocturnal comings and goings were not unusual the summer before Ryan and his friends left for college. There had been another farewell party for a classmate that evening, and it also wasn't unusual for the designated driver to taxi insufficiently sober passengers to our house for a recuperative overnight. Ryan was a volunteer with Safe Rides that year, and I was inducted into my role as Recovery Mom.

The next morning, I was on my way to the bathroom when a young woman I had never seen before, mascara ringing her eyes like a raccoon and hair matted to her head, suddenly exited. Freezing in her tracks like a startled doe, she stared at me in mute embarrassment, then quickly bolted through the door and disappeared downstairs. I woke up Ryan, asleep on the living room couch, and asked what was going on. The story, in brief: A neighborhood friend had brought his girlfriend over that night after his mother, shocked to discover them in his bedroom, had thrown them both out of the house. "Don't worry, Mom—they didn't 'do anything,'" he assured me. "I just gave them my room—they needed a place to sleep."

"Good God," I said, "Why didn't you let me know? At least put a note on the bathroom mirror, tell me her name?"

"She didn't want you to think she was a slut," he said.

Keeping her in the basement and failing to introduce her was the best way to make her feel that way, I told Ryan and our neighbor after the young woman departed later that morning. My grievance with them was not about whether anybody "did anything," but how crassly they managed to do what they did. I introduced them both to a lecture that began "under *my* roof": Any time they brought a female guest home, they must introduce me. Dignity required this, for me and for her. So did biology—the chances that she might need a bathroom sometime during the night were great, especially after a party with a lot of liquids.

"Gentlemen, girls will have clean sheets and towels in this house, whatever their condition upon arrival. And there are no sluts," I said. "Not at age eighteen. Never forget this principle of my faith: Treat other people as you would treat yourself. Girls therefore need introductions, bathrooms, dignity."

I WAS as unnerved by these episodes as my sons. Second-guessing myself—what was good advice, what was not—I knew that unconscious attitudes were bound to seep into any conversation about sex between me and my sons. Could a former "vessel of sin" teach her sons a wholly objective appreciation of human sexuality? The possibility was slim. Recognizing my limitations didn't mean I was relieved of the obligation to try to teach my sons everything I'd learned about sex so far. It only meant I shouldn't try to be their only source. It was much easier to reach this obvious reality than to follow through on it.

My experience in the dean's office taught me some of the most useful and most difficult lessons of motherhood. Both of my sons have mentioned how much they liked the guidance counselor at their high school, how they liked to drop by her office for chats because "she really understands us," as Darren once said. He did not mention the subject of these chats, and I suppressed the impulse to ask. Thinking about my honor student's hair falling out, I checked Darren's forehead for signs of recession. Then I moved clumsily through my feelings of jealousy and exclusion, reaching some measure of gratitude that he'd found someone to talk to who cared about him.

It was ironic that, having been privy to the inside facts of adolescent crises fifteen years ago, I became an outsider to some of the most important secrets my own sons harbored during adolescence. I thought about the difficult decisions that must have regularly come up for the woman who occupied the confessional at their high school, and I wondered what kind of grip she had on her car keys. If she recognized the myriad separation anxieties of both students and parents, she would keep that information in the strictest confidence.

AT MY own version of Ladies' Bridge recently, a discussion about sons and sex and responsibility came up at the card table during a long intermission between hands. A friend who is a few years ahead on the learning curve mused, "Do you ever want to know if your sons are good lovers? Do you ever wonder if they know how to satisfy their partners?"

Our foursome of middle-aged women received her questions with uncharacteristic silence. Mothers couldn't know this, it seemed, without inviting taboo thoughts, without imagining scenes that were risky to entertain, even at Ladies' Bridge. All of us knew by now what sexual acts satisfied women; we knew that our own youthful partners, who had been as inexperienced and frightened and ignorant as we had been, were mostly lousy lovers because pleasing women—if it even occurred to them at all—wasn't in the limited repertoire of the sex educators of our day; and we knew that we, personally, hadn't shared our own experiences with our sons. I found it challenging enough to teach young men to be responsible, to observe dignity. Did my friend mean to imply that mothers were also obliged to discuss techniques, to provide the next generation of women with partners who could send them to the moon? Couldn't those delirious trips to the moon—if both our daughters and sons had the language and self-esteem and encouragement to explore—be something they would figure out for themselves? And how would a mother ever find out if her son were a good lover?

"Did you ever ask your son?" I inquired.

"No," my friend said, and smiled. "I just wonder."

Epilogue
The Independence Room

It's all quiet on my Eastern front this night: I've camped out in a beach chair before the fireplace, a clipboard in my lap and feet to the flames, wondering once more where life will be taking us next. I've abandoned my backroom office to take advantage of the magnificent light show playing outside the picture window as a steady snowfall descends with manic frenzy under glowing pink streetlights. A heavy accumulation has already blanketed the street, immobilizing all traffic but a few dogged snowplows. Since early this afternoon, weather forecasters have been predicting the "worst blizzard of the century." I might be one of the few viewers still awake at 3 A.M., feeling oddly in sync with the weather.

I love blizzards, especially the worst ones. I'm awed by their tremendous power to reorganize human life, if only temporarily. Where reason and common sense fail to alter behavior, a blizzard compels everyone to slow down, abandon destinations, postpone deadlines. A "state of emergency" provides time for things we otherwise can't seem to do — go home from work early, check in on relatives and friends, commit kindnesses for strangers. We indulge the urge to build pots of slow-cooking chili, curl up on the couch with an afghan, maybe with an arm around someone we love. Blizzards are a precise metaphor for motherhood. In fact, for a great many Midwestern women, motherhood quite literally began in one. Chicago hospitals reported a sizable baby boomlet nine months after the historic blizzard of '65, suggesting that for many people domestic captivity had its sublime moments.

Except for the occasional thunder as a tree limb cracks and thuds to the ground, the night is almost spookily silent. The groan of trucks and the whine of planes are conspicuously absent—the annoying buzz of civilization always becomes louder somehow in its absence. Dutifully following advisory warnings earlier in the evening, I bundled up and made several trips out to the front stoop with a shovel to keep the doors free, being about as successful as the sorcerer's apprentice who tried to hold back a flood with his broom. A huge snowdrift has now claimed the front door, and I have surrendered, without much regret, to the cozy interior.

The television journalists obviously love blizzards too. They've all assumed their Natural Disaster Persona—loosened their ties and rolled up their sleeves, dressed down for the late shift in sweaters and jeans. Nobody wears a suit to a blizzard. I notice, too, the altered ethics of my profession: It's okay to abandon the pose of objectivity and to register emotion—to speak with urgency, express concern about the homeless, admire the heroism of common people, provide tips on how to survive without electricity. For a day or two, we get to hear about how everybody is doing, not just about the president and the Joint Chiefs of Staff. The issues are immediate and familiar: food, shelter, warmth, safety. For a while, we are all in this together: nobody's winning or losing on Wall Street; it doesn't matter, for the moment, whether Diana is right or Charles is wrong; Republican congressmen tried, God bless them, but couldn't get anybody to care about Clinton's sex life this week. In the democratic interior of a blizzard, nobody, however credentialed or personally entitled, is going anywhere. From my perspective, these states of emergency don't last nearly long enough.

ALTHOUGH THERE were no hazardous weather warnings when the nurse handed me the blanketed bundle nearly twenty years ago, there should have been, because I've been living in a state of emergency preparedness ever since. The total physical and emotional absorption of early motherhood whites out all other noise for a while. Nothing on this planet mattered more than the baby in my arms. In my initial euphoria, I imagined having the power to shape civilization with this mighty compassion. But like a snowfall that keeps coming and coming, a baby grows with relentless speed. Since that first flood of passion in the maternity wing twenty years ago, I've learned a great deal about the limits of maternal power. Doors have slammed shut here, and talk has periodically ceased; pain and tragedy have penetrated my defenses again and again. We've known the gale force of culture, biology, fate, and I can only feel grateful tonight: We are still alive.

"My nest empties this month," I told a friend last fall, expecting her sympathy and advice.

"If you're lucky," she said. "They could be back, you know. It's happened to the best of families."

"They can *do* that?" I asked, caught short once more by a possibility that wasn't mentioned in the baby books when I enlisted two decades ago: You could be lowering toilet seats for the rest of your life. I was rattled by a story in the *Times* about how the depressed economy has forced many grown children to move back in with their aging parents. The report was accompanied by a photograph of an unemployed young stockbroker, seated at the breakfast table next to his father, both men suited up and reading the newspaper while Mom stood behind them, holding a coffee pot. One almost hopes the woman is only posing for a photographer like the one at the *Fort Wayne Journal Gazette*, glued to the idea that if a woman doesn't look like a waitress, she must be a child abuser.

If this picture is true to life, I thought, then here is a woman having more than her share of bad mother days. This image should remind prospective mothers that "having a baby" could go on indefinitely, but it probably won't dissuade readers already inclined in that direction. We scan the newspapers, read the headlines about the depressed economy, dismiss the odds, and throw the dice for Let's Pretend. Like generations of mothers before us, we recite the game call: "It can't happen to me."

Settled into my empty nest for six months now, it's a little frightening to see how eccentric I'm becoming. Because I no longer have to worry about accommodating the fragile embarrassments of male adolescents, I'm wearing the recycled work outfit Ryan and Darren were loathe to encounter whenever they brought friends home from school. Their faces registered the same mortification I felt some thirty years ago when my mother wore one of the housework ensembles she had patched together from the discarded wardrobe items of her five children. Her favorite and longest running outfit—which regrettably coincided with my senior year of high school—was a pair of girl's junior-sized chartreuse toreador pants, flamboyantly embroidered, with a faded navy blue T-shirt still faintly imprinted with the acronym my nine high school friends adopted during a camping trip at Lake Geneva: "W.O.W." It meant, "Women of the World." We were seventeen. What did we know?

Imagine my chagrin when I brought four WOWs home one afternoon and found my cheerful, middle-aged mother wearing our sacred slogan while scrubbing the kitchen floor. At seventeen, I thought there was no possibility I would become my mother.

Tonight, however, I notice an uncanny resemblance. My work outfit is a pair of faded red warm-up sweats and men's athletic jersey with the logo of a once fiercely beaked Cardinal, now washed out to an unthreatening scowl after many wrestling seasons. Over the fleecy sweats my old black kimono fills in as a jacket, with large hip pockets to hold a copious supply of lead pencils, gum erasers, paper clips, and small yellow stick-'em pads. I fairly clink down the halls between rooms in this serviceable but unglamorous indoor attire. As May Sarton said in her later years, "Now I wear the inside person outside and am more comfortable with myself." Before shifting into this unorthodox apparel, I hadn't realized I was uncomfortable.

Like most women, I have been making unconscious adjustments in my own preferences and tastes to accommodate the family, usually before anyone had asked. I have now reclaimed my turf. Except for the news, the TV is rarely on; the radio dials have been reprogrammed to my favorite stations, the unnerving acoustics of heavy metal bands having been replaced with the emotive chords of Kenny G's alto sax. I can now work on my various projects, restoring my environment to the House Beautiful I abandoned years ago.

Above the fireplace, the collages and portraits of my still unfinished photo wall provoke memories of all the "gone people"— all the kids my sons have been, the moms I have been, the men I have loved. Like the snowflakes falling with relentless speed outside, altering the environment bit by minuscule bit, my sons grew and changed from day to day. I couldn't slow the sequence and halt the rush of nature. Motherhood is a constant experience in letting go. One way or another, the little people I once loved must leave.

"I THINK you better watch it with the candles," my sister Regina said during a visit a few weeks ago, pointing to my new arrangement of tea-candles on the mantle, next to the photographs.

"What do you mean—fire hazard?" I thought I'd been careful to contain the small flames in glass jars.

"No, I mean it kind of looks like an altar—like a Shrine to the Sons," she said. "You're not getting *holy* about motherhood at this late date, are you?" Regina, my sons' youngest aunt and closest pal in the family, loved them precisely for their unsaintliness. She thought the idealized arrangement on the mantle clashed with the actual facts.

I saw her point. I moved the candles, letting the pictures tell their own story.

Maybe it's the late hour, the eerie stillness of the night, the flood of memories provoked by the pictures, but the falling notes of Kenny G's sax hit me right in the throat tonight. I feel a swelling ache with each descending cadence, imagining these words behind each note: "Pleeee-ase, please-please-please-please . . ." Please what?

Please live honorably.

Please be happy.

Please commit joy.

Please be kind to yourselves.
Please know I love you.

LOOKING BACK is so much easier than trying to look ahead; the mistakes are clear, the deeds already done, the apologies and forgivenesses exchanged. Still, there was a lot of explaining to do on the computerized forms we had to fill out on the financial aid applications last spring, when our postnuclear family was subjected to the narrow grid of "tradition." The instructions carried the clear warning in bold type: "Do not send letters, documents, or additional data, for they will be destroyed." The folks at Princeton, with millions of requests to process every year, are not interested in any explanations from those who live outside the given boundaries. Whether or not the information was relevant to my sons' support, we were asked to provide IRS forms from a mother, a father, and any official step-parents. Forms designed for the "traditional family" were so confusing to the many single or remarried parents of graduating seniors that the high school staff held a series of workshops to help us translate ourselves for the computers in Princeton. Darren and I attended together.

"For the purposes of this form," the workshop leader said, "the definition of 'father' is the person who sits at your dinner table every night." Darren looked up from his notebook and gave me a quizzical look.

"Does that mean Carlos is my father?" he asked.

MY SONS have lived in half a dozen family structures by now, all unorthodox but with this common denominator: They were always in the company of people who loved them. Our last evolution, after Larry and I parted in the spring of '90, led to an apartment in a small bungalow on the western edge of town. In our ongoing trek into downward mobility, it was our most humble domicile to date. While Darren finished his last semester of junior high in Ann Arbor with Howard, Ryan and I spent two months plastering, painting, wall-papering, and hammering our way into the coziest and most comfortable nest we had occupied since their birth.

The main architectural advantage was a neglected basement that had once been a rec room and laundry, which Ryan and I reclaimed for his bedroom. We stained the paneled walls, carpeted the floor, and installed track lights to brighten a study area. The Independence Room, as I came to think of it, had two outside entrances—one through the garage, and the other through the cellar doors in the backyard. This meant that friends, perhaps with six packs, perhaps accompanied by guests of the female persuasion, could enter the room directly without encountering a parent (unless she happened to be downstairs doing laundry, which was rare, since everybody did their own according to need). Despite the humble decor and raftered ceiling, Ryan loved his new digs. Darren moved into the room across the hall from my office, but had designs on The Independence Room the moment Ry left for college.

Self-government, a "family value" ever since their alternative school in Fort Wayne taught us the wisdom of kid-made rules, was operative for The Independence Room as well. Since both kids were competently managing their school work, part-time jobs, and social lives, we were down to the minimum laws of home rule: Nothing illegal; no damage to the house; respect for the volume and noise requirements of your housemates and informing your friends of the same. Although we continued to talk about sex, alcohol, movies, entertainment, and parties, most of the decisions on those issues were largely their own now. When the Do Not Disturb sign was on the door handle to the basement, I did not. The Independence Room gave them both a chance to experiment, take risks, make mistakes while someone who loved them lived on the floor above.

Aware of our limited time together and taking almost nothing for granted, we entered Adrienne Rich's almost sinfully delicious vision of how satisfying living with children can be. Without fixed routines, without the jurisprudence of others, I entered the last, presumably most difficult passage of raising sons, when they became official members of the most frightening and violent segment of the population: The Male Adolescent. Ironically, it was during that same period that I felt enormously in charge of my life.

Transition periods are invariably fraught with embarrassments, but it was never remotely necessary to lock the liquor cabinet, as the advisory warnings in parent newsletters frequently recommended. The Independence Room took on the personality of each tenant. For Darren, it was a hacker heaven, a stereo-enhanced computer wonderland where he and his friends began exploring the global possibilities of the information highway. For Ryan, the unofficial senior class therapist, it became a safe haven for friends in trouble.

Working late one night I heard the garage door open at 3 A.M., and a desperate male voice began speaking loudly. Another voice, calm and questioning, gradually modulated the first. When both voices finally quieted down, I stood at the top of the stairs and whispered through the open door, calling the calm one: "Ry . . . everything okay?" He appeared at the bottom step in his boxer shorts, his hair still tussled from bed. "Yeah . . . it's Eddie. Had another fight with his dad," he whispered, then shook his head. I wasn't supposed to know Eddie's father was an alcoholic. I was never supposed to know anything that year. "He's okay—he's asleep now," Ryan said. "And don't worry. I just called his mom to let her know where he is."

I REMEMBER these scenes introducing me to who my sons are in their own world with gratitude now. Today Ryan lives on a campus 2,500 miles from home, and Darren is a thousand miles away as well. I'm "out of control" now. I have become unnecessary, the next plateau beyond powerless responsibility. Since I had no choice about sending my sons into a society where guns and drugs and violence are used every day, they needed practice with self-discipline—a quality that travels well, the best insurance I could imagine for their future. It seemed fairly absurd to lock the liquor cabinet and to demand chaperons for young men who would be living half a continent away the next year.

My friends tell me I wouldn't have been as willing to encourage independence if my sons had been daughters. I know that, as dangerous as the culture is to sons, it is even more dangerous to daughters. Without question, it would have been more frightening to launch girl-children into this threatening landscape. But I like to think I would have been an ally to their independence as well. Without preparation for the risks and responsibilities they would encounter, there could be no freedom. It helped to have been the sister of The Moon Man, my wild younger brother who tested Kay's patience throughout his teenage years. Now a Cleveland banker with distinguished grey streaks at his temples, a devoted father to two healthy children who simultaneously delight and frighten him, he says: "If my kids ever do half the crazy things I did, I'll kill them." In a few years, when his children reach adolescence, he'll be tempted to repress memories of his own youthful excesses and the many threats of Culver Military Academy. Since it has always been my job to record the messier facts of family history, I'll no doubt feel obligated to remind him: You can't become a mature adult without losing your innocence, again and again.

AFTER THE kids became more independent and my days were no longer chopped up into two-hour slices between car pools and bedtime rituals, I thought I would revert back to "normal" hours: work by day, sleep by night. But my muse must be a night person: a slow starter, she's fairly mute in the morning and still monosyllabic by afternoon. After nearly twenty years of working at night, I now usually have to wait for the stars to come out before I try to write. I was still regularly up at night when my sons reached adolescence, aware of exactly what time the car tires crunched into the driveway.

My thorough awareness of their nocturnal comings and goings, especially during the last years they lived at home, was often a royal pain to them. If they'd been drinking at a party, they knew they had no chance of slipping unnoticed into the bathroom to pray before the porcelain enamel. We suffered some of our most compromising scenes at night. Other times, however, my eccentric working habits permitted a rare and wonderful discovery: Teenagers, as sullen and monosyllabic as my muse was during the daylight hours, will talk for hours at night.

Our moods were nearly perfectly matched as well. A messy bedroom or abandoned soda can sighted that morning was nowhere on my mind by 3 A.M. I was usually coming back from a trip to the heart of what matters, often humbled by reality and in an exceptionally truth-telling mode. They were usually returning from some evening activity with friends, often wanting to share the laughs or the questions fresh on their minds. They would come into my office/bedroom where the lights were still on and lie down on the bed, shoes and sometimes jackets still on, and begin a lengthy recap. Since my judgments were soft and spongy at night and they were unusually confessional, we would talk then, as we never seemed to be able to by day, about jealousy, drugs, sex, AIDS, jokes, hurts, joys, friends, futures, dreams, and the question that baffled Freud most of his professional life: What do women want?

By accident rather than design, being awake until 3 A.M. allowed for some astonishing revelations. Just at the age when children retreat from their parents, we would slip periodically through that crack in time before dawn to recapture the intimacy of our past. We were so out-of-control that I had stopped giving rules to my sons almost entirely by then. Relying exclusively on the power of truthful conversation to inspire the desired behavior, all of us thrived under this less authoritarian arrangement.

Although my work as a writer means odd hours, a fleecy wardrobe, and sometimes a perilous grip on finances, I feel lucky that my professional life has been so relevant to my private life. Since I first began publishing personal essays in the Sunday edition of the *Fort Wayne Journal Gazette,* I have continued to write about my sons—not only because they were handy but because they fueled my passion to know, to name, to think hard, to be braver than I really was.

"How do your sons feel about your writing?" friends have asked through the years. Did they feel an invasion of privacy?

My sons hardly know privacy. But since all stories necessarily reflect the narrator's point of view, I've had to wonder now and then how closely my perceptions matched those of the subjects. My friend Phyllis Theroux, who covers much of the same personal journalistic terrain I do, once asked her youngest son after a riveting experience the evening before, "Justin, do you remember last night when I was singing you a song?"

"Yep," he replied.

"Do you remember how you felt or what you thought?"

Her question was followed by a short pause, during which she assumed he was trying to retrieve his feelings about the moment. Then he looked at her and asked, "Are you doing this for the *Post* or the *Times*?"

It was always a hazard for sons to live under the scrutiny of a mother who writes. My sons and I will never see our history quite the same way, even though we lived together for nearly twenty years. Our most memorable events invariably evoke different feelings in us. In the sad fall of 1980, for example, I extracted myself from a painful marriage and found a small measure of relief. My sons have missed their lovable father ever since. When the alto sax player blows his plaintive horn today, we all hear different lyrics.

OUR DEPARTURES from tradition may not look so odd in the future. The nuclear family of my own childhood—which followed the orderly, suburban routines of a full-time mother and bread-winning father, all of us seated around the dinner table by 6 P.M. every night—is rapidly becoming what my friend Sandra calls "the museum family." By 1995, according to Steven K. Wisensale, an associate professor of public policy in the School of Family Studies at the University of Connecticut, "80 percent of all school aged children will have mothers in the work force." The *New York Times* reported that "while families with two parents working outside the home had increased, real family income had dropped by about 8 percent nationally between 1973 and 1991." The disappearance of the full-time housewife has had dramatic consequences for a society that still refuses to acknowledge her unpaid labor, because there are few support systems in place to care for children and aging parents. Unless we stop having children and start expiring at an earlier age, the current arrangement of the culture "thrusts more and more people into care-giving roles when they already have jobs and their own families to support," the *Times* reported, adding that "75 percent of the people caring for older parents or other relatives are women." A study by the House Select Committee on Aging found that "a woman can expect to spend about 17 years caring for a dependent child and 18 years caring for an aging parent." It does not take a genius to see that the "traditional family" has not been a picnic for women. Trust me: Either women must obtain the power to structure our lives so these facts fit together, or we are going to have a nation of comatose women.

It sometimes appears that the most brilliant moves in my checkered career as a mother were complete accidents. My brothers and sister laugh when I say this because they believe that every accident of fate is an act of God. "Chance or what might seem to be chance is the means through which you shape your character," Paul said, quoting the philosopher Joseph Campbell. He illustrates this point for his students with the story of a Tibetan monk who suffered horribly during the Chinese invasions, yet later looked back on his torturers without recrimination, regarding them as instruments of his own destiny.

What did the story mean, I asked him, for a less holy, single mother standing on the brink of yet another risky career leap as the country sank into a deep recession and her sons headed for college? He thought a minute, then answered: "You are not now to lose your nerve."

INSTEAD OF the "normal" life I thought I was heading into twenty years ago, the photos in our family collages around the fireplace tonight record what Phyllis Theroux calls an interesting life: "It could, of course, be argued that an interesting life is less desirable than a peaceful, bump-free life; you would get no argument from me. I have been dragged toward an interesting life kicking and screaming," Theroux wrote. "But plot flows toward character, and one has to accept the results of the collision with equanimity if not grace."

Okay. I wasn't perfect. Sometimes I have been outright incompetent. Like Regina's young college applicant in Massachusetts, I am tempted to list under Honors and Awards that "I have never been arrested"—although I am haunted by the vague notion that maybe I should have been.

RYAN AND Darren were focused mostly on their own emancipation during the past few years, but all the same they were both a little worried about me as they left home. Unaware that I had a life that preceded and would follow my years with them, they knew me primarily as "mother." What would I do without that role?

"What are *you* going to do, Mom, after we're gone?" Darren asked.

"Me? I'm going to do every wild and crazy thing I can think of," I said. "Don't worry about me. I'll be fine."

Darren knit his thick brows, apparently trying to imagine what kind of wild and crazy things I might be contemplating. He looked puzzled. "Well, like, what have you left out?"

Well, like, . . . not much.

THE TWENTY years of nonreciprocal love invested in "having a baby" is strictly liquid capital, of course. It has to be spent now because we can't take it with us. The good news is that, perhaps because Ryan and Darren have had so much practice with long-distance relationships, their departures have not ended our intimacy. We still talk on the phone, with discounted rates and time zones working to their advantage since they have a mother who's usually up half the night. They call home often—sometimes even when they don't need money. I still get tremendous pleasure from these cheap thrills, along with the ones that changed my life. Perhaps it is unnatural to want the deep shudders of motherhood to quicken through me over a whole lifetime—maybe more than a lifetime. But this is what I like to imagine.

Motherhood is not a job I ever wanted to outgrow, but here I am, twenty years later: I have become unnecessary.

"Don't you hate it?" asked Carrie, the mother of two young girls. She is still in the stage of power, feeling indispensable and needed.

"Yes and no," I said. After two decades of daily involvement, I am as ready for separation as my sons. The mourning is accompanied by a peculiar satisfaction: Motherhood engaged me in all the passions I anticipated—and a whole lot more. I would amend Erikson's theory that most human beings don't achieve generativity—the long view, a sense of what's truly important in life—until very late in life. It can happen much earlier for mothers. Raising children accelerates the process of human development; it could be said that children make us prematurely wise.

I CAN'T know how my sons will turn out—whether they will become the "feminist men" most of my friends were predicting during their youth. Since children are products of their culture as much as their families, I'm grateful to know my sons love and respect me. They also love the *Sports Illustrated* swimsuit issue.

In the last two decades, millions of American women have changed not only their language and thinking, their professional choices and banking habits, but also the shape of the nonreciprocal gift that goes one way from mothers to children to grandchildren. Without asking anybody's permission—without anybody even noticing what we were doing—many mothers began teaching new conditions for love: no sexism, no racism, no violence, no gender entitlements. Whether these incremental, daily efforts over the last twenty years will amount to the Third Wave, as a new coalition of baby activists from Greenwich Village to Los Angeles are now calling themselves, remains to be seen. Change does take time, but even the "worst blizzard of the century" accumulates one flake at a time.